Prais
Bless Me Father,

"Imbued with compassion and humor, Dan's delightful memoir chronicles life in a loving but troubled family and a faith that brought both strength and profound guilt. These experiences, plus determination, ingenuity, and bumps along the way, launched him into a life of joyful purpose and meaning. What a gem!"

—Mary Webber MSW, Clinical Social Worker

"Intimate, authentic, riveting, *Bless Me Father* is the memoir of a young man coming of age on in the mid-twentieth century on the rugged, windswept northern American Great Plains. The story is familiar—a boy growing up —but its context is unique. Young Dan Geiger, son of pioneers, staunch Catholics, simultaneously carries his family's heritage and an abiding sense of ancient Indian spirituality in his bones. It is a story of a boy growing up on the last fringes of the American Frontier at a time of the quantum cultural change—from post-World War II to Woodstock.

Bless Me Father offers a glimpse into the riotous, often confusing, sometimes hilarious and even mystical adventures of a boy growing to manhood. In its essence it is nothing less than a spiritual journey of a soul. Experience the cross currents and riptides of cultural and personal transformation through the eyes of one remarkable soul who lived through these unforgettable times."

—Roberta Nowlin, teacher, singer/songwriter, author, *The Magic Apple Tree*

"There must be a ton of books on Viet Nam. This one stands out... because of the quality of writing, the location, Montana)... the culture, the deaths, the fears, the girls, and a reminder of how our culture changed from that point on. We had WW11/ Korea... but that was before this time... when America thought of itself as victors. But that changed in the 60's. And since then, the old culture of all Americans behind our military... and the divisions we see today. This is an excellent book on just how everything changed."

—Daniel Kelly, artist Japan

"Have you ever wondered what happened to Holden Caulfield from The Catcher in the Rye"? His spirit is alive and well in the Big Sky Country of Montana. *Bless Me Father, for I Have Sinned* picks up the journey of the boy that catches children in the rye field before they fall off the cliff. Montana is the setting for the next 50 plus years. The author recants his journey of trying to better the lives of children and adults during his professional and personal life. Keep in mind the setting during these times. There were no daylight speed limits on the highways. It was rumored that a sturdy young man with blues eyes could make a few bucks by adding to the gene pool of the Hutterites Colony.

This is a tale of life that shows the importance of religion, education, family, and profession. JMJ are the letters that often appear on the test papers of Catholic students—it stands for Jesus, Mary, Joseph. Placing JMJ on the papers may not improve the test score, but it couldn't hurt either. I suggest that you place JMJ on the flyleaf of the book as it may help you understand the heartwarming message of this book. Enjoy your read, you will find a great story that has many parts of you in it."

—Dr. Dennis Schulz, Professor of Habilitative Services Emeritus
Montana State Univ.-Billings

"Let's be clear. Dan is no monk. Yes, spiritual events have gripped his attention his whole life, but sacred moments scatter themselves among pranks, sports, muscle cars, insatiable wanderlust, a healthy relationship with friends and alcohol, and girls. Dan nails our generation's feelings about Vietnam – that callous Federal death threat to all draft-age guys. His 'friendships populate all six continents—from the Crow Indians in the U.S. to Arabs. Jews and Bahais in Israel and black-market contacts in Moscow.

Dan is a central figure putting himself out there. Starkly honest, a life like our own but he keeps us riveted through the brightest and darkest moments of that 'ordinary' life. The writing is unpretentious and clear. The story keeps moving. Mercifully, the guilt trips on tap won't make you squeamish. But expect to be surprised, entertained, and glad for the ride."

—Jack Dermody, Freelance Writer

Bless Me, Father, for I Have Sinned

A Memoir

Dan Geiger

Minneapolis

Minneapolis

Second Edition December 2022

Published by Wisdom Editions, 6800 France Av S, Edina, MN 55435.

10 9 8 7 6 5 4 3 2

ISBN: 978-1-959770-70-1

Cover and book design by Gary Lindberg

Bless Me, Father, for I Have Sinned

"I just dropped in to see what condition my condition was in."

Song: Kenny Rogers, Sony
Writer: Mickey Newbury

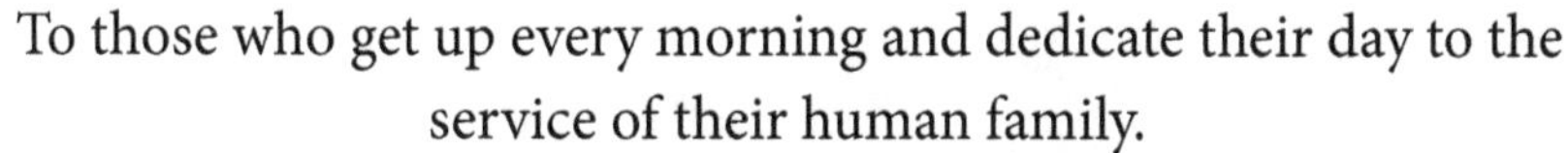

To those who get up every morning and dedicate their day to the service of their human family.

"Work done in the spirit of service is the highest form of worship."
—Abdu'l-Baha

Chapter 1

1962, Charley Gets Off Shift

"Okay, you guys can go home now," Father K says. "Don't let me catch you throwing eggs at cars again."

"Yes, Father," Glenn says with veiled sincerity, but his sly grin covers the lie. Of course, we will be throwing eggs again, why not? That's our job as seniors.

Glenn and I grab our books and head out the back door of Central Catholic High School. We'd been caught in an egg fight during lunch with our classmates, Gunner and Brick. They had managed to hide when the priests came by, but we were called into the principal's office for detention after classes.

"Jeez, I thought he'd never let us go," Glenn says.

"Yeah, it took two hours to copy that page out of the phone book. I was so fricking bored."

"No wonder my handwriting is so shitty."

Copying pages out of the phone book is standard detention punishment. We briskly walked the ten blocks to Glenn's house to be there before his dad gets home from work and wonders why we're late. Typical of "good" kids, we enjoy being mischievous but don't do any real harm.

Behind us, black smoke belches from the 506-foot-tall brick smokestack of the Anaconda Copper Smelter in Great Falls, Montana, a few hundred feet from the pristine Missouri River. The water of this great river, born in the Rocky Mountains, slices its way 2,500 miles down through the Great Plains of America and eventually to the Gulf of Mexico. Great Falls is known as the "Electric City" because of the five hydroelectric power plants built on each of the five waterfalls on the Missouri River, where it cuts between the city of Great Falls and the smelter town Black Eagle. Anaconda Company built this copper smelter here to take advantage of the cheap electric power needed to refine copper ore into pure copper ingots. While the smelter has been a source of income, most of the wealth created by it slipped into the pockets of "Copper Kings" William Clark and Marcus Daly. The rich got richer, and the poor stayed poor.

The day shift at the smelter is just ending, and Glenn's father, Charley, emerges after eight hours of stripping copper off electrodes. His blue work shirt and face are black with soot. His tired body eases into the driver's seat of his spanking new green 1963 Ford Falcon, which has been sitting in the warm October sun. He glances disgustedly at the driver's side recently pockmarked by a shotgun blast and mutters, "Those damn drunken kids at the drive-in."

An old army blanket covers the seat to protect it from his dirty work clothes. He takes his cap and throws it on the dashboard, exposing a forehead free of soot. He wipes sweat from his forehead with a sleeve, starts the car, listens to the six-cylinder motor purr, pulls the gear shift into low gear and eases the car out of the parking lot. He's worked hard to buy this new vehicle. The Falcon is a smaller compact, certainly not a Buick or a Pontiac, but it's new and shiny. He proudly drives south across the 14th Street Bridge on the Missouri River toward his home on the southeast side of Great Falls.

A fly buzzes against the inside of the windshield. He tries unsuccessfully to shoo it out the open window with his hat, but continues buzzing against the window. As he pulls into his driveway, the fly falls upside down on the dashboard, buzzes for a few seconds and dies. Charley picks up his hat and whisks the fly and some dust off the dash onto the floor.

Glenn was one of the first friends I made when I moved from Billings to Great Falls last summer to begin my senior year. We are in the basement reading *Hot Rod Magazine* when his dad arrives home.

Charley pokes his head down the stairs. "How you boys doin'?

"Okay, doing homework," Glenn answers.

"Good, you need to keep your grades up if you want to get into college."

"Yeah, Dad, no problem, I just have algebra tonight."

We continue to look through the magazine. Glenn and I have a hard time getting around to our homework. We both get Cs by doing the minimum amount.

"So, what are we going to do to get even with Gunner and Brick?" Glenn asks with his sly grin. "Those assholes got away today while we got detention."

When the two of us get together, we are always looking for a prank to pull on our friends. We also watch each other's back for retaliation. The egg fight was just one of a series of benign wars among our classmates.

"We'll get their asses tomorrow. I better get home, it's dinner time.

"Okay, see ya Saturday at Buttreys."

"Yeah, first day on the job. Is there much to know?"

"Nah, just sack groceries and carry them out. I'll show you how to do it."

"Seems like everyone from our class is working there—Gunner, Brick, you, me."

"Yeah, we'll have a good time."

"Okay, see you later."

I walk the six blocks to my house. It's not really a house like Glenn's but a trailer house that sits behind the Hi Ho Tavern and Bar in a small trailer court with seven other trailers. It's tiny, with no room to entertain a friend or have someone over for dinner. It's embarrassing when my friends see where I live. I wouldn't want to bring a date there to meet my parents. I mostly hang out at my friends' homes. Charley wants Glenn to go to college, but I've never had that discussion with my parents. No one in our family has ever gone to college, so it's a topic we don't know how to talk about.

Our trailer house behind the Hi Go Tavern

Glenn's dad, Charley, has worked at the smelter for twenty-one years, working his way up to the day shift after a long time on the graveyard shift. He has made a life for himself and his family. As with many of the blue-collar workers at the smelter, their house is not fancy but it is comfortable with two bedrooms upstairs and a half-basement where Glenn has made a bedroom for himself. The bank loan will be paid off in a few years, hopefully before Charley's tired body wears out. Many years of hard labor has taken its toll, and he's not sure how much longer he can keep this pace. Social Security is still a few years away, and he doesn't have much choice but to keep punching the time clock every day. Now in his early 60s, he got a late start having children and finding this job. It's a stretch to do this type of hard work, but he still has two kids at home. With copper prices strong, the smelter runs full shifts. It's a place where 2,000 blue-collar workers make a living but not an easy life. Charley has it better than his parents, who were poor farm laborers, but not much better.

With wheat prices high and local farmers harvesting hundreds of miles of wheat fields around Great Falls, life is good and was an inspiration for this song:

O beautiful for spacious skies,
For amber waves of grain,
For purple mountain majesties
Above the fruited plain!

It's a great time to live in Great Falls. Malmstrom Air Force Base, a few miles east of town, is home to 4,000 military transplants from around the country, providing some diversity to this white world. People of color brighten the city with their music, food and big city life. The city booms with numerous restaurants and night clubs that cater to black and white music lovers interested in jazz, big band, rock and roll and country western. It hosts seventy-two bars: Ambrose's Hi-Ho, The Barrel, Beano's, Brass Rail, Caboose, CartWheel, Cheerio, Cowboy, Earl's, Hank's, Joe's Place, Maverick, The Ranger, Stein Haus, Stockman's and Wally's to name a few. Most cater to the blue-collar community—mostly hard-working and hard-drinking men. The prevailing attitude among a lot of working men here is, "Damn it, I work hard and provide for my family, so I deserve to have a few cold ones after work." Unfortunately, a *few* often turns into *many*. Coming home drunk and late for dinner takes its toll on wives and kids, often to be played out in the next generation.

Some bars offer illegal gambling, and while it is kept hidden, it is not unknown to the local police who get paid off to ignore it. Each weekend, dozens of bands crank out live music around the city. Restaurants and bars bustle with business. We kids who are not yet twenty-one years old and mind our business can drink liquor in the local bars and clubs, some using phony ID cards and some by knowing the bartender—but most through indifference.

"What's wrong with drinking a few beers?" is a common mindset among the townsfolk, most of whom have been drinking since they were teenagers. The Great Falls Select Brewery, an icon of the city, advertises tours with free beer at 10:30 a.m. and 1:30 p.m., and it's not unusual to find folks from nineteen to eighty-nine enjoying a cold beer at 10:30 in the morning, some of whom had enjoyed late-night entertainment at local brothels the previous evening.

For a small city, Great Falls is also a family community with seventy-six restaurants, twenty-nine unions, seventy-four neighborhood grocery stores, thirty-six "mom and pop" motels, thirty-eight hotels or boarding houses for workers, eighty-two churches and four taxi companies—Diamond, Yellow, A&A and Black and White. Although Great Falls is the largest city in a four-state area of Montana, Wyoming, Idaho and North Dakota, on a good day, it barely counts 50,000 residents, a testament to the wide-open spaces of the West. But in the rural prairies around Great Falls, 150 Minute Man nuclear missiles are on alert to drop multiple atomic bombs on our arch-enemy, the Union of Soviet Socialist Republic (USSR). The Cold War is at its peak with the recent standoff between The US and the USSR over the Cuban missile crisis that occurred when the USSR tried to move ballistic missiles into our backyard. This spawned the building of backyard bomb shelters across America. Paranoia is seeping deep into the soul of our nation. I try not to think about it, but fear quietly follows me around.

Montana is the Wild West, and Great Falls offers wild opportunities for us kids just entering adulthood, a time when our focus is on the opposite sex, cars, smoking cigarettes, drive-in theaters, keggers, cruisin' the drag and getting served in the local bars. It's an opportune time to be a senior in high school. It's a time of innocence when life is simple and safe. There is action, fun and few cares, but soon an almost hidden undertow will wash lives out of this safe nest.

War!

Chapter 2

War Sneaks in the Back Door

While we continue to enjoy our senior year in high school, we have a gnawing feeling that we are coming of age only to be drafted by the local Selective Service Board. A low-grade anxiety hums in the background, and we try to block it out by still trying to be kids. By our eighteenth birthdays, we have to register the understanding that we could be drafted into the military when we finish high school. There are a few ways to avoid the draft: (1) become a conscientious objector and refuse on the grounds of freedom of thought, conscience or religion; (2) be or pretend to be homosexual; (3) fail the physical medical exam; (4) enroll in college; (5) have wealthy parents or political connections; and (6) move to Canada.

All these options have consequences. Most bright kids who can afford college or have wealthy parents or connections can avoid the draft without much difficulty. If you are poor, uneducated or black, the chances of being drafted are high. While blacks represent only 11 percent of the population, they represent 23 percent of the combat troops and 25 percent of combat deaths. If you live in poverty and lack education, you move to the top of the draft list. The class of '63 at Great Falls Central Catholic High School has a couple of advantages: (1) we are almost all white, and (2) we have some education. Glenn and I fall into this category.

* * *

As Glenn and I hang out in his basement bedroom, a conversation struggles to the surface.

"Did you register yet?" Glenn asks while looking down.

"Yeah, a few months ago on my birthday." I look down in the other direction. It's almost too hard to talk about, let alone look at each other. I don't think we want to see our fear reflected in the other's face.

"Mine's comin' up in a few months. Think we'll get drafted?

"Dunno, hoping to get into college."

"Me too, thinking of goin' to Missoula," Glenn says, retying his left shoe for the second time.

"I'll probably stay here and go to the College of Great Falls and keep my job at Buttreys," I say, staring out the 12 by 18-inch basement window and seeing nothing outside.

"I wanna get out of town, tired of living at home."

"Yeah, know what you mean. Ben and Larry said I could move into their duplex on 2nd Avenue with them. My folks' trailer is too small for me and my brother."

"Heard guys are being killed in Vietnam, and it's supposed to get worse." Glenn reties his right shoe.

"Yeah, for sure."

"All I know is I don't wanna have to kill somebody or get killed."

"Me too."

"Some of the Viet Cong are kids, I heard, like fourteen, fifteen years old." Glenn walks over and looks in the empty washing machine in the corner.

"Sure wouldn't want to shoot a kid."

"Me neither."

"My uncle was in World War II—said it was the worst thing, seeing people get killed."

"What you gonna do if you get drafted?"

"Dunno," Glenn says, still staring in the empty washer.

Eventually, Glenn managed to find his way into college, but lack of discipline and falling in love with billiards and beer led to failing grades and loss of his college deferment. Ironically, he was married for a short time and had a daughter, which earned him a deferment, but the marriage ended in divorce, and that deferment was lifted, so he got drafted. Glenn had a kind heart, and killing people, even in combat, just wasn't who he was.

* * *

A couple of years later, another classmate named Jim and I head down to the Stein Haus, a local pub.

"I hear Glenn and Barry are shipping out for Nam in a couple of days," I tell Jim. "Supposed to be at the Stein Haus tonight."

"Yeah, let's go see 'em."

Jim and I find them lined up at the bar with a few other guys. The first thing I notice is that Glenn's sly grin is missing.

"So, you guys shipping out soon?"

"Yeah, day after tomorrow," Glenn says. "Came down for a last beer on the town."

"How you doin' with this?"

"Dunno, going to spend tomorrow night with my folks and daughter. My mom isn't doing very well with this army thing. I don't know if we'll make it."

I can see Glenn is scared but can't find words to describe how he feels.

Barry says, "Hey, don't be talking that way—we'll make it."

Glenn and Barry have the same orders but different attitudes.

"I hope you're right," Glenn says.

"Gotta think positive, we'll make it, damn it," Barry counters.

"Easier said than done," Glenn says, studying the foam on his beer.

I remember Glenn as a football player our senior year when Central won the state championship. He was tough, and while not so big, he could hold his own against bigger players. He liked to play rough, but a moment later, he could flash a big smile and be courteous and kind.

Tonight, he is neither—just scared. I'm scared too. So is everyone else here. As I look down the bar, I see the empty stools of regular bar patrons missing in action—draftees all.

Barry is upbeat and sees himself as a survivor, while Glenn seems to have a subconscious death wish. Barry will return home to resume his life in Great Falls. Glenn might get his wish.

A couple of days later, Barry and Glenn ship out for Nam. I didn't hear from him but figured he was too busy to write. I saw his mom at the grocery store, and she said they had gotten some letters from him, and he was doing okay. Years later, I discovered this post on the Vietnam Memorial Virtual Wall from Keith, a classmate from Central, who saw Glenn when he arrived in Nam:

> In early August, I left HHC S2 with 4/39th in Dong Tam for Bearcat and DEROS. At the helicopter pad where I hitched a ride, the pilot said we might make a stop to pick up a KIA from the 2/39th. I put emphasis on "might," not welcoming the idea of descent into a kill zone in my last days, especially into 2/39th territory. They were, as I thought then, always getting their ass kicked. This means no disrespect to them, just respect for the VC and the fierceness of the battles the 2/39th got snared in.
>
> Soon the pilot began a steep ascent, climbing to at least 1500 feet, and I began to think we'd fly nonstop to Bearcat. Soon enough we began a steep descent, my stomach lurching as in a sudden elevator drop. We picked up the KIA: an Idaho son whose high school ring fell off his finger when his head bumped the chopper floor. We flew on to Bearcat, where we dropped him off at Graves Registration. I think I put his ring in his fatigue jacket, but my memory is never sure.
>
> After turning in my M16 and other gear, I was walking to Casual Company when someone called my name. I turned and saw a fellow Montanan from Great Falls, former

schoolmate from high school and college, Glenn. Small world! The irony of coming and going was awkward. He told me he was going to 2/39th. I had an instant foreboding, not telling him what I knew. We wished each other well.

From a schoolmate,

Keith

Chapter 3

1965, Glenn Comes Home

"Just got a call from Glenn's parents," I tell Jim. "He got killed in Nam." Jim and I ran around with Glenn our senior year, part of a loose-knit gang of innocent kids. Jim always rooted for the underdog and championed the poor and minorities—fought for justice in general. Like his businessman dad, he was a Republican, but over time left the party when it lost its way to greed.

"What, you kiddin' me? He just left? What happened?"

"I dunno, all his dad said was he was out on patrol and got hit by enemy fire."

Jim explodes. "Damn—screw the draft! It's them goddamn hawks that got us into Vietnam. I'm not going. They'll have to come and get me."

"I know. I'm scared shitless. I just got classified 1A because I didn't carry a full load of credits. They don't give a shit that I'm working full time and living on my own. They hate college students and think everybody should join the army. That asshole Tollefsrud, head of the draft board, is a stupid farmer who thinks we should kill all those commies even if many of 'em are women and children."

"Who are we to tell other countries how to live? I'm 1A too—thinking of going CO or to Canada," Jim says. "Pisses me off that Glenn got killed for no good reason—he was a good guy."

"Charley wants us to go down and identify the body. Says he and Gladys just can't do it. Let's go over there and see how they're doing."

We take my custom '53 Oldsmobile and rumble over to the south side of Great Falls. Glenn's dad and mother are second-generation Germans whose parents migrated to the US in the early 1900s as young adults. They moved to Great Falls from Bismarck, North Dakota, in 1941 when they got married. Glenn has two older sisters and was born in 1945. He would have been 21 on the second of June.

Everyone has a big party when they turn twenty-one and can drink legally, but Glenn won't see his party. I guess it doesn't matter because he was getting served in the bars when he was seventeen and buying beer for his friends. His heavy beard and dark eyebrows made him look older. When I was seventeen, I looked like I was twelve years old. Glenn would always make fun of my baby face, but he'd come up with the beer when I wanted some.

Charley's 1963 Falcon sits in the driveway of his small two-bedroom house. Small dents are on the side of the car from two years ago when we were spinning brodies in the gravel parking lot at the Four Lights, a local brothel where we went to "ogle the girls" but didn't have the guts to plunk down ten bucks to christen one's manhood. These brothels disappeared in the 1970s, but in '65 were still present in almost every Montana city.

That night, as the car spun around and around throwing gravel in a wide circle, Glenn laughed, diabolically mesmerized. He was trying to get even with the bouncer who had just thrown us out of the bar for causing a disturbance. The disturbance had happened after Glenn got into an argument with one of the girls because he didn't want to buy her a drink in exchange for a dance.

"Holy shit, there's the bouncer with a shotgun," Sig yelled from the backseat. Before anyone could say anything, a shot boomed out, followed by a splat of buckshot on the side of the car, creating those dents.

"Shit, he got me in the side of the head," Sig said, holding his ear. His window was rolled down about an inch—just enough for a buckshot pellet to sneak through and lodge itself behind his ear. "Get the hell out of here, that asshole is shooting at us."

Just then, Glenn came out of his dream world of being a professional auto racer. As another shot rang out, he steered the Falcon toward the parking lot exit. "That asshole! How am I going to explain this to my parents? I'm screwed. You'll have to come to the house with me, Danny. My parents will believe you."

I protested, "Believe *me*? Believe me *what*?"

"Just make up some of your sweet bullshit as you always do for the parents and teachers. They always believe you, just like Eddie Haskell on TV."

We sail across town, drop off Sig and Bob at their houses and then head for Glenn's place. The lights are still on. We get out of the car and survey the buckshot damage.

"Remember—come up with something good," Glenn reminds me. "I'm going to go back and get that asshole that shot at us."

"Yeah, right. Go back, and he'll just shoot you in the ass too."

Charley and Gladys are sitting in identical La-Z-Boys upholstered with crushed orange velvet with orange and black knitted Afghans draped over the back. *Sgt. Bilko* plays on the TV.

"Hey boys, did you have a good time at the drive-in?" Charley asks.

Glenn looks daggers at me, meaning *get me out of this*.

I begin inauspiciously. "Well, ah, err, Mr. Black, these guys that parked next to us at the drive-in were drunk and when they drove off, they spun gravel on the side of the car, so we tried to get their license number, but they tore off, and we tried to follow them, but they were going 90 miles per hour down River Road, and we were afraid to follow that fast..." I say all this in one breath.

"What the hell—did they hurt the car?" Charley shouts.

"Yeah, some small dents."

He runs out the front door and, in the dim of the porch light, examines the car.

"Damn it to hell! We just got this car and now this. Those SOBs." This is the first time I've heard Charley, a devout Catholic, cuss like this. With *hell*, *damn* and *SOB* all in a couple of sentences, he must really be mad.

"Yeah, Mr. Black, I wish we could have caught 'em," I say calmly. "Glenn tried his best, but those other guys were too drunk to catch. Driving like crazy!"

Glenn finally utters his first words since we had arrived home. "Yeah, Dad, they were drunk. If I woulda known it, I wouldn'ta parked next to 'em."

"Well, things could be worse. You could have gotten hurt or wrecked the car," Charley says, simmering down a little. "You're heading off for the service soon, and worse things could happen. Damn those kids! I'm glad you boys didn't get into that." Glenn and I look at each other, hoping he can't smell beer on our breaths masked by Black Jack chewing gum.

"Okay if we go downstairs?" Glenn asks, hoping to get us away from his dad.

"Yeah, make sure your homework is done."

"Okay. Can Dan spend the night? It's okay with his parents."

"Yeah, best you boys get to bed."

"Sorry about your car, Mr. Black," I offer. "I don't blame you for being mad at those drunk guys."

"Yeah, go on now."

Glenn and I head downstairs to the half-basement where Glenn has a bedroom he shares with the washer and dryer. Dangling by a wire cord, a bare light bulb barely lights the concrete walls. This isn't meant to be a bedroom, but it's a place where Glenn can hide from his parents. I make my bed on an old couch at one end of the room. Besides Glenn's bed, the only furniture is the couch, a small wooden dresser, a foldable card table and a folding chair. Two posters have been taped to the concrete wall. One is a game schedule for the 1962 Central football team, and the other is of Ann Margaret dancing in the movie *State Fair*. She is showing a lot of leg and a little cleavage, but it's modest enough that Glenn's parents allow it in their home. In the corner, next to a Maytag washing machine, is a pile of dirty laundry. The place smells like dirty socks.

"Boy, that was close," Glenn says. "I thought my parents would come unglued. Good story about the gravel at the drive-in. I can always count on you coming up with something. I don't think Eddie Haskell could have weaseled us out of that one any better."

I take this as a compliment "Yeah, I'm always getting you out of shit."

We lie there for a few minutes with the light off, reliving the shotgun blast.

"Holy shit, I can't believe he shot at us!" Glenn finally says. "I wonder how Sig's head is. The bleeding stopped by the time we let him off. Hope he's OK. If his parents find out, we're screwed."

"Think your dad will ground you?" I ask Glenn.

"Dunno. See what he says in the morning. Good story about the gravel."

"Yeah, no problem—you owe me."

"I'll buy you some beer someday."

At the time, I don't realize that these will be the memories that stick in my mind and create the myths of my life and my friends. Glenn and I argue a lot, but it's how we show our love for each other. It's also true with the rest of the guys and gals in our circle—we like to give each other a kidding and a bad time. An outsider listening to our conversations might think we're not close friends, but they'd be misunderstanding our "affection" for one another. Tomorrow, I'll remind Glenn he's an idiot for getting us thrown out of the Four Lights, and he'll call me a dumb shit for something I did to annoy him. In the end, we will be better friends.

Chapter 4

Knock on Door, Charley's House Funeral Parlor Waiting

We finally get up the courage to knock on the door. Charley opens it with glazed eyes and a gray pallor. Inside, Gladys is reclining in the same orange La-Z-Boy she was in two years earlier when the Falcon was hit with buckshot at the Four Lights bordello. A dozen crumpled tissues lie on the lamp stand next to her chair.

Gladys gets up and comes to the door.

"Thanks for coming, boys," she says, giving us each a half-hug—no, more like a pat on the back. Charley does the same. Germans are known for not hugging. It's the same in my family. Half a hug on very special occasions, but not too long or tight—gotta keep some distance with those feelings.

"Come in and have a seat," Charley says. "Can I get you boys a soda pop?"

"No thanks," we say, but Charley goes into the kitchen and returns with two bottles of Dr. Pepper, giving each of us one. We sit down on the couch across from Charley and Gladys, whose recliners face a dresser-sized black and white console TV. A rabbit ear antenna sticks out of the top with a six-inch square of tin foil fixed to the end of each ear. The orange and black knitted Afghans are still hanging on the back of each chair. It's quiet for a few minutes as everyone seems to be searching for something to say.

"Damn it, I worried about Glenn running around town with the car, and now I wish he was still doing that," Charley blurts out. He is just as mad as he is sad. He doesn't know what to do with his feelings but feel guilty.

Gladys just sits there pulling tissues out of a box covered with a blue knitted-yarn cover. She piles the tissues on the table as she blots her eyes. "I can't believe he's gone. Can you boys go down to the mortuary and identify the body? It's too much for us."

"Sure," I say, preferring to remember him as he was with that grin.

"Isn't fair he got killed."

"Nothing is fair."

"Yeah," Charley says.

"Tom O'Conner is at the funeral home now. Call him and let him know you're coming. We've been waiting two weeks for the body. We aren't sure it's him."

"Okay, we'll go down."

Jim and I head down to O'Conner's Mortuary on Central Avenue. The body has just arrived from Vietnam. Tom greets us in the reception room, and the smell of flowers and formaldehyde permeates our nostrils. He escorts us down the hall past a series of closed doors. I wonder what or who is behind those doors. He opens the last door where a silver-gray military casket sits with the lid closed.

Mr. O'Conner lifts the lid slowly. "Let me know when you want me to close it."

Glenn's head looks like it has been glued together by flesh-colored silly putty. The right side of his head does not match his left side. It's hard to recognize his face, but the hairy arms, chest and thick eyebrows are Glenn's. After about thirty seconds, we both say, "That's enough," and Mr. O'Conner slowly closes the lid.

"Is that Glenn?" he asks.

"Yeah, that's him," I confirm, "but he hardly looks like a person."

It's evident that Glenn has gone through a huge trauma as if his spirit has been blown away, leaving only a paper shell. I'm glad his parents didn't see him like this. He looks scared, probably the way he looked most of the time during battle. Bravery is bravery, but at some point, there is an initial shock when you leave this physical world—I'm pretty sure of that.

Back at Charley's, Gladys asks, "Did you see him? Was it him?"

"Yes, it was him. We know it's him."

"Should we have the casket open for the funeral?" Charley asks.

"Let's just remember him as we knew him," I say, not wanting them to know how awful he looked.

Gladys breaks into tears, "Yes, I'm going to remember him as he was."

Charley rants, "Damn the war! A bunch of kids getting killed for nothing. We think we need to fight every Commie in the world. Now what's going to happen to Glenn's baby daughter? She won't have a dad. If the generals and hawk politicians had their sons dying in the war, it wouldn't have ever started. They don't give a shit about anyone but themselves."

"Sorry for you and Gladys," I say. "It's not fair, I agree."

We get up to leave, but Charley says, "Wait a minute," then goes down to the basement. He returns with a couple of rolled-up posters, a pocketknife and a yoyo. "Here, we cleaned out Glenn's room, but these were left in a drawer. You guys can have them."

"Thanks, it'll be nice to have something to remember him by," Jim says.

I put the knife in my pocket. It will follow me around for the next fifty years or so until it finally ends up in my desk.

Gladys sits frozen in her chair. I go over, lean down, give her a hug around the shoulder, and she grabs my elbow and hangs on.

"Bye, Mrs. Black. I'm so sorry," I say.

She just nods her head to let me know she heard me.

Charley walks us to the door and gives us a pat-on-the-back hug. "Sorry, Mr. Black," we both say almost in unison.

"Yeah, boys, thanks for coming over and going down to O'Connor's. It means a lot to have you help us out. You're good boys."

We say goodbye and cruise Central Avenue for an hour. The radio waves from fifty-thousand-watt KOMA, a station in Oklahoma City, bounce off the atmosphere to Great Falls some 1,400 miles away and blast out "I Can't Get No Satisfaction" and "You've Lost that Lovin' Feeling" as our emotions move between anger and sadness. My '53 Olds cruises down the street, its twin chrome exhausts rumbling a sadness that matches our hearts.

"So, what are we going to do?" Jim asks. "Who is going to get killed next? It's just a matter of time. We've got to get out of the draft. Fuck the draft!"

Feeling glum, we drive down to the Stein Haus. Art, the bartender, can sense our moods and clunks two longneck bottles of Hamm's Beer down on the bar and says, "It's on me."

"Thanks, was just up to see Glenn's parents."

"Musta been hard."

"Yeah, didn't know what to say."

"Nobody does, it just ain't right."

The next morning, we read a four-inch, single-column story on the front page of the *Great Falls Tribune* that states, "Falls Man Killed in Vietnam." The brief article mentions that it is not known where in Vietnam Glenn was killed, that he was a member of the 39th Infantry Division, is survived by his parents, daughter and two sisters. It mentions he was a member of the Great Falls Central football team. This will be the only mention of his death other than a small notation under the O'Conner Funeral Home's announcement of the pending burial.

"I can't believe they didn't say more about him," I tell Jim.

"Maybe we're getting too used to people dying in Vietnam," Jim suggests.

"Yeah, does it even matter anymore?"

Chapter 5

Funeral, Glenn Finally at Rest

"Seems like half the town is here," I say to Jim.

"Yeah, everybody is coming."

"Too bad you have to die to get this much attention."

The six of us are waiting to carry the casket into the church. All we can do is make small talk, but nobody knows what to say.

It's 9:30 on Saturday morning at Holy Family Catholic Church on Central Avenue. Cars line the streets, people walk toward the church, the September sun basks, autumn knocks on winter's door, leaves turn a dozen shades of yellow and orange, insects look for a warm place to hide, squirrels stash nuts, migrant birds gather and talk about the upcoming trip south while the local birds brag of staying and make fun of the snowbirds.

The O'Conner Mortuary hearse has been parked in front of the church since nine in the morning when the pallbearers received instruction on carrying the casket. We pallbearers line up, three on each side as it rolls out the back of the hearse. We carefully lift it and carry it up the stairs. It feels heavy, like our hearts. Gunner, Fred, Greg, Jim, Sig and myself—all classmates of Glenn—wear sport coats with neckties.

In the sanctuary, we set the flag-draped casket on a chrome stand with wheels. On top of the casket, Tom O'Connor places a spray of flowers and a picture of Glenn in his sergeant's uniform. A nearby table displays memorabilia of his life—pictures spanning infancy to his most recent army photograph. The pictures show him playing sports, being with his friends, fishing and drinking beer. Some show him as an innocent child just like his daughter is now.

We wait outside in the sun for an hour while people stream into the church—Glenn's parents, friends, teachers, acquaintances at the grocery store, friends of friends and people just sad about a young father giving up his life, a life that had just begun. I stand near the confessionals and wonder who will be going to confession today. Probably not the generals, the politicians, the president, or those who didn't take a stand to keep our young men from dying in their war.

At ten o'clock, the church bells ring as the priest sprinkles holy water over the casket. He then wafts sweet-smelling smoke by swinging an incense burner on a brass chain. The ornate burner clangs against the chain as it swings. The priest blesses the casket and nods for us pallbearers to slowly push the casket-on-wheels up the aisle. Following closely behind are Mr. and Mrs. Black and other family members. They file into the front pew. We leave the casket at the foot of the altar and take our seats. The Catholic Mass takes an hour as the congregation goes through a ritual of changing positions between sitting, standing and kneeling.

Before communion, another classmate says a few words, and the priest gives a sermon and remembrance of Glenn. "Glenn was an asset to our church, community and country," the priest says. "He served bravely to protect our country." But he leaves out the part about Glenn serving to protect our country from an enemy halfway around the world, the elusive Commies.

The sermon goes on, but the priest struggles to justify Glenn's death. He knows it is impossible, but it is his job to make things seem better, so he tries to provide justification in different ways. They all fall flat like stale pancakes. In the end, he pitches eternal happiness in heaven, the standard fallback position when we can't make sense of tragedies. This might work in Glenn's favor, but what about his baby daughter, who would never know her father?

After an hour of rituals, we finally rise, silently push the casket out of the church, lug it down fourteen stairs and slide it into the hearse. Mr. O'Connor slams the door shut, and we move into the rear seats of a Cadillac limo reserved for pallbearers. The immediate family gets into an identical black limo behind us.

Our vehicle, heated by the September sun, feels like a greenhouse. The driver, Tom O'Conner, pushes buttons on the driver's door, and the six electric windows slide open with a high-pitched whine. From the seat behind Sig, I notice a small buckshot bump behind his right ear, courtesy of the bouncer's shotgun.

The hearse slowly drives off, leading a string of cars that stretches for several blocks. We wind our way south on 26th Street and cross the busy highway of 10th Avenue South, where oncoming traffic patiently waits for the entire procession to move through. We continue south for another mile to Mount Olivet Cemetery, which sits like an oasis of trees and grass on a brown autumn plain.

A pesky housefly bumps against the inside of the windshield, looking for an escape route. Occasionally the driver attempts to shoo it out the window, but it continues to bump against the glass. As we turn into the cemetery, the fly quietly falls onto the dashboard and stops buzzing. The driver picks up a packet of extra memorial leaflets and smashes the fly for good measure. I wonder if this fly is a relative of the one that died on Charlie's dashboard.

The hearse parks near a mound of dirt camouflaged with a piece of carpet that looks like fake grass. It sits under a square awning protecting a hole in the ground. Standing at attention about forty feet to the side is an honor guard, seven US Army soldiers in dress uniforms facing their commanding officer. It's a full military funeral with a Three-Volley Salute. We carry the casket to the grave and place it on two canvas straps connected to a chrome frame.

Hushed conversations waft through the waiting crowd.

"He was so young."

"Heard he left a baby daughter."

"His mother must be taking this hard."

"Damn war anyway, what we trying to prove."

"Heard he played football for Central."

"Are those pallbearers his classmates?"

"Nice day with the sun out."

"Lot of people showed up today."

It takes about ten minutes for all the cars to park and their occupants to gather around the grave. The priest opens his Bible, and there is silence except for the "chirr, chirr, chirr" of a robin. Once again, the priest says a few prayers, sprinkles holy water on the casket and delivers a few final words of comfort. Then a lone bugler plays the sad melody of "Taps"—the military song also known as "End of the Day," or in this case *end of life*—and it travels across the cemetery. The haunting sound penetrates our bones, chills our hearts and stiffens the hair on the backs of our necks.

The officer shouts a command to prepare the honor guard for the legendary Three-Volley Salute. "Ready Arms," he yells to the seven soldiers who bring their rifles across their chests. "Aim"—and they point them up at a forty-five-degree angle over the casket. "Fire," he finally shouts, and the seven rifles crack the autumn air and our hearts. Seven empty brass cartridges eject from the rifles, spin into the air and the sunlight.

Again, the officer commands, "Ready, Aim, Fire," and the seven rifles crack once more. Then, he gives the order for the final and third round: "Ready, Aim, Fire!" The rifles crack and launch the spent cartridges, which land on the grass. Our ears ring, our eyes flinch, our heads spin, our hearts whimper and our noses are affronted by the noise and the stench of gunpowder. Perhaps, this was reminiscent of what Glenn had experienced in those final moments of bravery, terror and sudden disorientation as he passed from this physical realm to the spiritual realm the priest was talking about.

Two additional members of the honor guard position themselves at each end of the casket. They carefully pick up the corners of the draped flag, step to the side of the casket and carefully fold the flag into fourths lengthwise and then into a triangular shape. The final fold reveals the stars on the flag. Lifting up the neatly bundled triangle, one of the soldiers slowly and deliberately walks over to Mr. and Mrs. Black, salutes them in slow motion, places the flag gently onto Mrs. Black's lap and briefly whispers condolences. Mrs. Black melts into a puddle of sorrow.

The casket is slowly lowered into the grave. Dozens of mourners pick up a handful of earth from a small mound, ceremonially drop it into the grave and then brush their hands together to remove the soil and maybe the guilt of this tragedy.

Over the next ten minutes, people filter back to their cars in small, hushed groups. We file back to the limo. Again, I sit behind Sig and stare at the buckshot behind his ear. The limo slowly creeps down the loop road narrowed by mature elms and pines along the sides. I look back and see the honor guard digging spent cartridges out of the grass and a maintenance worker walking from a storage shed with a shovel.

Chapter 6

Bless Me, Father, for I Have Sinned

That Saturday night after the funeral, I find myself at St. Ann's Cathedral waiting in line for confession. It's been two years since I've done this—figured I had never killed anyone, so why bother? I wonder if Glenn would have to go to confession for killing some nineteen-year-old Viet Cong. Is it a sin for a soldier to kill in war? Maybe if it is a "just" war, it's okay, but what if it's an unjust war? And who decides what is just and unjust?

Confession is always an interesting time. People line up to confess their sins, and the priest conveys forgiveness and a guarantee of heaven. I can't imagine God waiting for a signal from the priest that these folks have met the requirements for forgiveness. What would that sign look like—the high sign, thumbs up, thumbs down, a cutting finger across the throat, squashing a bug under the thumb? I look at the people in line and wonder what dastardly things they could have done to have brought them here.

As a kid, we had to make up sins for confession. Standard sins were things like: I disobeyed my father and mother, I fought with my brother, I picked my nose in church. These were serious enough to count but not too much to get oneself a long penance, or worse yet, get us sentenced to eternal damnation. As we got older, we started confessing more serious things: impure thoughts about the opposite sex (something we did not have to make up); and worse, touching yourself in an impure manner (a nicer way of saying masturbation). The very worst sin was touching a girl in an impure manner. This could range from snapping a girl's bra strap to actually unhooking it.

To obtain forgiveness, we had to do a voluntary self-punishment. Called a penance, this was a prescribed number of prayers ordered by the priest. Greater sins required a higher number of prayers. Disobeying your father and mother usually rang up a penance of three Hail Marys; impure thoughts might require three Lord's Prayers. Any kind of impure touching could require a rosary or two, which could take up to an hour to recite. After confession, you didn't want to kneel for that long in church because other members of the congregation might run a stopwatch on you to figure out the gravity of your confessed sins. I would always finish my penance later, chancing that if I got in a car wreck before doing it, I could be doomed to eternal damnation, which meant suffering in the flames of hell—which, by the way, are 100 times hotter than anything on earth. I had many unanswered questions, of course. What would be the penance for murder? A million Hail Marys? When soldiers kill in battle, do they have to say a penance for murder?

I decide to go to confession here at St. Ann's because I don't know any of the priests, so I could be anonymous. I don't know why I'm even here. I haven't killed anyone this week, but I'm pissed off about Glenn's death and don't know anywhere else to go. My turn to enter the booth comes. I close the door behind me and kneel facing a small window covered with a curtain. The priest behind the window slides open the privacy shutter on the window, and I can see a faint shadow of his profile behind the curtain. We can hear but not clearly see each other.

"Bless me, father, for I have sinned," I said and immediately wonder why I need another person to forgive me, especially some guy who thinks he has special powers. What should I confess? Maybe that I called Glenn an ass for getting us kicked out of the Four Lights or that I was speeding over the 35 mph limit on 10th Avenue South? It all seems irrelevant considering the tragedy of Glenn's death, so I default to my age-six routine and say, “I disobeyed my father and mother three times since my last confession.”

“Anything else?” the priest asks in disbelief.

“Nope, that’s it.”

“I absolve thee in the name of the Father, Son and Holy Ghost. Say three Hail Marys.”

The priest closes the shutter, probably wondering, “Who in the hell was that wise ass?” I wonder if he gave me thumbs up for not having any big sins, or maybe he secretly gave me a thumbs down and later will be laughing it up with the bishop at dinner over bottles of Great Falls Select beer, saying, “I can’t believe that dumb shit thought he could get away with that fake confession. He’ll burn in hell for sure.”

Leaving the confessional, I look at the people standing in line. There are older women, young kids and parents. What could they possibly have done to require their confessions? I’m tempted to say, “Anyone here commit murder? No? Just as I thought. You can all go home.” Stepping outside, I say to myself, “That’s the last time I’ll ever go to confession.”

I’ve come a long way from the time I felt a calling to be a priest. At the time, it seemed like a great idea. I could have been the guy sitting behind the curtain forgiving other people’s sins. Now I’m resenting that guy behind the curtain.

When I was a freshman at Billings Central Catholic High School, Father Henry, a priest from the Passionist’s Order, had facilitated a boy’s retreat. It was here where we talked about *boy stuff*, but unfortunately, we never got into any of the good stuff like sex, which was the biggest thing on every boy’s mind. Father Henry talked about “finding your vocation,” by which he meant recognizing one’s calling to become a priest. “Does he have a vocation?” was the term he used to mean “Does he want to be a priest?”

At that time, I had convinced myself I had a “vocation.” Perhaps many Catholic boys who have contact with priests and help with the celebration of Catholic Mass wonder what it would be like to be a priest. Priests have a lot of influence in the community and, in many ways, guide and even control the lives of their parishioners. As in every profession, there are good priests and not so good priests. Back then, I thought I could be a good priest, but tonight I'm headed in the other direction—to the Stein Haus for a cold beer.

Chapter 7

Wally's Crew

On the way from St. Ann's to the Stein Haus, I drive by Wally's neighborhood grocery store just a block from Central Catholic High School. During our final year at Central, some of the seniors known as "Wally's Crew" would sneak over to the store for lunch consisting of a cigarette, a Moon Pie and a bottle of RC Cola. Sometimes we would dump a small package of Planter's salted peanuts in the bottle of RC and swig them down with the pop. The food at the school cafeteria is okay, but nothing beats a Lucky Strike cigarette for lunch.

Tonight, the store is closed and dark, but I can still imagine the guys hanging out around the corner beyond the sight of Central and the eagle eyes of Fr. Reitz and Fr. Kabeary. If we were caught, we'd surely be assigned to detention. After school, if I were going by the principal's office, I would look through the window to see who had been caught that day doing something they weren't supposed to be doing. I rarely had detention, as I usually managed to escape being caught or weaseled my way out of it with my Eddie Haskell line of bullshit.

I remember one time when Glenn and a bunch of us senior boys were standing outside the front door during one of our lunch hours. He and Sig were arguing about which car—a '63 Chevy Corvette or a '63 Ferrari XKE—would win a race from Great Falls to Helena, a distance of ninety miles. The first twenty-six miles is to the small town of Cascade, then the road cuts across a flat plain of wheat fields and continues down a winding road for forty-six miles along the Missouri River through Wolf Creek Canyon to an open plain for the last twenty miles into Helena.

"The Ferrari might corner better through Wolf Creek," Glenn insisted, "but the Corvette would get so far ahead on the straightaway to Cascade that the Ferrari would never catch it." He then took a swig of RC Cola followed by a drag off a Lucky Strike and blew the smoke at Sig.

Sig countered, "You're so full of shit. The Ferrari would be on the Corvette's ass all the way to Cascade, and once they got into Wolf Creek, it would eat the Corvette's shorts for breakfast on those curves."

"Yeah, but the Ferrari wouldn't even be able to get its engine started because they're made of shit, and by the time it got to Cascade, the Vette would be miles ahead." Glenn flicked his cigarette into the traffic on First Avenue North. The first car missed it, but the draft created by the vehicle's passing threw the cigarette into the air, where it died in a shower of sparks.

"Only in your dreams, Glenn," Sig answered.

The argument then switched to which car and engine would win in a quarter-mile drag race—a 1963 Dodge Ram Charger with a 426 cubic inch Hemi engine or a '63 Chevy with a 427 cubic inch engine. Sig stirs up Glenn by saying, "You probably think a Dodge 426 could beat a Chevy 427 in a quarter mile."

"Yeah, easy."

"See, you're full of shit on that one too. The 427 would clean up—it's got more torque and horsepower."

"You're the one who's full of shit! Chevys can't beat anything."

With that, Glenn won this argument in his own mind.

Chapter 8

Stein Haus, a Second Home
Nothing Under the Christmas Tree

I abandon the memories of "Wally Crew" and continue to the Stein Haus, wondering if Glenn was right about the Corvette—and was he right about going to Vietnam and getting killed? And I wonder if *I'm* right by dodging the draft. Like so many young men, Glenn was drafted to support the Vietnam War. The US would soon have half a million troops in Vietnam and required a continuous supply of draftees to replace the wounded and killed. Because Glenn had gotten divorced, he had become eligible for the draft.

Did he do the right thing, going to Nam? I always wanted to do what was right. Was it right to join the army? Was it right to dodge the draft? Was it right to just be passive? Most of my life, I tried to do the right things—please my parents, please my teachers, please my friends.

At the end of my freshman year at Billings Central, with the help of Fr. Henry, I convinced myself I should become a priest. So at age fifteen, I left my parents' home in Billings and traveled 1,500 miles by train to the Passionist's Seminary in Warrenton, Missouri, which was dedicated to preparing young boys for the priesthood—the furthest thing from our real interest, girls.

I stayed there for my sophomore and junior years of high school. At the end of my second year, I leave the seminary and finish my senior year at Great Falls Central. My parents had moved to Great Falls while I was a junior. At Great Falls Central, I encouraged the belief among the nuns and priests that I might still have a future as a priest, thinking that such a delusion might help me get through school.

There were several reasons I thought it might be good to become a priest: to please my mom; to gain some prestige and self-esteem; to attract attention from the priests and nuns; just plain old-fashioned guilt; and, of course, to get a new Oldsmobile. Most of the priests in Billings drove new Oldsmobiles, courtesy of the Don Ryan Oldsmobile dealer. Maybe the real reason, though, was so I could hear confessions of other people and give the thumbs up or down.

If somebody in our family of four boys needed to be a priest, why not me? I had spent most of my life covering up my insecurity by looking good on the surface. It was a tough job—never making a mistake, being the model child and not causing any problems for the family. It was difficult and exhausting to always look good. I felt that if I caused problems, our family would fall apart.

My parents dearly loved each other but struggled with their own issues. Both came from families who had rejected them. My dad, who came from a family of ten, was kicked out of the house at the tender age of fourteen—not because of any wrongdoing but just to make room in the nest. My mother had struggled to maintain her identity in her birth family and was abused by a very controlling brother and an alcoholic father. My parents escaped their families and sought refuge in their marriage. But they brought the trauma of their childhoods into that marriage and passed it down to their four sons.

My brothers didn't seem to be interested in becoming priests. Each of them found unique roles in keeping the family together. My oldest brother, Gene, was the hellraiser and rebel. He liked to look good and was obsessed with his hair and clothes being perfect. He slept with his head hanging over the edge of the bed so his hair wouldn't get messed up. Gene worked at an early age and helped my parents with family expenses, but he made up for it by borrowing money from our parents until they died.

It was common in those days for kids to work. Lots of poor families produced child worker bees to support the family. With his rebel behavior, Gene distracted my parents from the family's dysfunction and their own marital struggles. I remember him often coming home drunk and getting into arguments with Mom and Dad. He never admitted his problems and lived his life in denial. When I tried to talk with him about family issues, he'd look at me like I was from another planet. Though he was successful in business, he squandered his money until finally, when he was in his seventies, he and his wife were homeless. They lived with my wife and me for a year, and while it was good getting to know him better, it was hard to watch him get drunk most days.

Gene was older than me by eight years and left home when I was just ten, so we had little contact after that. In his eighties, he found himself without friends and living with a wife who had Alzheimer's and three unmarried alcoholic sons. Our relationship eventually deteriorated when he moved to Nevada.

My next oldest brother, Arne, was the clown and the optimist. He kept everyone laughing and feeling upbeat, and this also distracted my parents from their struggles. But Arne also grappled with insecurities and a lack of self-confidence. He worked very hard at looking happy. Like Gene, he started working at an early age and gave most of his money to the family, but unlike Gene, he was happy to contribute.

I remember that after Arne had children, he'd often stop at St. Ann's Cathedral on his lunch hour and kneel before the altar, obviously trying to find the strength to get through the day. Later in life, he became emotionally stronger, always working to think positively. He was once given a nice car—"an answer to prayer," he told me—and when it was destroyed by a drunk driver with no insurance, he said, "I'm sure this is part of the Lord's plan to make me stronger." He enjoyed many years in service to his fellow humans, volunteering at church, visiting prisoners in the county jail and praying with them to make it through struggles. He tried hard not to gossip or judge others. In this way, I believe he was a true Christian who lived the life rather than just talking about it.

My younger brother Steve was a sick child. His heart problems and rheumatic fever diverted Mother's attention away from her own struggles with depression and her strained marriage. She coddled Steve physically and emotionally, which hurt him more than helped him. Later in life, he had difficulties holding down a job and paying his debts, eventually filing for bankruptcy. He believed that he was somehow above the law, or at least deserved to be.

Steve's fundamental brand of Christianity seemed to strengthen his sense of self-righteous indignation. Unlike Arne, he became a Christian of many words but no visible actions. When he wrecked my '53 Olds while I was in basic training for the Air Force, my mother continued to coddle him by urging me to quietly write off the car and not cause him the emotional stress of taking responsibility for the loss. Many years later, when Steve and I spoke about the incident, he still could not admit fault or offer an apology. He went into narcissistic rages in which he blamed his wives entirely for the failure of their marriages. When we disagreed on even the smallest of issues, he'd send me long messages ranting about how he was right and victimized by my stupidity. I finally blocked his emails and phone calls. Eventually, I came to understand how my own co-dependency had prevented me from speaking my mind to him.

By helping my brothers financially and emotionally, my mother set them up to be dependent. They borrowed money from her until she passed on, all the while breaking promises of making things right. My parents were extremely frugal, saving every penny and often going without things we would've loved to have. She would frequently ask me to pray for my brothers or help them financially. I wondered if she ever asked my brothers to pray for me. I finally resigned from the role as model child and caregiver—I was fifty-five. At last, I was able to tell her that my siblings were adults and could take care of themselves.

My mother managed the family finances and made most major decisions. She wrote the checks, paid the bills and kept the family cash in her purse. My Dad just went along with her to keep the peace. Mom complained that Dad had difficulty making decisions, but when he tried to assert himself, she'd resist. In general, I suppose we were the typical American family, somewhat dysfunctional but managing to survive and have some happy times.

We all contributed to the family finances, but in the early years, my older brothers contributed more because of their ages and higher income. In grade school, I worked as a field hand hoeing weeds between rows of beans for fifteen dollars for a week comprised of six ten-hour days. At the end of each month, the farmer would pay my parents for my labor, and they would give me a small allowance, usually a dollar for spending money. Later, I had a paper route, and the bulk of my earnings went to the family. In my adult years, I helped my parents financially so they could continue giving money to my brothers. I resented this for years, but I finally came to peace with it by understanding they were just doing what they thought was best.

Despite my mother's struggles with depression, she had an acute intuition. A good example occurred in mid-August 1959 when our family had been driving most of the day, and we were anxious to get to Rock Creek Campground near Hebgen Lake in Montana.

"We're almost there," Dad reassured us.

It was early evening when our '53 Pontiac finally pulled into the campground. I was fifteen, and my brother Steve was ten. We jumped out of the car and began exploring. The campground was almost full, so we were anxious to find a spot.

"Here's a good place to camp," I shouted. "It's by the creek and in the shade."

"Yeah, looks like a good spot," Dad agreed.

"I don't know," Mom said. "I don't think it's a good spot. We should find another place for the night."

"There are more camp spots along the creek," I said.

"No, I think we should find another *campground*," Mom explained.

I protested. "But we like this one."

Dad offered his support for staying. "Yeah, it's late, and we're getting hungry."

"We can have a snack and look for another place," Mom said, consoling us.

"But we really like this one," my brother pleaded.

Mom's face grew serious. "No, we need to go. You boys get in the car."

"Really, it's too late," Dad said. I could tell his resistance was fading.

Mom insisted, "No, we have to go now, Frank. If you don't drive, I will."

We reluctantly piled in the car with my dad behind the wheel and headed down the road. After driving for a while, Mom said, "We can stay at Bill and Lois's tonight. We can get there before dark."

"Why can't we camp out?" we all asked, almost in unison.

Mom was staring out the window. "I don't know. It's just better this way. You can camp in their backyard."

"That's not camping," I complained, hoping the disappointment in my voice might influence her.

She shook her head. "You'll just have to make the best of it."

A couple of hours later, we arrived at Bill and Lois's. They give us a warm welcome, and Lois dished up some leftover chicken while Bill helped us put our blankets in the backyard for our make-believe camping.

Mom and dad allow us to stay up late. Steve and I were lying there looking for shooting stars when suddenly we were bounced a few inches off the grass as if a giant had just shaken the backyard. The house door slammed open and shut a half a dozen times.

Dad ran out of the house. "You boys okay? It's an earthquake."

"Yeah, the ground bounced us in the air."

"Just stay where you are, we'll be okay."

Mom, Bill and Lois all raced out of the house in their pajamas. As they stood in the backyard, an aftershock almost knocked them off their feet. The shocks continued for a few hours. At about six the next morning, Mom and Dad came out of the house.

"Wake up, boys, and come into the house," they said with some urgency.

In the kitchen, we found Bill and Lois listening to a radio newscaster who said, "Last night at 11:37, an earthquake with a magnitude of 7.3 hit the Hebgen Lake area, causing a massive avalanche of rock, soil and trees and completely burying Rock Creek Campground. It is believed all those in the campground have been buried alive. At this time, officials estimate about thirty people have perished. The avalanche completely filled the Madison River Canyon and has damned the river, causing rapidly rising waters to threaten homes in the area. The Army Corps of Engineers has warned people to stay away from the area because the dam created by the landslide may break at any moment and flood the valley below. People are being evacuated at this very moment."

The kitchen was quiet. Mom was sitting at the table with a blank stare. "St. Christopher must have been with us last night," she finally said. "I knew something wasn't right."

Later we learned that twenty-eight people had perished. Nineteen were still buried under ninety million tons of rock. The massive landslide had blocked the Madison River and created a new lake now aptly named "Quake Lake."

Today, whenever I stand near the visitor center at Quake Lake and look down on Rock Creek Campground, now covered by several hundred feet of rock, I think of the nineteen people buried there. I think of my mom and St. Christopher and have gratitude for my mother's intuition and fortitude.

Chapter 9

Still Nothing Under the Christmas tree

There were good memories of childhood, too, like cutting a fresh Christmas tree each year from the pine-covered hills near town. One of those occasions has stuck vividly in my mind where I live it almost in real-time.

"Wear your snow pants and buckle up your boots, the snow is deep," Dad tells me as we prepared to hike into the juniper and pine-dotted hills on the outskirts of town. Soon, my wool pants were pulled on, suspenders fastened, then my boots, pant legs tucked in, five buckles snapped, flaps on hat tied around my chin, coat buttoned to the top, mittens on, ready to go.

When I was nine, I saved up a few nickels and dimes from helping my brother Arne deliver papers in our small town of Bridger, Montana. I was born in St. Vincent's Hospital in Billings, forty-six miles from Bridger, but spent my early childhood in this small community buried in the middle of remote Montana.

It was Christmas, so my Dad, my brother Arne and I slog through deep snow a mile into the sandstone cliffs and hills outside town to cut a Christmas tree. Here, juniper trees cling with root fingernails to sandstone boulders in a perpetual battle with the winds that roar through the valley. I wonder, "How do those junipers grow in rock? Are they cold?"

"Follow in my tracks," Dad says as he breaks through the deep snow. I trudge along, breathing heavily and snow rolling up to my waist at times.

We look at several trees and find one about ten feet tall, just able to fit in our living room. Dad saws away for a while, then stops and says, "Here, you can saw for a while." I don't realize it, but he has saved the last few saws for me. Quickly, the tree flumps on its side, blowing a snow cloud into the air and covering us with ice crystals. We cheer. No one seemed to notice that we look like snowmen.

"Good job," Dad says, "tie the rope on it." We walk single file with the rope strung over our right shoulders, leaving a trail of footprints and scattered pine needles. The tree is right behind me, and I feel like I'm pulling it by myself.

At home, dad made a tree stand from two-by-fours nailed in an X and then fastened to the bottom of the tree, which he finally stands in the corner of our tiny living room.

"Smell the fresh pine!" he says with a satisfied grin.

We string popcorn on a long cotton thread with my mother's sewing needle. "Here, thread the needle, make it wet in your mouth," Mom says. But before she can finish, I have it threaded.

She smiles. "Guess I didn't have to tell how to do it." I've watched her thread dozens of needles as she darned socks, patched pants and made old clothing good for another season.

With the tree up, we cut folded paper, then, when unfolded, reveals intricate snowflakes. We color them with Crayons and hang them on the tree. Next, we unpack glass Christmas ornaments that are wrapped in old newsprint and carefully hang them too. A string of "bubble lights" that look like candles is clipped to the branches with bobby pins. The bubble lights are sealed glass candles filled with colored alcohol with a small light at the base. When the lights become warm from the bulb at the bottom of the "candle," the alcohol starts to boil, sending air bubbles streaming up the glass tube. We fasten a few real candles to the branches with the intention of lighting them on fire for a few minutes on Christmas Eve without burning down the house. Standing precariously on a chair, Dad tops the tree with a silver star. Finally, we drape the tree in tinsel, shiny strands of lead foil that would later be banned as a health hazard. The manger scene with the baby Jesus is set up under the tree, and I move the animals and figurines playfully around, making sure baby Jesus is comfortable.

From my meager savings delivering newspapers, I had bought presents for everyone in the family. The gift I remember the most was a big purple bottle of perfume for my mother that I bought at the local Rexall Drug Store for twenty cents. I can't imagine how it smelled or if she ever used it, but it was perfume.

Finally, Christmas Eve comes, and it's time to open presents. "Here, Mom, I got this for you," I say, handing her the wrapped perfume bottle.

"Thanks, it smells good," she says, dabbing some behind her ears.

"And this is for you, Dad." I gave him a used Prince Albert tobacco can I had found and filled with wooden matches. "You can light a fire if you get cold." Dad's job was repairing railroad tracks in the dead of winter.

I finish handing out crudely wrapped presents for my three brothers and wait for my present, thinking maybe it is hidden behind the tree. To my dismay, there isn't a single present for me. I'm hurt, but I didn't say a word, quickly rationalizing the situation—my mother is sick, my younger brother is also sick as usual, my Dad is busy working and we are poor.

I sit and watch everyone else open their presents and keep telling myself it is okay that I didn't get a gift. I don't want to complain and cause more problems for the family. Even at that young age, I believe it is my job to help people. Maybe that's why I wanted to become a priest later in life.

* * *

I successfully repress this Christmas memory, but thirty years later, I find myself driving to a therapist appointment and wondering why I had scheduled it. I know something is wrong, but I don't know what. I'm trying hard to understand why I am so unhappy and angry, and then that Christmas scene from 1953 flashes into my mind.

I park behind the therapist's office, hoping no one will see me. After all, I am now a counselor myself, so it would be unseemly to let anyone know I might have my own issues. I slide through the back door, and Marian, my therapist, is surprised to see me sneaking in that way. Marian is a colleague, but we were not close friends. Today is a professional visit.

"Well, Dan, why are you here to see me today?" she asks.

"The only thing I can think of is something that came to mind when I was driving here. I don't think it's a big deal, but that's all I can think of." I don't know how to explain my feelings. All I knew is that something is not right in my life.

"So, what's this memory?"

"Well, when I was nine years old at Christmas, we had hard times. My family was poor, and my youngest brother was sick. I had saved a few cents, and I remember buying all my family small presents. Some just cost a nickel or so. I bought my mother a bottle of perfume for twenty cents. When we opened presents on Christmas Eve, everyone got a present except me. But that was okay, I knew, because we were having a really tough time."

Marian looks at me. In a kind voice, she says, "If that had happened to me, I would have been devastated."

I immediately grow frustrated at her response and repeat, "You don't understand, things were tough—my mom was sick, my dad was working hard, we were poor, and it was okay that I didn't get a present."

Marian quietly repeats, "Nevertheless, if that had happened to me, I would have been devastated."

I become even more upset with her. "You're not listening! Things were tough, my mom was sick, my dad was working, we were poor. That's why I didn't get a present."

For the third time, she gently says, "If it were me, I would have been devastated."

I leave in a huff, convinced that Marian is a lousy therapist who wasn't listening to me. It is three in the afternoon, so I skip work and go home. At five-thirty, my wife Joyce arrives home from work and discovers me on the bathroom floor weeping—the kind of deep, aching cry that tears one's heart in two.

"What's wrong?" she asks.

Between uncontrolled sobs, I mutter, "I didn't get a Christmas present."

It seems that finally, at age forty, I am beginning to tear down my veneer of always looking good. I am beginning, I think, to become human—someone who doesn't have to know everything, someone who can feel things and not have to cover it up. Someone who can make mistakes, who can begin healing his heart. It has been twenty years since I was stumbling through life in Great Falls burdened by the military draft, work, religion—and still wondering who I was. But on this day, weeping on my bathroom floor, I am starting to learn how to live rather than stumble.

Chapter 10

Back Home to the Stein Haus Pizza That Makes You Drip

The drive from Wally's to the Stein Haus is only ten minutes, but many memories of my childhood in Bridger and my encounter with Marian, my therapist, are flooding through my head. I pull into the parking lot of the Stein Haus, where I know almost all the patrons.

The Stein Haus, modeled after a German beer parlor, welcomes patrons with a wooden sign hanging over the door with the words "Stein Haus" and a large beer mug carved into it. The bartender, Art, is a fatherly figure to many of the guys who live at the Stein Haus between their jobs and college studies. College kids, businessmen, blue-collar workers, retired folks and a few guys from the Air Force Base (or Jet Butts, as we call them) make the Stein an eclectic hangout. About one-quarter of the patrons are local women. It's a safe place for females to have a beer. Art doesn't tolerate bad language or making an idiot of oneself. If you do these things, you'll find yourself thrown out and barred from coming back. Beer is cheap at thirty cents for a sixteen-ounce glass or twelve-ounce bottle. A pitcher is just a buck. No hard drinks or fancy wine here, just cold beer.

Food is simple at the Stein Haus—a thick, dripping pastrami sandwich on a fresh, steamed rye bun for a dollar is dinner for many. Art offers two other snacks—fresh-popped corn served in an almost-red-hot wok and still popping for twenty-five cents, or a brown bag of roasted peanuts in the shell for fifteen cents. And then there is the pizza—pizza from heaven. Pizza that should require one to go to confession for being so decadent. It comes from Howard's Pizza next door and slides through a small window behind the bar. The Stein Haus Special is a monster pizza covered with cheese, green peppers and spicy, greasy Italian sausage. To eat a Stein Haus Special properly, one must pick up an overloaded slice by the crust and fold it lengthwise to keep it from hanging down and dumping the grease-enriched topping back on the platter. Then enjoy the grease as it runs down your throat and down your arms and drips off your elbows.

The Stein Haus, long and narrow with a bar down the right side, is home to many regulars. They sit slouched over the bar with beer bellies hanging over their low-hung jeans. There are three categories of bellies—the belly where the owner can still see his own belt buckle, the sow belly when the person can't see his own belt buckle but others can, and the slop belly where other people cannot see the belt buckle. The slop belly is the ultimate accomplishment.

Walking down the bar, one can almost recognize the regulars from the rear by the ass cleavage revealed by blue jeans sagging in the rear. For me, this is a disgusting way to recognize the regulars, of which Kid Shelleen, the Little Professor, Mo, Willy, Gooch, Babe, Ricky and Jay are a few. Several tables line the left side of the bar and circle around the fireplace in the back. Usually, women or guys with dates sit at the tables.

Tonight, I step through the door to the rapid-fire sound of popcorn exploding against the lid of a hot wok. The smell of popcorn and hot pastrami comforts me like a mother cradling a baby. I saunter down the long bar, diverting my eyes and trying not to recognize anyone from what's sticking out the back of the bar stools.

"Hey Kid, Willy," I nod as I go by. We know each other well and don't need to say much in greeting.

"Jay, what about the Packers, they gonna win?"

"Should, especially if it's cold at Green Bay."

"Yeah, they love that cold shit."

In the back, a round fireplace in the center of the room sucks out smoke from burning logs and cigarettes. Nine patrons sitting around the fireplace drink beer and throw spent peanut shells into the round hearth. As I walk to the men's room, shells crunch beneath my low-cut black Converse All Star tennis shoes. In the restroom, I wait my turn at the urinal behind a guy wearing the same skintight jeans pegged at the legs six inches above his low-cut black Converse All Star tennis shoes. He leans heavily against the wall over the urinal, steadying himself against the wobbles from too much beer and trying not to pee on his shoes. I read the graffiti on the walls—crude jokes, a bad sketch of a naked lady and phone numbers. "Call Susie for a good time" was probably scrawled by a guy dumped by his girlfriend and trying to get revenge.

I crunch through the shells on my way to the end of the bar. Art pours three beers at a time from taps that offer Great Falls Select, Hamm's, Olympia, Rainier, Lucky Lager, Budweiser and Miller High Life. In his late forties, Art has wavy black hair parted in the middle and wears a starched white shirt with the sleeves rolled up one fold. He moves around behind the bar with the agility of a boxer. There is a rumor he won several championship bouts in his youth. Art likes his patrons and watches out for them. He particularly likes college kids and, on occasion, sends us home to study if he knows we have a test the next day. "Get your asses out of here and go home and study or you'll end up being a bartender like me," he admonishes us. On holidays, he cooks up a free turkey dinner for college kids and others who don't have any place to go.

I tried to get served alcohol here when I was eighteen and had two phony ID cards showing I was twenty-one. One was a green Circle K Construction ID card hand-drawn and typed on a typewriter. The other was a Montana driver's license with a number 1 cut out of the white pages of a phone book and hand pasted-over the 4 in the last digit of my birth year, 1944. When I laid them on the bar, Art took a quick look and asked, "How old are you, son?"

"Well, err, ah…" I could never lie for some reason, "I'm eighteen." Actually, with my baby face and peach fuzz, I looked like I was twelve. Eventually, my baby face will pay off when I'm in my sixties, and some of my friends are wrinkled and bald.

"Okay, son, here's how it works," Art said. "You get served today, but when the cops are making the rounds, there's no beer. And don't be bringing any underage girls in here. No monkey business. Got it?"

"Err, yes, sir."

"So, what are you drinking?"

I looked down the bar and saw two guys drinking Hamm's Beer, so I said, "Gimme a bottle of Hamm's," and dropped a silver dollar on the bar.

Art grabbed a cold bottle of Hamm's by its narrow neck and clunked it on the bar in front of me, picked up the dollar and flopped seventy cents change back at me in one smooth move. Because Montana is a silver producing state, silver dollars were the main Montana tender in the 60s with few paper dollars available. Everyone always had a half dozen silver dollars sagging down their pockets.

I took a drink out of the bottle and celebrated quietly in my heart: *Yes, now I can join my buddies at the Steiner.* They are all sitting at the other end of the bar waiting to see if I get served, not wanting me to ruin a good thing for them. Now I can join them. Most of us are under twenty-one.

* * *

Today, like three years ago, Art clunks a bottle of Hamm's on the bar at the same time I sit down on the stool.

"Glenn got killed," I tell Art.

"Yeah, I heard."

"You in the service?"

"The Big One."

"Was it worth it?"

"Depends on the war. Not many of them are good ones. The Big One was good in the sense that we won," Art replies. "Everybody has to decide for themselves. I served because we were under attack, but nowadays, we just seem to think we are under attack. This Vietnam thing could be a big mistake," He shakes his head.

I plunk a fifty-cent piece on the bar for the beer, take a sip and drop the two dimes change into the Red Ball Machine, a crude gambling device that has five tennis balls bouncing around in the bottom. There are five rows of five holes each. The object is to have the balls line up purely by luck. At the drop of a dime, all five balls bounce up in the air, looking for a place to land. I hope to hit the four corners and win ten bucks but instead end up losing all twenty cents. No luck today. I sit back down at the bar.

"No luck? So whatcha gonna do, kid?" Art asks.

"I dunno, got to come up with a plan."

"A plan for what?"

"A plan for life."

"Might not be a bad idea."

I think, *Where is my life going? I've got a job and a few credits at the College of Great Falls but no real plan.* I figure I need to get a college education. I'd be the first one in my family. My dad worked hard labor all his life, first as a farm laborer and then as a janitor for the public schools and now as a janitor for the College of Great Falls. He was taken out of school at fourteen and from that time was on his own.

My mom worked the farm fields, too, and then was a seamstress in our home. The small table in our trailer house was always covered with clothes and her portable sewing machine. She was an accomplished seamstress who could transform old double-breasted suits into stylish single-breasted suits.

I learned to work hard from my parents but always felt ashamed to live in a trailer house. My mother tried to make it sound better by calling it a mobile home. Thirty-five feet long and eight feet wide, with

280 square feet, it was cozy, to say the least. My brother and I shared a bedroom just two feet larger than the bed. It had a small closet and a shelf where we displayed a couple of model cars, a coral and maroon '57 Dodge and a turquoise '57 Chevy. We were poor, but that fact mostly escaped me until I became older and could look back on wearing patched clothes and cardboard in our worn-out shoes, thinking that was normal.

As a kid, poverty is blind—it's a time when life is fun, when you can do anything and everything and are afraid of nothing. Flying is a real possibility. Years later, I remember poverty being hard on my parents, who wanted to give us more but didn't know how to do it. College for their kids was beyond imagination, so there was no talk or encouragement to go to college. So now I'm in college, taking a few credits, working at Buttreys grocery store as a carryout boy, drinking beer at the Stein Haus and wondering what to do about the draft board breathing down my neck.

And now, Glenn is gone—gone like that fly on Charley's dashboard. So here I am, barely twenty-one and trying to avoid the draft and without any real plan for my life.

Suddenly, I have a plan.

Chapter 11

Pawn to Bishop, Checkmate

"Hi, I'm Dan Geiger, I came to see the bishop," I say.

"I'll tell him you're here," the secretary at the office of the Catholic Diocese of Great Falls says. She looks like a nun without the habit—hair in a bun, black plastic glasses, grey dress below the knees, flat shoes and all business. I wonder if she has ever had a boyfriend.

It's been a week since I was sitting in the Stein Haus wondering what to do, and now I have a plan. The bishop is my ticket out. I'm wearing a navy-blue blazer with brass buttons, a Gant blue oxford shirt with a narrow black necktie, brown khaki slacks and penny loafers with a copper penny in the slit. My hair is trimmed above my ears, and I'm on my best Eddie Haskell behavior. The Bishop knows my parents, who are devout Catholics, and I'm hoping to ride out of Dodge and the draft on their reputation. I just have to make a favorable impression.

"Okay, you can go in now," the secretary says. She is not wearing perfume, or if she is, it is Office of Olay.

She leads me into a stately office filled with heavily carved and upholstered wood furniture. A large framed photograph of Pope Paul VI on the wall behind the bishop seems to be looking over the cleric's shoulder, almost like God keeping an eye on things.

"What can I do for you today, son?" the bishop asks from across a massive desk. He wears a black cassock with small red buttons and narrow red trim around the collar. A silver crucifix hangs on a silver chain. His grey hair is combed back, and he wears wire spectacles.

I sit about six inches below him on an upholstered chair, gather my thoughts and say, “I’ve been doing a lot of praying lately and feel that I have a vocation to be a priest.” Having a “vocation” is church lingo the bishop can identify with. It means you have a “spiritual calling” to be a priest.

“And what makes you think you have a vocation?”

I take a deep breath and rattle off what sounds like one sentence. “Well, I went to the Passionist’s Seminary in Missouri my sophomore and junior year of high school but then came home my senior year to think things over. I think I was too young in high school to know if that’s what I really wanted, but since I’ve had some time to think it over, I feel I’m ready now. I keep seeing myself helping people to find the true way, maybe even going on a mission to work with poor people.” I end the monologue when I run out of breath.

“It sounds like you have been doing some soul searching.”

“Yes, I thought about it a lot. I’m trying to make a plan for my life.”

“It takes time to understand a calling to be a priest. I remember having to go through the same thing.”

I had assumed that all priests or bishops didn’t have any doubts about their vocation. “I’m thinking it’s time to make a decision,” I say.

Our conversation continues for about a half-hour, and I seem to be saying all the right things. He listens to every word I say and seems convinced I could be the next St. Daniel or whatever.

When it is his turn to speak, he says, “I can send you out to the Benediction Seminary in Richardton, North Dakota, for your first year.”

The word North Dakota sends me into shock. North Dakota—the brunt of all my North Dakota jokes and the land of nowhere. Suddenly I’ve just been sentenced to a year in prison. I’m trying to stay focused on my long-range goal to beat the draft. Maybe God is finally fed up with me and getting revenge.

When I recover, I switch to the real reason I'm here and say, as casually as possible, "Oh, I'll need a letter for the draft board with the war going on and all."

"Come back tomorrow at three o'clock," the Bishop says, "and I'll have the letter. You're a fine young man and will be a great asset to the Diocese."

"Uhh, thank you. See you tomorrow."

As I leave, I am thinking, *Fine young man indeed. Do I really have a vocation? Probably not.* I lost my vocation some time ago when I attended the seminary in Warrenton, Missouri, during my middle years of high school. At the end of my junior year, visions of girls danced in my head. The pull was too strong then, and I forgot about my vocation. I wondered what happened to a vocation when it got lost. Does someone *find* my vocation blowing down the street on a windy day and pick it up, or does it end up falling behind someone's refrigerator and getting covered with lint to be discovered years later? Will I find it again, or do I even want to find it?

As I drive off, a North Dakota joke shoots through my head.

Question: What's the most popular pick-up line in North Dakota?

Answer: Nice tooth.

The next day, at three o'clock sharp, I'm at the bishop's office to get my letter stating that I am a certified seminarian and exempt from the draft. The bishop comes out of his office and hands me the letter.

"Good luck, my son. See you at Christmas."

"Okay, see you then."

I jump in my '53 Olds and speed down to the Draft Board office. Lars Tollefsrud, head of the Draft Board, sits behind a desk looking like Scrooge before enlightenment. A retired Norwegian bachelor farmer, his sun-reddened face contrasts with a white forehead where his hat has protected it from the sun for seventy years. His hair is shaped like the billed hat that hangs on a hook by the door.

Tollefsrud, a pro-war Lutheran farmer, is not happy to see the letter. He reads it twice and seems perturbed that I'm requesting a deferment, but even worse that I'm going to be a Catholic priest. In his view, the Lutheran Church is the one true church and, of course, I know for a fact the Catholic Church is the one true church—or so I've been assured by priests and nuns ever since I was a small child. Basically, everyone was going to hell except the Catholics. Even as a child, it never made sense to me that God would condemn almost everyone because they weren't Catholic. Furthermore, if each church thought it is the one true church and each was correct, then everyone else was going to hell but that one church.

And what about those folks who are not Christian—they certainly are going to hell, right? Jews, Hindus, Buddhists, Muslims—none of them have a snowball's chance in hell. This thinking never made sense to me as a child and makes less sense now. If God is all-just, then he would be just for all. If only a few selected souls are included in God's justice, then God would be kinda-just, or semi-just, or 76 percent-just, but definitely not all-just.

On this day, however, I accepted the traditional Catholic belief that Lutherans are going to hell, and since Lars is Lutheran, it is comforting to know he's one of those going to that hot place.

"So ya goin' to the Catholic college?" Lars says, scrutinizing my letter from the bishop.

"Yes, sir. I'm going to be a priest."

"Well, we'll see about this."

Lars painfully searches for my file through one of the numerous four-drawer filing cabinets lining one wall of his office. Each drawer is labeled with pieces of paper cut into two-inch by two-inch squares tucked into a holder marked with a leaky-ink pen with part of the alphabet. He pulls out a squeaky drawer marked "G-Gr," removes a manila folder and shuffles back to his desk. He sits down, adjusts his glasses, takes them off and polishes them on his shirttail, tucks his shirt back in his pants and reluctantly opens my file.

I try not to squirm for twenty minutes, which seem like six hours. He slowly scrutinizes my file with a furrowed brow, turning each page like it is glued to the next page. He then shuffles to a bookcase with stacks of forms on top, picks up two copies of a form and returns to his desk, where he removes a piece of carbon paper from a desk drawer. He sandwiches the carbon paper between the two forms, taps them on his desk to make sure the edges are even and slowly threads them through a green Underwood manual typewriter one agonizing click at a time.

Then he lines up the first box on the form and types achingly slow, with one finger. After filling in seven or eight boxes, he removes the forms and erases a mistake on the original and carbon copy with a large brown eraser that seems to rub a hole in the paper. He then taps the forms and carbon paper on the desk again, excruciatingly feeds them back into the typewriter and begins methodically to type again. Carefully reading down each row of keys, he finds the proper key, puts his finger on it, looks back up at the form and pushes the key down.

I can't possibly imagine how he could make a mistake with this typing method, but he does. Incredibly, he goes through the same correction process four times until crumbs of eraser rubbings litter his desk like mouse turds. Soon, the forms look like they have been attacked by moths.

After the forms are finally completed, he signs each one and leisurely searches through a tattered cardboard box on his desk for an ink stamp, taking time to read each one backward by looking at the red rubber rather than the stamp's name printed on the handle. He slams the stamp on an ink pad and then onto the forms, imprinting "2D-ministerial deferment" across the page, then signs the stamped document and gives me the copy.

He stamps "2D-ministerial" on a new draft card, signs it and hands it back to me. During the process, he has looked up at me three times with frustration and disgust. I worry that he knows my deceptive plan to avoid the draft.

"Here ya go," he says, handing me the new draft card.

"Thank you, sir."

I waltz out of the office and head directly for the Stein Haus, skipping confession at St. Ann's Parish. What would I say there, "Bless me Father for I have sinned, I duped the bishop and made fun of Lars?"

I waltz into the Stein Haus and lay my draft card on the bar like it was an ace of spades. I say to Art, "Read 'em and weep, I'm 2D."

"Yeah, 2D, too dumb?" he says, laughing. "Congratulations. You're now a priest. This one's on me." He clunks down a bottle of Hamm's for me. It's four o'clock, and I begin a ten-hour celebration at the Stein Haus with my friends. They all filter in except for those who are MIA, Glenn and the others who are in Vietnam.

At two the next morning, the Stein Haus is closing. I pour myself into my car and take 1st Avenue South home. Three blocks later, at the corner of 1st Avenue and 5th Street, a red blinking light on a cop car jars me out of my ten-beer daze. I pull over.

"Driver's license."

"Yes, officer. Here," I try to look sober.

"How fast were you going?"

"Uh, between 25 and 30."

"I clocked you at 32. What's the speed limit?"

"Err, 25."

"What's the hurry?"

"No hurry, just distracted thinking about my buddy that was killed in Nam. Had a few beers with my buddies at the Stein Haus, kind of a wake for our buddy."

"Who's your buddy?"

"Glenn Black."

"Yeah, heard about him. Take it easy and go home. If I see you driving around again tonight, I'll give you a ticket."

"Yes, officer, thanks."

"Get home."

I am thinking, *Boy, that was close!* Drinking and driving were pretty much accepted in the 60s. Even the cops partied and drove home. If you didn't hit a tree or another car or were going 60 mph, you could usually get off if you were polite. It crossed my mind, though, that maybe I shouldn't have gotten so shit-faced that night.

I drive home and think, "Thanks, Glenn, for getting me out of that one."

I wonder about Glenn and my other buddies who went to Nam. They served the country and weren't really appreciated by the general public. Many of them fought a losing battle with the Viet Cong, the American public, and in some cases themselves. They call it a Catch-22. My older brothers volunteered before the war to get out of small-town Montana. One went to Germany and enjoyed two years of independence and drinking German beer. The other went into the Air Force and spent four uneventful years in Texas. My younger brother and I both joined the Montana Air National Guard, he for six years and me for thirteen.

Chapter 12

You Were On My Mind, Patty, Summer of '65

"So what's the deal with Laura's cousin, Patty?" I ask my buddy Mick who is working at the smelter for the summer.

"She's from Terre Haute, here visiting Laura for the summer. Seems like a nice gal, nice bod."

"Can you line me up?"

"I'll talk to Laura tonight, but you'll owe me."

"Owe you what?"

"I dunno, something. I'll just hang it over your head."

"Yeah, right. Just get me the date."

Mick is dating Laura, a big-chested gal whose cousin, Patty, is visiting for the summer. Patty isn't as big busted as her cousin, but she has a nice body.

Mick is driving a '55 Plymouth four-door sedan that looks like a tank. My '53 Olds got wrecked by my younger brother, so I'm leeching off my friends for transportation. I came home one day to find out it had been totaled when he got in a wreck with another driver. I asked my mom if we could get the car repaired. She just said there was nothing we could do and not to expect my brother to pay for it.

I was out of a car. It wasn't fair, but my mother didn't want to hold my brother responsible, so I just dropped it. He was the brother who was sick as a child, and Mom would continue to enable him into his adulthood. The car was a classic custom—dark metallic blue, lowered, beefed up hydromatic transmission, eight cylinders, chrome reversed rims and dual exhausts.

I never saw it again.

* * *

The next night, Mick and I pick up Laura and Patty for a double date to see *Cat Ballou* at the Twilight Drive-In Theater on the west side of Great Falls.

Patty turns out to be beautiful with short blond hair, a petite body with a nice figure—and she smells heavenly, which may be needed if my deodorant fails. I'm torn between being polite and respectful and giving in and just letting my eyes glue themselves to her breasts. Of course, in the back of my head, Catholic guilt is playing over and over like a 45-record stuck in the same groove: "Shame on you, you draft-dodging seminarian. Shame on you for having impure thoughts. Shame on you for looking at her breasts, etc., etc., etc."

I try to look her in the eyes while I stumble over my nervousness and make awkward conversation. "So, you and Laura are cousins?" *Duh*, I think to myself, *of course they are cousins.*

"Yes, my mom and Laura's mom are sisters."

"So, you from Terre Haute?" *Duh, I already knew this too.*

"Yeah, I come to Great Falls every summer to visit Laura."

After a little more conversation, I realize Patty is just as nervous as I am. Once we realize this, we both relax.

"So, Mick is your best friend?" she asks.

"Not at all. He's on the bottom of the list, but he has a car."

From the front seat, Mick says, "I heard that! Keep badmouthing me, and you'll be walking."

So, that begins the night, Mick and I giving each other a load of crap with Laura and Patty laughing at our antics. I've learned it is easier to clown oneself out of uncomfortable situations than actually deal with them.

We stop at the Stein Haus and pick up two six-packs of Big Sky Beer and a bag of fresh popcorn. The beer is a buck for a six-pack, and a big bag of popcorn is twenty-five cents.

"Got a hot date?" Art asks me.

"Yeah, we're going to the drive-in."

He slides the six-pack into a tight-fitting brown bag and then slides another one on top of it. "Behave yourself and treat them girls like ladies," he says. We wait a few minutes for a rattling wok of popcorn to finish popping, and then Art pours it into another brown paper bag. The bag is spotted with grease by the time we get back to the car.

At the drive-in, Mick and Laura are cuddled up in the front seat, but I notice Mick has the rearview mirror focused on me and Patty. Telling him to move the mirror would be too obvious, but I'll get even with him later. Maybe this will be the favor he thinks I owe him.

I put my arm around Patty, and she snuggles up to me. I'm committed to keeping my arm around her for the entire two hours of the movie, even if it becomes permanently paralyzed. While Patty likes to snuggle, I can tell she is not "easy," which makes me like her more. I try not to put too many moves on during our first date, but as I feel her bra through her blouse, I think about unhooking it. We make out a little but nothing too heavy. She smells like Heaven of Olay—sugary, sweet, sensual, soft, feminine, womanly and many other things I try not to think about. She soaks into my lungs, my clothes and my being. I'm afraid if I take one more breath, I might explode.

After the movie, we cruise Central Avenue, honking and yelling at friends and making idiots of ourselves like every other person out here. At midnight, we take the girls home to Laura's house. Patty and I pause at the front gate for a goodnight kiss.

"You're a good kisser," she says.

"Yeah, um, ah—you too. Wanna go out again?"

"Yeah, I'd like that." She has a syrupy look in her eye that drowns out my Catholic guilt for a few moments.

"I'll call you tomorrow," I mumble.

"Great. Night."

"Night."

She says "night" as in "nigh, nigh lover boy," or so it seems to me.

Back in the car, Mick says, "Hey, what was going on in the back-seat?"

"You should know with the mirror on me the whole time."

"That was for your protection. I figured you needed a chaperone."

"You pull that stunt again, and I'll break off that mirror for good."

"So, did you fall in love?"

"No, but I think I fell in *like*."

"I think you fell in *lust*. You definitely need a chaperone."

"My shirt still smells like Patty, so don't touch it."

So begins the summer of '65. It's June 7, and I don't have to report to the seminary until August 28. In the meantime, it's the summer of good times. "When I Woke Up this Morning You Were on My Mind" by the We Five plays on the radio and repeatedly in my mind. I try not to fixate on Patty's bra clasp. Finally, I wash her sweet scent out of my shirt.

My buddy, Jim, also gets a deferment through the bishop, and in ten weeks, we are both heading for The Benedictine Abby in North Dakota. Jim may be more serious about his vocation, but I'm not sure.

I'm enjoying my job at Buttrey's working with some of my friends—Brick, Gunner, Ben and Larry. While we get our work done, we also goof off and play pranks on one another and the older workers like Alan and Jerry. Those two are married and in their 30s, which seems old to a twenty-year-old kid. They like us but occasionally rough us up for our wisecracks. I nickname Jerry "Cock Nose" and Alan "Pecker Neck."

A tinny "box boy on check stand eight" crackles over the store's PA system. I hurry from the canned goods aisle where I'm stocking shelves to check stand eight where Alan is checking out a shopper's groceries.

"I'm on it, Pecker Neck," I whisper to Alan so the lady customer can't hear.

"I'll get you later," Alan whispers back.

Alan isn't happy with this nickname, and he and Jerry will occasionally catch me in the stock room and give me a "Dutch rub," which consists of rubbing their knuckles on my head until my scalp is almost raw. While it hurts, it is one way we show affection. Later in life, I will realize these two co-workers were actually mentoring us young kids—keeping an eye on us and teaching us boundaries and how to work. The Retail Clerks Union guarantees us eighty cents an hour and a fifteen-minute coffee break every morning and afternoon. Most mornings, we are hungover from a stint at the Stein Haus or the Cartwheel Bar and need to jump start our day with a cup of coffee, a Bear Paw pastry and a cigarette. Brick has a York, an odd brand of cigarettes, and the rest of us enjoy a Marlboro.

Chapter 13

Wreck of the VW, Sinned Again

"That was a great show," I say as the movie *What's New Pussycat?* ends. Mick and I are doubling dating again at the Twilight Drive-In.

"Yeah—so funny," Patty says.

"Hey Mick, remember that time we raced Pete from here to the Burger Master?"

"Lucky we didn't get killed."

"Yeah, I almost won."

As we leave the drive-in, I remember last year when I raced Pete, who was driving a '63 Cadillac Deville convertible from his dad's Cadillac dealership. I was driving my parents '62 Volkswagen bug. Quite a contrast! The hood on the Cadillac was as long as the whole VW. Long fins made it look like a yacht out of water. The race was across town to the Burger Master Drive-In, a local hangout known for the Ramp Burger, Flying Saucer Pizza Burger and the Green River soft drink.

The rule of the race was to drive on alleys only, with the exception of using the bridge to cross the Missouri River on 15th Street. As we started, I cut off Pete at the exit of the drive-in theater because his Caddie couldn't get traction in the gravel parking lot. I stayed ahead of him on the way to the 15th Street bridge by weaving back and forth and not letting him pass. This continued across the bridge, but as soon as we crossed the bridge, he passed me on the right by driving on the sidewalk.

Things were going pretty well—I was able to keep up to the Caddie by running stop signs—but finally, the race ended for me when I slid into the side of a car at an intersection, smashing the front end of my parents' VW. It was still drivable, and after the police wrote me a ticket for not yielding the right-of-way, I drove home to face the music.

I slowly idled through the trailer park behind the Hi-Ho Bar and parked the car next to our mobile home. The house lights were still on. My mother was sitting at the table modifying a double-breasted suit into a single-breasted style. My dad is playing solitaire across the table from her. This being a Saturday night, my curfew wasn't until midnight.

"Hi, Mom, Dad."

"You're home early. It's only ten-thirty."

"Yeah, had a little accident with the VW."

"What?" Dad asked with alarm. "An accident? What happened?"

"Um, I hit a car on 20th Street."

"Is the car okay?"

"Not really, the front end is pushed in."

They both rush out the door for a look.

"Damn it to hell anyway," Dad said. "I can't believe it. Now we need a new bumper and hood." This was the worst swearing I'd ever heard from him. He rarely cussed.

"I'm sorry, it was an accident. I didn't see the other car."

"Did you get a ticket?"

"Yeah, the other car was to the right of the intersection, so it was my fault, I guess."

"How much was the ticket?"

"I need to go to court on Monday and pay fifteen bucks."

Mom shook her head. "Well, that's coming out of your pocket. And don't plan on driving for a while. You best get to bed now."

For the next few weeks, I was on my best behavior—doing the dishes, my homework and other chores without even being asked. After a couple of weeks, they seemed to forgive me, and I was allowed to drive the VW again, now with a new bumper and hood. I drove a little more carefully after that.

Chapter 14

Summer of Dating Patty Too Short, Almost Sinned

As the summer flies by, I take Patty down to the Stein Haus, where Art, doing his job as the bartender, asks me how old she is.

"Well, err, ah, she's not quite twenty-one." It's still difficult for me to lie to Art.

"I told you not to be bringing in those underage girls."

"But she'll be twenty-one in a month," I whisper so she can't hear me.

"Okay, you can drink here tonight as I know the cops won't be coming in, but when they're making their rounds, you can't bring her in here."

On occasion, two policemen would show up in the bar with flashlights and check IDs. Underage kids would pretend to go to the restroom and then slip out the back door. Sometimes, other cops would be waiting for them in the alley. The local bars would bribe cops for information about when they'd make their rounds. The police were known to look the other way for other offenses, too, like gambling and prostitution. Drugs were just beginning to come on the scene, with marijuana the most popular but alcohol still rules.

Mick, Laura, Patty and I spend the summer double-dating and listening to the We Five sing "When I Woke Up this Morning You Were on my Mind and making out. The end of July finally comes, and Patty returns home to college in Terre Haute.

Our first call goes like this: "Hey Patty, how you doing?"

"Good, getting ready to start college."

"Me, too."

"Are you still going to the seminary?"

"Yeah, don't have much choice now with the draft and all."

"I wouldn't want to see you go to Nam. Do you really want to be a priest?"

"Not really, but I'm committed with the bishop at this time. You know, priests don't have girlfriends, or they're not supposed to anyway. I'm not sure about this part of being a priest. I miss our time together."

"I'd hate to see you give all that up," she says. "Being Catholic—I never understood it either." Then she whispers, "You're a good kisser, hate to see that go to waste."

"Too bad you live so far away."

"Yeah, next summer is a long time off. I'll be thinking of you."

"Me too. Take care and good night."

"Nigh nigh, Dan."

"Nigh nigh to you too."

I realize I went from being in *like* to being in *lust* to being in *love*. I'm not really sure what love is, but I feel crazy inside—a good crazy.

Patty and I won't see each other again, but for years whenever I would hear the We Five sing "You Were on My Mind," my thoughts would flash to her snuggling up to me and those delicious kisses… lips luscious as cream puffs.

Years later, I see her cousin Laura.

"Hey, good to see you again. That was a good time double-dating back in the day with Mick and Patty."

"Yeah, funny times."

"How is Patty doing?"

"Good," Laura said. "She asks about you now and then. Said she wished that priest thing hadn't gotten between you. She was hoping for a first time with you."

"What, you mean a first time for her?"

"Yeah, I think she would have saved herself for you."

"I didn't know about that. I was trying to be nice."

"You know what they say—nice guys finish last."

"Yeah, damn it."

I missed my chance with Patty. I try not to let my imagination go back to that time, but as you can see, I still fondly recall the smell, the sweetness, the softness.

Chapter 15

Birth of the Eyeball

"How are we gonna get to "The Abbey," I ask Jim. We need transportation to North Dakota, where we will begin our sophomore year at the Catholic seminary at Assumption Abbey, known as "The Abbey." This will be my second try at seminary after quitting Passionist's Seminary in Missouri.

"Dunno, maybe we should buy a car," Jim answers. "I saw a '49 Ford sitting in the parking lot of the IGA with a For Sale sign. Let's go look at it."

We find the car, and a sign in the window reads "$60 Cash" with a phone number. We go to the courtesy counter in the store and use the house phone to call the number.

A gravelly voice answers, "You got cash?"

"Yeah, can you come and meet us. We're at the car now. Do you have the title?"

"Yeah, see you in ten minutes."

Cash and title exchange hands, and the seller wheezes "Thanks" and takes another drag off a Lucky Strike. His greased-back hair glistens in the sun but not in a good way. I wonder what went on in his car. After he leaves, I check the trunk for a dead body.

At the Great Falls Saving and Loan, where Gunner's mother works, we get the title notarized in our names. A few minutes later, we are cruising up Central Avenue, proud owners of a green '49 Ford four-door sedan. It runs well but burns oil, so we head over to Frenchy's Refinery and buy a five-gallon can of re-refined oil for two bucks. This should last the rest of the summer.

This is the last weekend before heading off to the seminary, so a half dozen of my buddies head south on Milligan Road for a camping trip on the Smith River. Mick, Jim, Gunner and I are in the '49 Ford with Sig. John and Mike are in John's maroon '52 Desoto. We take six loaves of Wonder Bread, a quart of mayonnaise, two pounds of bologna, four onions, two heads of iceberg lettuce, a bottle of Ranch dressing, bottles of ketchup and mustard, five pounds of wieners, six pounds of hamburger, four dozen eggs, three 32-ounce cans of tomato juice, a bottle of Tabasco sauce, a pound of Morton Salt, a can of black pepper, three cases of Big Sky Beer and a cast iron frying pan. We don't know it yet, but the next day we will drive ten miles back to Ulm for more beer.

We find a nice spot along the pristine Smith River and set up camp for the weekend—a couple sleeping bags, some blankets and pillows, and a campfire. We're here to party, fish a little and keep the campfire burning all weekend. The nights are cool, so we hover around the fire as the damp ground creeps up through our sleeping bags, and every small stone and stick feels like a dagger. The Milky Way pours sparkling molten lava over us. The river gurgles, the wind whispers, the willows wave, the air smells earthy and meteors scratch silver lines in the sky. We huddle together in a small dot surrounded by an immenseness that we little notice, numbed as we are by years of growing up in Montana. A city dweller suddenly deposited here without warning might be gripped with agoraphobia, panic crushing them with the weight of the place. While our subconscious minds explore the hidden reality around us, our conscious minds tend to dwell on more mundane things as we ramble on a variety of topics.

"Hey, what happened when the cops pulled you over for speeding after that kegger at Ryan Dam," John asks Gunner.

"He got me for fifteen bucks," Gunner says, "but he didn't smell my breath to see if I was drunk."

"You were lucky—pretty shit-faced that night, if I remember."

"Yeah, I was real polite, so he let me go."

"Wasn't that the night you tore your car door off backing into a parking place at the Steiner?"

"Yeah, still can't open that door. Managed to get it shut, but now it's all jammed up."

"Still trying to get into Laura's pants?" I ask Mick.

"None of your business. It's a work in progress."

"Keep me posted."

"Yeah, right."

"So, you and Jim heading out for the sem?" John asks.

"Yeah," I reply, "can't believe it's in North Dakota, but that's better than Nam."

"I still got my deferment at the University of Montana," John says.

"Keep your grades up, or you'll end up in Nam."

"I might try studying more this semester."

"So, you think you want to be a priest?"

"I dunno—not sure of the whole church thing. Always had a hard time with the nuns and that."

"Yeah, they were pretty hard on us, but then we pulled some shit."

"I guess they were just doin' their job."

"Hey, Dan, still in lust with Patty?" Mick asks.

"Don't get me thinking about her, I won't be able to sleep tonight."

"Yeah, you need a chaperone."

Most of the conversation is about past escapades—girls, teachers who rapped us on the knuckles with a ruler, car wrecks, getting drunk, belching, farting and, of course, girls. At two in the morning, we are deep in our sleeping bags, still looking up at the stars and still talking and farting. Finally, around three o'clock, it gets quiet as everyone falls asleep. The summer sun peeks over the horizon around five-thirty, forcing us to crawl deeper into our bags to keep from being blinded.

The light is relentless. Around eight, I hear a "pop" as Gunner snaps a pop top off a can of beer, pours it into a plastic cup and tops it off with tomato juice and Tabasco sauce.

"Red Eye, anyone?" he asks, offering this famous hangover cure.

Mike stirs and mumbles, "Yeah, I need one. Who crapped in my mouth last night?" He is referring to the bad taste left from drinking beer all day and smoking cigarettes.

Hungover, we pull ourselves closer to the smoky fire, light up cigarettes and medicate our hangovers with Red Eyes.

After about an hour, we are beginning to heal. Sig throws three pounds of hamburger and a couple of chopped-up onions in the big cast iron skillet. Once the hamburger is browned, he cracks a dozen eggs on top, doses it with salt, pepper and Tabasco sauce, stirs it and serves up a hearty, cholesterol-filled omelet. It slides down our throats, and we burp, fart and light up more cigarettes.

I open the trunk and pull out four quarts of paint that I got at a garage sale for ten cents each. It's time to customize the '49 Ford. Sig and John are the artists in the group, and the first order of business is painting a bloodshot eyeball on the chrome bullet in the front grille of the car. Once this is done, we decide to name the machine.

"How about The Flying Bloodshot Eyeball," I suggest. That name is a natural, and John paints it in large, black letters. The name is so long it takes the entire length of the car to print it out. Now, the '49 Ford is becoming an icon. Sig paints roaring flames coming out of the front wheel wells and streaming down the side of the car. We add a coral-colored racing stripe down the center, beginning with the front bumper and ending with the rear bumper. We know the color is coral because it says so on the paint can. Coral is a sickly pink color. With the tires and rims in matching coral, the The Flying Bloodshot Eyeball is alive. John brought his .22 pistol, and we take turns shooting bullet holes in the doors and fenders— the frosting on the cake. Luckily, we manage only to shoot the car.

Chapter 16

Going to Hell, or Is It Just North Dakota?

"How much oil in the trunk?" Jim asks.

"Five gallons. I filled it at Frenchy's." Jim is referring to the five-gallon can in the trunk.

"Okay, that should last us for a while."

"I'll pick you up at seven, so we can get an early start."

The happy summer of '65 is coming to an end. We depart for the Abbey and a life of priestly virtues. "When I Woke Up This Morning, You Were On My Mind" is still going through my head as I thought about Patty. I should have worked harder on that bra clasp.

We head southeast out of Great Falls for a place so remote we wonder if it really exists or is just a figment of our imagination. We have 521 miles of mostly barren, deserted highway ahead of us. The Eyeball cruises down Highway 87 South, a narrow highway with no shoulders that takes us to Highway 10, another narrow road ten years before it was transformed into Interstate 94. It heads east into North Dakota, a land that devours us like a whale swallowing Jonah. We seem to be going into the bowels of an endless horizon. I somehow feel lost, wondering if the road will just end at nothing at all. I guess I'm lost in many ways—lost in war, lost in the Church and now lost in time and place.

"Where in the hell is this place?" I ask Jim.

"I dunno. There's nothin' out here."

"Maybe we're lost."

"Seems like it."

"I wonder if we'll ever get there." I look hopefully at a Montana highway map torn at its multiple folds. "Map says the road goes there. Hope it's right."

We pass a farm where an American flag and a North Dakota state flag hang from a pole in front of the farmhouse. I wonder if we are in a foreign country.

* * *

An endless line of barbwire fence has been following us for hundreds of miles, and suddenly I'm beginning to feel fenced in, not so much by the wire but by the land. The Eyeball continues to toss up and down the gentle slopes of an endless prairie accentuated here and there with a few crumpled hills, waving grass, wind beating at anchored sagebrush, sandstone boulders peeking out of the grass, unidentifiable animals in the far distance, eagles soaring overhead and snakes slithering off to the side.

After twelve hours of floating on this barren sea of grass, a beacon appears on the horizon.

"There it is," Jim says, pointing toward the distant horizon. "The Abbey. See it? On the left." A stately cathedral rises above the prairie like a lighthouse shining a beam of hope, safety and shelter—a lifeline out of this stormy sea of land.

"Yeah, we made it," I sigh.

It's September 8, 1965, as Jim and I roll into Richardton, North Dakota, the hometown of the Benedictine Abbey and Seminary, located in central North Dakota somewhere between nowhere and beyond. Richardton, population 796, is home to 796 Catholics. Down the road seven miles, the little town of Taylor has 622 Lutherans.

The great Benedictine Abbey rises on the flat prairie, a Renaissance sculpture. Built in 1907 with large cut stones and brick, it consists of a twin spire cathedral, monastery, seminary, cafeteria, junior college dorm, classrooms, power plant and farm. Here, pious Benedictines live in quiet solitude, pray, meditate and run herd on a hundred testosterone-charged boys who think they have a vocation to become celibate Catholic priests.

As we cruise Richardton's main street, we notice Frank's Bar and note it for future reference. Not that we will be doing any drinking in there. After all, we are under the strict control of the monks.

We pull into the parking and look for the dean, Fr. Louis. His office is in the original Abbey, an imposing brick and stone structure. On one corner of the campus is the cathedral with two spires topped with crosses reminiscent of European design. On another corner is the monastery. We pass through an eight-foot-high double door that swings on huge iron hinges and walk down a wide hallway with a twelve-foot ceiling. We find a door with a brass nameplate reading "Father Louis – Dean of Seminary."

We knock and hear a deep voice say, "Come in."

Fr. Louis sits behind a massive wooden desk reminiscent of the Bishop's desk. He wears a black robe with rosary beads as a belt. By looking at his huge hands, we assume he's about six-and-a-half-feet tall.

"Fr. Louis?" I ask politely.

"Ya sure, so you da boys from Great Falls?" he asks in a heavy North Dakota German accent.

"Yes, Father, we just got here. The bishop asked us to give you these letters." We hand him our letters, and he smiles.

"Good, I've been expectin' you. I'll go over some of da basic rules, and then yous can unpack and get settled. First, yous boys are seminarians, so yous will be expected to set an example for the other boys wit good behavior. No drinkin', girls or leavin' campus without permission. Understand?"

"Yes, Father," we answer nearly in unison.

"Mass every morning at six, study hall at seven with breakfast at eight. I got some bad news for yous boys. As there isn't room in the seminary dorm, yous will have to live in Schnell Hall with the regular college students. It'll be tough being away from the other seminarians, but yous will have to make the best of it."

I've been so busy counting the number of times he has said "Yous" that I almost missed the fact that we get to live in the regular college dorm. He doesn't realize he is talking to two guys who may have just lost their "vocation" and are thrilled to hear this news.

"That's okay," I say, trying to hide my delight. "We'll make the best of it."

"Oh, that car you're driving," Fr. Louis says, "Seminarians aren't allowed to have cars. Go unload your stuff and bring me the keys."

"Okay, we'll bring them later," I tell him.

We drive across campus to the college dorm, unload the car, park it in front of the dorm and walk back to return the keys, knowing we can easily hotwire the car with a half-dollar coin anytime we want. It's a simple matter of reaching up behind the dashboard and shorting out the terminal that sends current to the electric starter.

Jim and I settle into a single room with two beds, two desks, a single sink and a medicine cabinet. I'm not sure Jim wanted to room with me, but we ended up together. For me, it was mostly about financial reasons as the bishop was paying for a double room.

At dinner, we sit with six other students at an eight-foot table. The first thing I notice is the East Coast accents. Several students from the East Coast have been sent to this remote place by wealthy parents frustrated with their juvenile behavior, naively hoping this Catholic college in the middle of nowhere will shape up their delinquent sons. I say "sons" because this is an all-male school—no girls allowed.

Driscol from Philadelphia has actually danced on Dick Clark's American Bandstand TV show and will attempt to bring a couple of Montana hicks up to the Dick Clark dance standards. Rick, in the room next to us, is a bodybuilding fanatic whose arms are the size of my legs. He's compulsive about exercising but good-humored. We kid him almost to the point of his breaking us in half. Bob, his roommate from

Glasgow, Montana, is an intellectual type with thick glasses that slide down his nose. He knows every song by Roger Miller and goes around singing his favorite:

> Ain't nothin' but a fool would live like this
> Out all night and runnin' wild
> Woman's sittin' home with a month old child
> Dang me, dang me,
> They oughta get a rope and hang me,
> Hang me from the highest tree,
> Woman would you weep for me.

Malley, from Bryn Mawr, Pennsylvania, is a rich kid who drives a new '64 Pontiac Bonneville. He doesn't much care about being here and has been sentenced to this prison by his parents. He wears penny loafers, khaki pants and Gant shirts.

Danny, from Miles City, is the son of a lawyer. Catholic and Irish, he drinks like a fish.

Don and Rich, across the hall, are from Billings and are focused on how to smuggle beer into their dorm room.

Lucky comes from St. Mary's, Montana, a small tourist community at the entrance to Glacier National Park. His dad owns the town.

In all, about a hundred misfits live in the dorm and all have one thing in common—they are all stuck in Nowhere, No Dak, at the height of their testosterone production with no girls in sight.

Chapter 17

It's Not Prison, But First Breakout

"Has Father Louis said anything about skipping Mass?" I ask Jim.

"No, I try to hide from him."

"Me too. Wonder if he's on to us."

"Dunno, afraid to find out."

"Can't believe it snowed last night."

"Yeah, I thought Great Falls had shitty weather, but this is worse."

"I have to give No Dak credit. It holds its own to Great Falls with the wind."

It's late September, and the first snow of the winter falls. It's not too unusual to get snow this time of year, although it usually lasts only a few days. Not this year, though. The snow sticks, then piles up a few more inches on top of that, covering the windswept prairie with just a few brown weeds and wheat stubble sticking up here and there. Autumn took a bye and skipped to winter.

As the weeks pass, Fr. Louis seems to have forgotten Jim and me. We are supposed to go to Mass every morning but rarely make it. Quietly, we slide out of the seminary lifestyle and into the wild life of a small community college. Saturday night is always a big night watching TV in the day room of the dorm. Shindig, a rock and roll dance show, shows the Beach Boys performing their most recent hit, "Do You Wanna Dance?" As the weeks go by, we watch The Righteous Brothers,

Lesley Gore, Bo Diddley, Sonny and Cher, The Ronettes, and James Brown.

While we're watching James Brown on screen, a short, wiry Italian named Driscol tries to teach us a few good dance moves, and we start dreaming of impressing girls. The only girls in town are at the girl's high school but getting to them is like trying to break into a prison. The nuns who guard the school make Bonnie of Bonnie and Clyde look like a piker. I swear they have Thompson machine guns under their habits. After Shindig, we watch The Sergeant Bilko Show.

One day, I see a poster in the local grocery store window advertising Joe and His White Jacket Trio playing at the community center in Gladstone, another tiny community fifteen miles west of Richardton.

"Jim, we got to fire up the Eyeball and go to the dance," I say.

"Do you think it will start?"

"Dunno, let's see."

It's the end of November. The brown spots on the prairie and the wheat stubble have long disappeared under a couple more feet of snow, which moves constantly, slithering, scurrying and skulking across the landscape. The temperature reaches zero each night. We walk out to the car and look around to make sure Fr. Louis is not around. He never is, but worrying about him makes us nervous when we take the car. The Eyeball, like a faithful dog, has been resting on its front paws for days waiting for its masters to return.

I slide a half-dollar coin behind the dashboard and connect two terminals on the back of the ignition. The flathead V8 slowly turns over and fires, then backfires and starts running on a couple of cylinders, sounding as if it has a head cold. As the engine warms up, it quits coughing and then runs a little more smoothly. Driscol, Don, Lucky, Rich, Jim and I head out for Gladstone, aka Happy Rock, leaving a trail of white vapor that quickly crystallizes in the biting air.

We are on the trail of Joe and His White Jacket Trio—and girls, of course. We navigate the country road pinned in by a wall of snow on each side like guard rails. The defroster breathes tepid air on the windshield, clearing a small half-circle on the driver's side. The rest of the windows grow white whiskers. We take turns shaving the frost off the windows with a plastic scraper bearing an image of a Flying Red Horse.

In Gladstone, we find the community center walled by three-foot drifts and a plowed parking lot strewn with a couple dozen idling cars that create their own weather system, a cloud of ice crystals glittering under a single yard light on a telephone pole. A black-on-white 1962 Impala spews white vapor out of its dual exhaust pipes and beer cans out of its windows as three farm boys inside quaff cold ones on an even colder night.

Joe and His White Jacket Trio are stage center. Living up to its name, each wears a white sport jacket with a pink carnation in the lapel. It seems corny but somehow complements the large grain bins across the street. The trio plays country western songs—Joe on the guitar, Joe #2 on the bass and Joe #3 on the drums. The first three songs are "Four Strong Winds" by Bobby Bare, "Orange Blossom Special" by Johnny Cash and "Stop the World and Let Me Off" by Waylon Jennings. The music is amateurish, but there are girls, and they are interested in the new college guys in town. Several girls stand together on one side of the dance floor, and a couple of dozen guys gather on the other side. A dozen couples are dancing. One gal, who is wearing jeans and a western shirt with her hair in a ponytail, agrees to dance with me. I hope she doesn't have a big farmer boyfriend.

"Hi, I'm Dan. What's your name?"

"Sherry."

"So, are you from Gladstone?"

"Yes, and you?"

"From the college at Richardson." She seems impressed, probably because she is a senior in high school, and I'm a big man on campus. We hit it off, but there is no place to go for privacy except behind a three-foot snowdrift or the back seat of a '49 Ford with no heater.

Sherry lives on a farm outside Gladstone and dreams of going to nursing school in Grand Forks. "I hope your dream comes true," I tell her.

"Thanks, I'll be the first one in my family to go to college. My parents never had much schooling. Been farmers all their life."

"Yeah, me too. I'm the first one to go to college, but mostly to beat the draft."

"Whatcha wanna do when you finish?"

"Maybe help people, like be a counselor or psychologist."

"Sounds good, people need help. Why not be a priest?"

"I dunno—not sure about the Catholic thing. I like some things about it, but some things don't make sense."

"Yeah, I know. We have to go to church. My parents don't give us a choice."

"I guess they think that's good for us. Maybe they're right."

"Yeah, maybe."

We enjoy a few close, slow dances. She is sweet and soft. I could dance with her all night.

At midnight Joe stops playing, and everyone heads out the door. Sherry and I steal a quick kiss.

"That was nice," she says.

"Yeah, it was." I seemed to have established myself as a good kisser, but it's not getting me anywhere.

Sherry leaves with her girlfriends. I fire up the Eyeball, and Jim and I head down a dark country road toward Richardton. "When I woke up this morning, you were on my mind" is running through my head. I never see Sherry again. It's too complicated to have a girlfriend in the middle of nowhere with nowhere to go at ten degrees below zero. Best I can do is remember that last kiss.

Punks: Driscol, Dan and Rich

Chapter 18
Bless Me, Father, for I Have Sinned, Again

"You boys get your homework done?" Frank asks. He's the owner and bartender of Frank's Bar.

"Yeah, just here to play pool."

"Not much to do in this weather. Worst I've ever seen."

"Yeah, worse than Great Falls."

"You boys keeping up on your studies?"

"Yeah, not much to do but study."

"That's good. I didn't get schooling. Don't take it for granted."

I hope I can remember his advice tomorrow.

Frank lets us drink beer in his bar and play pool even though he knows we aren't twenty-one. It's the only place in town to go except for our dorm.

December brings more snow, and now it's drifting up to the windows on the first floor of the dorm. Ropes have been strung along the sidewalk between the dorm and the cafeteria so we can find our way during the frequent blizzards. It's just a block between buildings, but it would be easy to get lost in zero visibility. Before making the trip, we wrap towels around our heads and peer through narrow tunnels in front of our faces to keep from getting frostbite. Wind blowing, ice crystals biting, snow blinding, students baying and belaying down the rope. The wind chill is minus twenty degrees on a warm day.

In the meantime, the beer continues to flow into the dorm as we pass the time playing cards, studying and keeping an eye out for the priests. At mealtimes, I see the seminarians sitting together and wonder what their life is like without beer and frolicking at the community dances.

Chapter 19

Do you Wanna Dance? Oops Bless Me Again Father

"Everyone is supposed to meet in the cafeteria," Don says, sticking his head into our dorm room."

"What about?

"A lecture from Fr. Richard on behaving ourselves at the dance in Bismarck."

We all head to the cafeteria. Once a year, St. Mary's Girls College in Bismarck, sixty miles away, hosts a dance for the boys from Richardton. It is a very proper dance, well supervised and devoid of any hanky-panky.

During the lecture, Fr. Richard, our dorm supervisor, warns us, "You guys behave. No fighting, and no drinking, and treat them girls like ladies."

Everyone murmurs, "Yes, Father," and nods his head—even Malley, who has hidden a couple of bottles of Everclear liquor in his car. Twice a strong as vodka, Everclear is 95 percent grain alcohol and will take the paint off your car and the shine off your soul. His mission is to spike the punch bowl at the dance with this tasteless, odorless hell in a bottle.

We arrive at the dance at about 8:15, trying to look our best and not be nervous. These are college girls, the first we have seen in several months. The music is provided by a nun spinning 45 rpm records on a small turntable connected to one tinny speaker. She plays the "Name Game" by Shirley Ellis, "You've Lost that Loving Feeling" by the Righteous Brothers, and "The Eve of Destruction" by Barry McGuire. I must say her taste in music is better than Joe and His White Jacket Trio. I assume she is playing records contributed by the students.

The crowd is quiet, with all the girls bunched into a corner like sheep retreating from wolves. The boys in the other corner are circling, each of them trying to figure out a way to separate one girl from the flock.

A punch bowl filled with orange Kool-Aid and sparkling water with a two-pound lump of vanilla ice cream on top sits on a table covered with a white table cloth surrounded by clear glass cups. On the table is a large bowl of greasy, glistening potato chips with a bowl of clam dip next to it. A large tray is stacked high with triangular tuna fish sandwiches made with Wonder Bread and laced with chopped dill pickles. Another tray is heaped with orange Cheetos that match the color of the punch.

After about twenty minutes, Malley walks by me and mutters, "Touchdown," meaning the Everclear has landed in the punch bowl. A half-hour passes, many cups of punch have been consumed, the girls are circulating and the guys are on the move. In our Everclear-enhanced minds, we guys are all God's answer to women. Even the nun chaperones, also victims of the spiked punch, are giggling in the corner, and the nun DJ has turned up the volume. Lucky is eating Cheetos by the handful, and his right hand is bright orange along with the back of his right pants leg. I wonder if an unsuspecting girl will end up with the back of her dress painted orange, the result of dancing with him.

I ask a gal named Sally to dance so I can try out a few moves Driscol taught me. Either I'm good, or the Everclear has distorted our perceptions of reality, but we strut across the dance floor doing The Jerk.

"So, how do you like St Mary's?" I ask Sally.

"Not that great. No boys—and boring."

"Yeah, the Abbey is the same way. No girls."

"I heard you guys are pretty wild."

"Really? Where did you hear that?"

"Oh, a birdie told me," says Sally. "I like wild guys."

With this encouragement, I take my cue, and we do the Mashed Potato out the door of the gymnasium and down the hall unnoticed by the nuns. Little do I realize it's time to go to confession—a different kind of confession.

"In here," she says, pulling me into the chapel. It's dark, and we find our way into the confessional booth. This time it is not, "Bless me, Father, for I have sinned," but "Bless me, Father, for I am sinning." We land in the priest's chair with Sally on my lap. As we fumble around in the dark, I am thinking, "Bless me, Father, for I have sinned—I've gotten inside a girl's bra in the confessional."

I imagine the priest saying, "This is worse than murder. Two million Hail Marys every day for the rest of your life."

At half past-ten, we strut back into the dance a bit rumpled. By this time, the punch bowl is empty, and the speaker is cranking "Land of a Thousand Dances" by Cannibal and the Headhunters. For a moment, I think of Glenn missing these times of our young lives. I say goodbye to Sally, and we kiss at the front door of the gym.

"Nice kisser."

"Thanks, you too."

Jim and I pile into the car and head back to Richardton. I never see Sally again. I had rung up another sale as a good kisser, but it does me no good. It's just too cold to have a long-distance girlfriend during a North Dakota winter.

Infamous Confessional

Chapter 20

Hell Actually Freezes Over the Winter of '65

"Stay together."

"Jim, you back there?"

"Yeah, don't get too far ahead."

"Don, you still with us?"

"Yeah, right here."

"Stay together."

A bunch of us are on our way from the dorm to the cafeteria about a block away. We belay ourselves with gloved hands to the rope strung between the two buildings about 200 feet apart. For the past couple of months, we have used this rope during the blinding blizzards that happen a couple of times a week. We work our way toward the cafeteria, yelling to each other to stay together.

The noon sun is hidden by a six-foot blanket of snow driven by wind that creates a horizontal blizzard. The needles of ice penetrate our coats, puncture our faces and sandblast off the baby fat.

The harsh winter punishes us with a chill factor of minus forty degrees and visibility of just ten feet. It is the beginning of the worst winter in the history of North Dakota—the historic blizzard of March 2-5, 1966, with thirty-eight inches of snow, winds of seventy miles per hour and drifts up to forty feet. Eventually, nine people would die and tens of thousands of livestock. The state would be paralyzed for weeks.

After what seems like climbing Mount Everest, we arrive at the cafeteria with frost and ice welded to our eyes, noses and mouths. We seize cups of coffee, huddle around a table and wait for the ice to drip to the floor. We are now just a few hundred feet from the dorm, but the cold has cut through our heavy winter coats and blued us to the bone. A person would only last about an hour if they were lost out there.

"North Dakota! Maybe we should have joined the Army," Jim quips. We all know it is a joke, but it provokes a second thought. I think of Glenn for a minute, wondering what he would be doing now if he were alive.

With spare time on our hands, our minds wander to possible practical jokes to play on one another. Don and Rich live across the hall from me and are easy targets. One day I fill up a wastebasket with a mixture of water, ketchup, mustard and other condiments from the cafeteria and lean it against their door at a forty-five-degree angle so that when they open their door, the contents will slosh into the room. I wait for almost an hour, listening for the slosh, before I finally hear their door open.

"Shit, what the hell! Who did this?" Don yells out to his roommate Rich.

"We gotta get whoever who did this," Rich yells back.

I almost have to lie down I'm laughing so hard. I listen for any clues about who they think did this but can't hear anything helpful. At dinner, I sit with Don and Rich, hoping to hear them talk about the incident, but they are mum.

A few weeks later, I am watching TV in the day room with a few other guys. It's Friday night, and we are watching *Route 66*, *Twilight Zone* and *The Alfred Hitchcock Hour*. About ten o'clock, I go back to my room. As I open the medicine cabinet in the bathroom to get my toothbrush, two sparrows fly out and into my face. I'm horror-struck, and if I weren't young and in good health, would have suffered a heart attack, I'm sure. The confused birds are flapping around the room, so I open the hallway door and shoo them out. They fly up and down the corridor, but there really isn't any way out. Don and Rich emerge from their room, laughing hysterically.

"So, you thought you could get away with the wastebasket trick?" Don asks gleefully.

"Okay, we're even." I acknowledge defeat. "Help me catch the birds."

Our attempts are futile, and soon Don retrieves two tennis rackets from his room and hands me one. He positions himself at one end of the hall with me at the other end. Rich shoos the birds toward Don, who promptly whacks one of them into the next world. "15-Love," he shouts. "My point."

Don's whack sends the other bird toward me and whack, it's 15–15. I've tied the game, but I feel a tinge of guilt—the same kind of guilt I had when I shot a sparrow with my BB gun at age nine.

"Okay, tie game," Don says.

I agree it's a draw. The birds lay lifeless in the hallway.

I think of Glenn.

Chapter 21

Second Breakout, Escape to Great Falls

“Grab some clean sheets from the laundry room for the Eyeball,” I tell Jim.

“Got ’em. Anything else?”

“Yeah, need to tell everyone to bring the blankets off their beds. It’s going to be colder than shit driving in this weather.”

“Hope we can get the Eyeball started.”

“Yeah, it’s been sitting all week.”

After four months of incarceration in a prison whose “walls” are an impassable land moat, we are finally paroled for good behavior—or despite undiscovered bad behavior. It’s time for Christmas vacation and home for the holidays. Fr. Louis gives back the key for the Eyeball with a lecture to be sure to return it when we get back. Four of us will make the trip home—Jim and I plus Lucky and Danny.

The thermometer looks as blank as the landscape as the mercury huddles for warmth at the bottom of the tube. Drifted snow and thick frost blanket the countryside, making the Eyeball almost invisible in the parking lot. We scrape the windows clear. Our faithful companion, The Eyeball, groans, sputters, belches, gasps and pops as a couple of cylinders fire and begin to pound life into the engine. After five minutes of shivering, it begins to warm up and finally purrs like a skinny cat on a cold day.

With fresh, white bedsheets "borrowed" from the laundry covering the car seats, we set off on the 521-mile journey to Great Falls. We pile in the car, tucking blankets around ourselves. The car heater wheezes a hint of warm air, enough to keep a half-circle of windshield clear of ice. Our rations include a bag of potato chips, a sack of salted peanuts in the shell, bologna sandwiches with mayonnaise on white bread, two quarts of A&W Root Beer, two six-packs of Dr. Pepper, a first aid kit and a pint of Jim Beam.

We turn the car onto Highway 10, heading west. The five-degree temperature and a wailing wind create a wind chill of thirty-five degrees below zero—and a haunted feeling. The highway dances with snow jetting sideways across it, creating a "white-out" or ground blizzard. While the sky is blue above, everything below the hood ornament disappears into the silver-grey ice crystals.

The Eyeball pushes ahead with Jim at the wheel—through Dickinson and then on to Beach, North Dakota, on the Montana border. Today, it takes more than a pint of Jim Beam to imagine anything named Beach in this part of the country. The Eyeball slips and slides down the highway on worn tires slick as the ice under them. A piece of cardboard covers the radiator to keep the engine warm. The Eyeball snorts ahead.

We are all shivering as the storm leaks through cracks around the doors and windows and powders us with snow.

"My fucking feet are freezing," Lucky says.

"Have another cigarette, it'll warm them up," I say.

"When we gettin' to Miles City?"

"A couple more hours, hang on."

"You and this fucking car, I could have walked faster."

"Here, have a swig of Mr. Beam," I say, passing the bottle to the backseat.

Lucky takes a swig, lights a cigarette, squints out the window and says, "Fucking North Dakota."

Blankets stuffed around the doors help keep us warm, but the car is basically unheated. It looks like the inside of a freezer and smells like

Cheetos laced with cigarette smoke. We constantly scrape the windows to keep up with the heavy frost gathering on them. Frost grows like a stubby beard on all the metal parts around the windows and doors. Behind the wheel, Jim peeks out the six-inch clear spot on the windshield.

An approaching snowplow creates a tornado that tries to suck us underground as it passes. I glimpse the driver's troubled face flash by. Drifts creep across the road, like tentacles of giant squids from *20,000 Leagues Under the Sea*. The Eyeball fights back. It has survived the Blizzard of '65 this far, and it's not going down now. It booms through foot-high drifts, sounding like a baton hitting a bass drum and throwing up a huge cloud of white snow behind us. "Is that all you got?" it seems to yell at the storm.

We pass mile after mile of barbed wire fence, which at times disappears under snowdrifts and reemerges like a snake burrowing through the snow. In places, telephone poles look like toys on a model train set overrun with twenty-foot drifts of snow. A cow, stationary in a snowdrift, stares at us with blank eyes, telling us not to worry. It has probably spent the last couple of months in this position and will be here until spring, or until coyotes or ravens discover a waiting meal. It won't be the last cow or horse we see that won't ever enjoy spring. Besides frozen animals, we are pretty much alone out here.

Telephone poles overrun by twenty-foot drifts.

I told my parents not to worry; the drive would be easy. I was wrong.

We forge the Missouri River over a narrow steel bridge and enter Glendive, a small cowboy town on the Montana/North Dakota border. The Eyeball brakes and slides into the Take a Break diner, where we relieve ourselves and warm up with coffee, french fries and burgers.

Our waitress is in her 30s with a brown, Twiggy hairdo, short skirt, skinny legs and a smile that makes us squirm. Seems like every waitress we encounter stirs us up. It doesn't take much. Everything that could be pent up in guys separated from women for months is doubled with us.

"Where you boys headed?" the waitress asks.

"Great Falls."

"Be careful, it's bad out there. You got a ways to go."

"Yeah, we're taking it easy."

"Coffee?"

"Yeah, and fries and burgers."

"Sure, hon, anything else?"

I think of lots of things—a date, smell her perfume, hold her hand—but I keep my mouth shut.

"No, thanks."

Lucky buys a pack of Lucky Strikes and smokes three during our short break.

Refreshed and relieved, we head out the door.

"You boys come on back again."

"Yeah, sure."

We head to Miles City, home of the world-famous Bucking Horse Sale. Since I'm driving, Jim reminds me, "Dead Man's Curve coming at us soon."

"Thanks, don't want to end up like one of those crosses."

I'm referring to the white crosses the American Legion places on Montana highways wherever there is a fatality. In 1965 there were 340 highway fatalities in Montana, a state with a meager population of 700,000. Drunk driving, no seat belts, no speed limit and a cowboy bronc rider attitude thins the population at a disturbing rate of double the more populated states. The highways are dotted with hundreds of white crosses. Dead Man's Curve is a cemetery. Dropping off a high plateau into the valley, the narrow road snakes left and then right like a whip trying to shake a bulldog clenched to the end.

Peaking the plateau, I downshift into second, the Eyeball furrows its brow, we begin our descent and reduce speed to 25 mph, 20 mph, 15 mph… Ahead is an "S" shaped skating rink.

"Going too fast," Jim warns.

"Yeah," I say, riding the brakes gently as we slow down to 10 mph.

The fog in the car dissipates as everyone stops breathing. We slide quietly past the first group of crosses and then past the second group and can see the straightaway ahead.

"Man, any slower we would have been parked."

"Yeah—will make a good story later."

"Hey, Lucky. Miles City ahead."

"Holy Crap, we were damn near killed coming down that hill. Get me to Miles City and outta this car."

* * *

Each May, the main street of Miles City is corralled off from traffic, creating a street paved an inch deep with flattened beer cans. It fills with raucous country music bands, boot-scootin' dancers, brawling cowboys, tight-jeaned cowgirls and hard-drinking. No sissy or foofoo drinks allowed, just good ole whisky shots and beer chasers. At the fairgrounds across town, the Wild Horse Rodeo bucks and broncs as buyers look for good rodeo stock. The special horses that are considered athletic and know how to buck bring the high prices. The Miles City Bucking Horse Sale is known worldwide as the best place to buy good bucking stock.

The town overflows with cowboys wearing crushed hats with sweat rings, greasy chaps, scuffed boots, Wrangler or Levi jeans draped and tattered over spurs, and silver belt buckles the size of turkey platters. For many, it's their annual trip to town. Some look like they just crawled out from under a rock or fell off a horse. It's a time of whiskey drinking, fistfights, chasing cowgirls and riding bucking horses.

Today, the frozen Main Street is quiet, with a few cowboys braced against the wind with colorful silk bandannas wrapped around their necks. Their cowboy hats are pulled down snugly to keep them from blowing off and rolling down the street like tumbleweeds.

The 600 Café is full of customers looking for a warm place to hide from the weather. Owned by the Grenz family since 1946, it caters to cowboys, cowgirls, bankers, grocery clerks and truck drivers. Men in cowboy hats sit at the counter and in booths drinking stout coffee and talking about the rigors of farming and ranching. Breakfast is served all day, with the favorite being a plate piled high with fresh biscuits drowned in sausage gravy, a half dozen slices of steak-thick bacon, a pile of crisp hash browns and three fried eggs.

Across the street, the Range Riders Bar features a red neon sign with a cowboy riding a bucking horse. It's a rough bar—a good place to pick a fight with a whiskey-drinking cowboy and a good place for us to avoid trouble.

We continue down Main Street and stop at Danny's parent's home. It's taken us seven hours to travel the 197 miles from Richardton, a whopping twenty-eight miles per hour. By now, we realize that Lucky's feet are seriously cold. He takes off his shoes, and his feet match the blue living room drapes.

"Here, put them in this warm water, not too hot," Danny's dad tells Lucky, setting a basin of water in front of him.

"Ow, that hurts," Lucky says.

"Go slow, a little at a time."

Soon, Lucky's feet are warm and pink again—crisis passed.

"I told you dumb shits my feet were cold," he says, annoyed as he lights up a cigarette.

We realize we can't make it to Great Falls that day, and Danny's father insists we spend the night. "You can all sleep on the floor in the basement," he tells us. "Bring in all those blankets."

We make up beds on the basement floor, and Danny's mother cooks us spaghetti, which we wolf down. After dinner, we head down to the Red Rock, a local night club, looking for girls. Danny knows the local girls because he went to high school here.

A local rock band at the Red Rock pounds out "Wooly Bully" by Sam the Sham and the Pharaohs, "Downtown" by Petula Clark, "You've Lost That Lovin' Feeling" by the Righteous Brothers, "My Girl" by the Temptations, and of course, "You Were On My Mind" by the We Five. We find a few girls to dance with, but most are taken by the local cowboys. We avoid fights over girls and mainly spend the night drinking beer and listening to the band.

The next morning, we leave for Great Falls. The wind is gritty and sandblasts the side of the car with ice crystals. Our next stop is Forsyth in eastern Montana, and then it's a hundred miles to Roundup on a deserted country road punctuated by a couple of wide spots. One boasts a post office (closed) and a bar, the only remaining evidence of life before this part of the world is reclaimed by nature.

Ten hours and 315 miles later, we crest the Belt Hill and begin our descent into Great Falls, still about twenty miles away. The Big Stack at the Anaconda Copper Smelter looms in front of us like a lighthouse on a sea of shifting snow. The wind continues to scream across the prairie. It has not missed a beat since we left Richardton two days ago. It's the winter of '65-66, and it has taken us seventeen hours to drive 521 miles, an average of thirty miles per hour—without insurance, of course.

"Whoopi do, we're finally fucking here," Lucky says.

Chapter 22

Time Off for Good Behavior, Christmas Break

"It's good to have you home," Mom says. "We were worried about you driving in this weather."

"Yeah, I missed you guys," I confess. "There isn't much to do in North Dakota."

"How were the roads?"

"Okay, some snow here and there."

"When I was a kid there, the winters were really bad. They say this is like the old days." Dad says.

"Yeah, it's been a hard winter. Good to be home."

My mother believes I have found my "vocation," that I am leading the life of a good seminarian. My Dad doesn't say much but seems glad I haven't been drafted into the army. He worries about me, but then he worries about lots of things. He's a natural talker and likes making new friends. My buddies think my folks are the best parents in the world. It will take me a few more years to see them that way. Right now, they are just parents who don't understand me—but then no one does.

After visiting for a while, my mother says, "The bishop's office called. He wants you to come in and see him before you return to the Abbey."

I had almost forgotten about the bishop, and a feeling of guilt comes over me as I think about facing him. "Sure, mom. I'll go down to see him next week."

"So, what do you think of the seminary?" she asks.

"It's okay, made some new friends. Jim and I are rooming together."

"What about studying to be a priest?'

"Well, that's okay too," I say, trying to avoid the fact that I'm not sure about this whole Catholic thing. But I'm not going to say anything to upset my parents, who are devout Catholics.

The next night at the Stein Haus, several of my friends are earning life credits in beer drinking, sports and girl talk. I walk in, and Rick announces with a megaphone voice, "Oh, look—here comes the priest. Bless me, Father, for I have sinned."

"I have no idea what you're talking about," I tell him. "At least I have a vocation—unlike you heathens."

"Yeah, right, you're the one going to hell. On a more important thing, how is the Eyeball running?" Rick asks.

"Great. Only took us seventeen hours to get here and froze our asses off with a shitty heater, but we made it."

"Hail to the Eyeball!" Rick raises his beer glass.

"Yeah, it always comes through."

It's ten o'clock and time to leave the Stein Haus and look for girls.

Chapter 23

Saved again, This Time By a Wink

"Let's head up to the Wheel," I tell Gunner.

"Okay, see you there."

We each have our own car in case we meet some girls. That way, we can take them home separately.

At about ten o'clock, our standard procedure is to move from the Stein Haus to the Cartwheel Bar where there is live music and a chance to meet girls. Curly Greaseman, the owner, welcomes us. His name is really Creaseman, but we call him Greaseman because he combs his silver-grey, greased hair over his ears in a ducktail. He is about twenty years older than us but married to Marlyss, one of our classmates, a beautiful blonde. We always wondered how he managed that.

A local rock band blasts out "I Can't Get No Satisfaction" by the Rolling Stones, "Crying in the Chapel" by Elvis Presley and "Help Me Rhonda" by The Beach Boys. It's difficult to see through the blue haze of cigarette smoke, but I spot Sandy, a girl I dated a couple of times, sitting at a table. A guy from the Air Force base is trying to get her to dance. She seems annoyed and tries to ignore him, but he's persistent. I decide to rescue her.

"Hey, Sandy, wanna dance?" I ask.

"Dan! I would love to dance," she says, grabbing my hand and pulling me onto the dance floor. "Thank God you came along, that guy and his friends are creeps. They've been bothering me and my girlfriends all night."

We both remember enjoying our dates a couple years ago. "So, I heard you're going to be a priest," she says. "That's a shame."

"Well, uh—I'm thinking about it. You know, with the draft and all. Did you hear Glenn got killed?"

"Yes, I felt so bad when I heard. What a waste."

"Yeah."

"So, you're havin' second thoughts about the seminary?"

"Yeah. Even about the whole religion thing. You go to church?"

"Sometimes, to please my parents."

"Me too. I don't like the guilt thing and Catholics thinking they're right about so much stuff."

"Yeah, I know what ya mean."

I walk her back to her table and sit with her as the Jet Butts watch from the bar. Her girlfriends decide to leave, tired of being harassed. "Can you give me a ride home?" she asks.

"Sure, be happy to."

Just then, Wink, an old buddy with a body like a fireplug and a reputation as a tough, stops by the table and says, "Hey Dan— back in town? Heard you're going to be a priest. Does the bishop know you're here drinking at the Wheel?" He winks. Maybe this is where he got his nickname "Wink." Rumors have it that Wink spent some time in jail, but he never talks about it. I realized a few years ago, though, that I wouldn't want Wink as an enemy, so I've always gone out of my way to be his friend. We haven't done much together but chat in bars over a beer.

Wink says, "So, let me know how the priest thing goes. See you around."

"Sure," I agree. "Let me know if you need a 'get out of hell free card.' I've got connections now."

He laughs, "Yeah, I probably could use one."

Sandy and I dance to "Feelings" by Morris Albert. It is always the last dance of the evening, slow and close, the last chance to find someone to give a ride home and maybe make out with. The bartender flicks the lights, announcing it is two o'clock—closing time. The night has gone quickly with Sandy.

We head toward my car. "Want you to know I got a new car," I say.

"Really, what kind?"

"You'll see."

She sees the Eyeball and starts laughing until we realize the two Jet Butts are waiting in the parking lot for us. I shove her into the passenger door of my car, push the lock button down and slam the door.

The two Jet Butts are blocking me from getting into the driver's side when I hear Wink say, "You Jet Butts got a problem? I mean, now *you* got a problem—me. Now hit the road." The Jetters divert their attention from me to Wink.

"Get in the car and take your girlfriend home," Wink says to me, opening the door. Before I can get in the car, the two Jetters come after Wink and within seconds are both lying on the ground groaning, one holding a nose sprouting blood and the other in a fetal position holding his crotch.

"You boys have a good night," Wink says, then turns to me and says with a laugh, "Can I have that 'get out of hell card' now?"

"You bet, anytime. I owe you."

"Don't worry about it, take care of that gal. Hey, nice car. I like the bullet holes." He slams the door, slaps the roof and waves us out of the parking lot.

The next two weeks go by fast. Sandy and I go out a couple of more times just to have fun. We're good friends and enjoy hanging out together and making out a little.

"You know, Dan, you're a good kisser."

"Ah, um, err—thanks, you too.

"Would be a shame to see that go to waste."

"Umm, yeah."

Once again, I have second thoughts about being a priest and wasting those kisses. Two girls have told me I'm a good kisser. I must be doing something right—or maybe something wrong with this whole priest thing. I want to do the right thing, but what is right, staying true to the Church or myself?

I remember my mom telling me once, "You know, life is about family, raising kids."

I can't imagine having a family at this point in my life, but it sure feels good to be close to a girl.

Chapter 24

Pawn to Bishop Second Round

"Okay, the bishop can see you now," his secretary tells me, looking over the top of her black-rimmed glasses.

It's Tuesday afternoon, and I'm waiting in the bishop's foyer for my two o'clock appointment. His secretary escorts me into his office, and I try not to look like a liar.

"So, Dan, how did the first semester go?"

"Great. I really enjoy Latin and Theology," I tell him, thinking that is what he would like to hear.

"Good to hear. I always enjoyed Latin. What do you like about it?"

I stutter, then say, "Well, I like how it is more exact than English. And I like knowing the origin of English words from Latin."

"Yes, it gives a better understanding of English. How about theology?"

"I like Thomas Aquinas's idea that religion and science can co-exist in harmony."

"Sounds like you're developing a good philosophy of your own."

I can't believe I'm carrying on a mature conversation with the bishop. Maybe I'm not so dumb. I leave out the part that I'm just barely earning a 2.0 grade point average. For some reason, I've always been a C student despite not reading the textbooks or going to class.

"So, how are you feeling about being a priest?"

This question almost knocks me out of my chair, but thanks to the high back and side arms, I'm not thrown off. How do I feel? What's feelings? I want to object to the use of the word "feelings," but I'm sure the Pope in the photograph on the wall would shout out, "Objection overruled—answer the question."

I take a deep breath. "Well, I think my vocation is important, and I'm understanding the importance of it more each day," I answer like a true politician by not answering the question and keeping my distance from any feelings because I know they are probably too painful to acknowledge. If I were to acknowledge my true feelings, I would blurt out my anger, tears and feelings of hopelessness for Glenn, the war, my fears, my life.

The bishop accepts my answer, and I check to see if my pants are on fire.

"Okay, keep up the good work. See you next summer."

"I'll let you know when I get home."

I worry that the bishop can see right through my bullshit and could pull the plug anytime on my deferment.

I jump in the Eyeball, which I'd parked out of sight because I didn't want him to see me driving a "party car," as some people called it. I fire it up and head down to the Stein Haus.

"Hey, it's the priest!" Art addresses me as I walk in. "Did you come to hear confessions?"

"No, just to check up on you guys for the bishop." The Catholics sitting at the bar all laugh, and the protestants all have a blank stare, not knowing they are going to hell for not being Catholic.

Chapter 25

Back to Nowhere, Dakota

Christmas vacation slips by quickly. I see old friends, catch up with my parents, buy another five gallons of oil from Frenchy's Refinery, and find a couple of used snow tires for five bucks to replace the bald ones. Saturday morning, January 3, we load up the Eyeball and head for Miles City to pick up Danny.

Rolling out of Great Falls, Lucky complains from the backseat. "We need a new fucking car. We'll freeze to death in this piece of shit." I pass the Jim Beam to the backseat.

"Here, take a pull of Beam and enjoy yourself."

On the hundred-plus miles of Highway 12 from Roundup to Forsyth, windmills brace against the ruthless prairie wind, some whirling, some stilled with dangling blades waiting to be put out of their misery. Over three hours, only two rusted pickup trucks crawl by us and disappear in the rearview mirror.

A third pick up unexpectedly appears, moving in our direction like a snail. I slow down from forty to twenty-five, looking through his snow dust to see if I can pass. It's a 1948 Ford F150 with a bale of hay and a German shepherd in the back. The driver, blurred through our frosted windows, wears a grey cowboy hat with a dark sweat ring around the crown. As we pass, he nods but appears annoyed that we're in such a hurry.

Idle chatter fills our car, creating more frost on the windows and door frames.

"Wonder how far Forsyth is."

"Wonder if it's still there."

"Wonder if we're on the right road."

"Gotta be, no other roads out here."

"Only one way to go, straight ahead."

"Where's the Beam?"

"Windshield needs scraping."

"Is that deer over there?"

Suddenly, the highway morphs into seven blocks of Main Street in Forsyth. The only warning is a "Welcome, Home of the Dogies" sign. "Dogie" is slang for an orphaned calf, as in "Get along little dogie." It's a one-sided Main Street with the Northern Pacific Railroad tracks on the south side of the street. The north side boasts the Speedway Café, Hotel Howdy, Ben Franklin Five and Dime, Blakesley Bar, Buffs Bar, Masonic Temple, Lefty's Bar, Forsyth Drug and Fountain, JC Penney, Vaughn Ragsdale, Hub Western Wear, Town Bowling, City Barber, Roundup Room Lounge, County Courthouse and Roxy Theater playing *The Alamo.* It will be another fifteen years before the Interstate 94 bypass sucks the lifeblood out of the community and leaves remnants of a western culture that will cling on for years.

We stop at the Speedway Café for burgers, fries and hot coffee. The waitress looks older, probably in her late thirties. She wears tight cowgirl jeans, boots and a white blouse that shows some cleavage when she bends over the table to pour coffee.

"What can I get you boys?"

"I'll have coffee and a burger."

"Sure, Honey. And what about you, Sweetie?" she asks Jim.

"Well, err— the same."

I guess waitresses have the liberty to call customers, "Sweetie, Honey and You Boys."

"Where you boys coming from?"

"Great Falls, on our way to Richardton."

"Oh, you going to the college there?"

"Yeah, back to school after Christmas break."

"You going to study to be priests?"

"No, the regular college," I say, making it clear we are available.

"Priests—that would be a waste of good-looking guys like you."

We wonder what an older woman would be like. She flirts with us just enough to get us hot and bothered, giving us something to talk about for the next two hundred miles.

We continue driving on, and somewhere outside Beach, I hit a patch of ice and the Eyeball spins a 360-degree circle, skidding into a snow-filled ditch. The engine kills, and it takes a minute to realize we are still alive.

Jim says, "Let me behind the wheel." I crawl out of the driver's seat, shaken. Jim fires up the Eyeball, rocks the car back and forth using first and reverse gears. The Eyeball begins to inch forward. Soon we begin moving, and Jim continues to drive down the ditch for a few hundred feet. When we have enough momentum, he steers the Eyeball back up onto the highway, and we are off again.

"Piece of cake," he says.

"The Eyeball always comes through."

"Hail the Eyeball."

The Eyeball smiles and puts its head down into the wind.

We finally pull into the Abbey late that night for our second term. The next morning, we voluntarily return the car keys to Fr. Louis as a goodwill gesture but keep a half-dollar coin in reserve in case we need to connect the terminals and hotwire the ignition.

Chapter 26

Hell Still Frozen Over

"Haven't seen the ground since September," I say to Jim.

"Yeah, snow is piling up. We walked up on the barn roof yesterday."

"No shit, I can't believe this."

The winter of '65–66 has North Dakota in a deep freezer with the door open just a crack so we can see more snow continue to accumulate. We haven't seen the ground since October 4, 1965, almost four months ago. Residents have been shoveling snow off their roofs to keep them from collapsing. Shoveled snow from sidewalks creates walls that look like a giant gopher has tunneled down each street. At the farm behind the college, sheds and a barn are inundated by immense drifts where the snow has flowed around.

Farmers are hard-pressed this winter to feed and protect their livestock. Ten of thousands of cattle and sheep have already succumbed. The National Guard drops hay to stranded cattle from helicopters and C-130 transport planes. It's not Vietnam, but it's a war for survival against the brutal winter.

The small town of Shields sits in a valley on the Cannonball River about a hundred miles southeast of Richardton. Only the steeple on the church is visible above the snow. National Guard helicopters bring in food and airlift residents out for medical emergencies.

Meanwhile, our faithful companion, The Eyeball, refuses to surrender to the brutal winter. It escorts us on our rounds of the country dances. We continue to hit the high spots of North Dakota nightlife—Taylor, population 793; Gladstone, 239; Halliday, 188; Mott, 721; New England, 621; and New Salem, 947.

Winter in Richardton

Chapter 27

Beergate

"I just can't believe the snow," I say to Jim.

"Yeah, now it's frozen like a rock."

"Yeah, you can almost drive a car over the drifts."

In April, the door on the deep freezer opens wider and allows us to peek into spring. For the past seven months, the white prairie has seemed to flow like a mighty river from north to south, fed by an infinite snow machine hidden somewhere near Santa's North Pole. The constant wind has shifted and shaped the landscape to look like an abandoned planet, but now the spring snows are heavy and wet, freezing this mighty river into a tray of hard frozen custard. The wet snow clings to everything and brings down stately cottonwood trees along the streets in town. Power lines stretch like rubber bands and eventually break, snapping the town into darkness for days.

The spring sun gradually shrinks the mounds of snow covering the lower windows on the dorm, allowing us to peer out of our cave entrance. Each day, red Budweiser and blue Hamm's beer cans begin to sprout like Easter lilies from the huge drift that runs the entire length of the dorm. For the past seven months, beer cans have been chucked out the windows, swallowed by the snow monster. Unfortunately, none traveled more than a few feet. By May, a flourishing crop of beer cans is ready for harvest.

It's the first Saturday of May, and I return from breakfast to find my room turned upside down. A raid! The black robes, seeing the beer cans outside the dorm, search every room looking for contraband beer. They find no evidence in my room because I was smart enough to drink in the rooms of my friends.

"What the hell happened?" Jim asks.

"Goddamned Gestapo pulled a raid."

"Oh, shit, there's going to be some guys in trouble."

We run across the hall to Don and Rich's room and find them packing their suitcases. Their room had served as the local pub for the dorm.

"Busted," says Don, throwing stuff into his suitcase. "They have us on the three o'clock train to Billings. Guess my deferment is down the drain. My parents are going to kick my ass. I don't know what I'll tell them. My dad isn't pretty when he's mad. I don't know what's worse, my dad or the draft."

"Me too," says Rich, stuffing clothes into a footlocker. "They didn't give us a chance to say anything." Rich is more scared than pissed. I'm scared, too, realizing how close I came to getting caught.

"I'll drive you down to the station," I offer.

"Yeah, if we're going out, then let's go out in style in the Eyeball," beams Don.

We load up the Eyeball and drive in silence to the train station as the reality of Don and Rich getting kicked out sinks in. Two tickets are waiting for them at the ticket window. I hate to see them go. We had a lot of fun messing with each other, and we bonded over crazy things like sparrows, following ropes across campus in storms, and trying to find hot girls in a frozen tundra. I'm almost envious of them going home to civilization. Maybe they are the lucky ones escaping from the priesthood—but not so lucky walking into the jaws of the Vietnam War.

"You guys take it easy and good luck with your parents and the draft," I say sadly.

"Thanks, and take care of the Eyeball—it showed us some good times," Don says. "Hey, what happened with you and that gal you waltzed out of St. Mary's Gym that night we dumped the Everclear in the punch bowl?"

"Nothing I would tell in a confessional."

"You dirty dog!" Don shouts. "So that's where you disappeared to. You're going to hell for sure—but it will be worth it."

Don and Rich board the train and yell back at us, "Don't let the bastards get you down," then flash the peace sign. We flash it back, but inside we are scared and sad.

We return to the dorm and see Fr. Robert supervising a dozen guys picking up beer cans. As soon as he sees us, he says, "You guys help us here," pointing at the half-block-long snowdrift gleaming with aluminum. The priests have rousted everyone out of their rooms to help. We're like a chain gang from a 30s movie in the south but without the striped prison suits.

We hadn't seen Fr. Louis much during the year. I think it was easier for him to let us slip through the cracks rather than try to supervise us from a distance. He belongs to the Benedictine Order, and we're under the auspices of the Bishop of Great Falls, so he doesn't have a vested interest in us.

Fr. Louis, at six-and-a-half feet tall, is intimidating just by his sheer presence. He enjoys academic studies—he's a student of history—but has little interest or knowledge of practical matters like mechanics. He had heard about a raid with firecrackers on the seminarian's dorm and came by to find out if Jim and I knew anything about it. Perhaps he knew our penchant for practical jokes.

We overhear him saying to Fr. Robert, "Did you find any beer in Dan or Jim's room?"

"No, their room was clean. They didn't seem to be involved."

Fr. Louis looks pleased and comes over to Jim and me. "I'm glad to hear you boys are behaving and weren't mixed up in this."

"Yeah, we try not to hang out with the guys that drink," we lie.

"I see your car has moved since last fall. I made it clear to you boys you couldn't drive. Do you have a second key?"

"No, we gave you the only key," I tell him, which is the truth, so it won't have to be confessed later. "We had to push the car back to make sure the bearing in the wheels didn't freeze up over the winter." Of course, *this* lie will have to be confessed someday.

"Oh, okay—just don't be driving it." Fr. Louis walks off.

"Man, that was too easy. I can't believe he fell for that." We both stand there and give a sigh of relief.

Chapter 28

The Incident, Is This a Sin?

"I heard Fr. Louis and the seminarians are doing some kind of a dig looking for Fr. De Smet's camp," Jim says.

"Wonder where they are digging?"

"Dunno, let's try and find out."

Saturday morning, May 14, 1966, finds the North Dakota prairie revealing brown patches of dirt between white drifts of snow. The sun has finally taken the edge off winter, and bits of green grass sprout on the south side of hills. It has been nearly eight months since we had last seen the ground. Fortunately, everyone has survived, including our faithful companion, the Eyeball.

With spring arriving at last, the seminarians have been with Fr. Louis on an excavation looking for evidence that Fr. De Smet, a Belgian Roman Catholic missionary, traveled through this area and camped here on his way west in the early 1840s. Chatter pours from the seminarians' table during breakfast about this exciting project. For some reason, Jim and I don't identify with the seminarians, mainly because we are living a life of sin in the college dorm while the bishop is paying the bill. Luckily for us, our consciences are operating at an all-time low, and as a last resort, there is always confession to save us from hell. The seminarians are local North Dakota boys—naive, sheltered and not of the world. We don't have much in common with these nerds, but they are perfect targets for practical jokes.

After breakfast, the seminarians and Fr. Louis noisily ride a yellow school bus to the site, a location where Fr. Louis thinks Fr. De Smet camped on his journey to Montana over a century ago. Fr. Louis loves the history of the West and dreams of connecting Fr. De Smet with this part of North Dakota.

Jim and I watch as the bus pulls out of the parking lot. "Let's follow them," Jim says.

"Yeah, good idea."

We jump in the Eyeball, and I hotwire the beast into life.

"Hurry up, don't lose em," Jim yells. "Stay back, so they don't see us."

We follow the dust trail of the bus down a gravel road. After about ten miles, it turns off the road and travels a quarter-mile across the prairie.

Before the turnoff, Jim says, "Pull over here and hide the car. We'll walk to the top and see what's goin' on."

"Okay, keep low. If Louie sees us, we're screwed," I say.

We steal up the knoll and crawl the last fifty feet until we can peer over the top and look down on the group.

"Look at 'em, what a bunch of losers," I say. "We should pull some shit on them. Those 'holier than thou' seminarians—glad we didn't have to be in the dorm with 'em. It woulda killed me."

"How could we screw with 'em?" Jim says.

"Maybe fake some relic of De Smet."

"Holy shit, I got it!" Jim says, trying not to shout in excitement. "I've got the crucifix my aunt gave me. We could make it look old and fool 'em with it."

Suddenly, we are on a mission. Hurriedly, we retreat from the knoll and head back to the dorm. In our room, Jim grabs his crucifix. "Look at this beauty. It's made of brass—how can we make it look old?"

"Vinegar and salt," I shout, remembering my high school chemistry.

We head to the cafeteria and grab a salt shaker off a table. In the kitchen, Leroy and Bill are doing prep work for dinner, and the manager isn't there.

“Hey, Leroy, got some vinegar? We need it for a science project.” Leroy could care less why we would want vinegar.

“Yeah, here. Take as much as you want.” Leroy hands us a quart.

On our way out, we grab a plate from the serving line and make a beeline back to Jim’s room, where we mix the vinegar and salt on the plate and put the crucifix in it.

“How long will it take?” Jim asks.

“I dunno. Maybe a couple days.”

The next morning, we eagerly check the crucifix, and while it’s a little tarnished, it doesn’t look old. On the third day, the brass plating is coming off, and the figure of Jesus is turning black. On the fifth day, the crucifix is corroded enough to look like it had been buried for a long time.

“Looks like 1840 to me,” Jim says, holding up the crucifix. “Do I look like Fr. De Smet?”

“No, you look like an asshole who is going to hell.”

Friday night after dark, Jim and I cruise down the dirt road toward the site. “Turn here,” Jim yells. “You almost missed the turn. That’s the knoll we were on.” He points out the window.

We drive about a quarter of a mile until the headlights shine on a square pit dug down about twelve inches into the level prairie and surrounded by white cotton string stretched around four corner pegs.

“Kill the lights,” Jim says. “We don’t want some farmer driving by and catching us.”

“So, what do we do now?”

“Bury it just below the surface,” Jim says, bending over the edge of the pit so as not to leave footprints. “Make it look like it’s been there forever.” He digs down about two inches. Using his hand to scrape away the loose soil, he puts the corroded crucifix into the small depression and covers it up. We pat the dirt down until it looks like it hasn’t been disturbed.

We slowly drive back to the road with the headlights off, then tear back to the dorm and quietly sneak into the parking lot. Back in Jim’s room, we laugh it up.

"Those dumb asses, they'll probably think they discovered the pyramids."

"We can't tell anyone," Jim warns me. "Not even our friends. If word gets out, we're screwed."

"Okay, a pact—no one else knows."

On Saturday morning, the seminarians board the bus bound for the site. We follow the trail of dust, park behind the knoll and crawl until we can peer over the top through last year's foot-high prairie grass. The ground is wet from melted snow, and after two hours, the fronts of our pants and jackets are wet. Things are quiet about a hundred yards from us.

"I wish those dumb asses would find it," I say. "What's taking them so long?"

"Yeah, after all, they're professional archaeologists."

After another hour, we are getting cold and hungry. We hadn't thought to bring anything to eat. Suddenly, we hear the booming voice of Fr. Louis reverberating across the prairie. "We found it, we found it," he shouts out, holding the crucifix high above his towering frame.

"Holy shit, they found it!" I say. "Let's get the hell out of here before we're spotted."

When we are out of sight and can run, we slop in the muddy prairie on our way back to the car. We jump in the Eyeball and hightail it back to the dorm, fearing that we will be caught but laughing hysterically.

In our rooms, we change into dry clothes, hoping no one had seen us. We wash our jackets and pants in the dorm laundry and wait for them to dry.

"Remember, don't tell anyone," Jim reminds me.

"Yeah, I got it. No one."

Malley stops by and asks, "What you guys doing today?"

"Not much, just getting some laundry done."

"Hey, does Fr. Louis ever say anything about you having a car?" he asks.

"No, we gave him the keys. That keeps him happy."

"So, I heard Louie is out doing some archaeology dig or something with the seminarians," he says.

"Yeah, we heard something about that but didn't pay much attention," Jim says.

That evening in the cafeteria, there is a great buzz around the seminarians' tables about the big "find." Jim and I eavesdrop, trying not to laugh.

William, the seminarian who actually uncovered the crucifix, is bragging to the others, "Yeah, I was just scraping away the dirt and noticed a gold shine and kept brushing away and this cross showed up. I called Fr. Louis, and he came over and then got all excited and started yelling, 'We found it, we found it' over and over like he discovered gold or something."

Another seminarian chimes in, "He wants to publish an article for some magazine. I guess it would make him famous."

Hearing this, Jim and I look at each other and mutter, "Oh shit!" under our breaths.

"What are we going to do now?" I say.

"I dunno, but it's getting out of hand with the article and everything. Louie is going crazy," Jim whispers.

We go back to my room and try to figure out what to do. Jim suggests, "Maybe we should go talk to Louie and tell him what happened."

"If we tell him he'd kill us and then send us home to the draft."

"Yeah, that's a dumb idea, but we can't let him write that article. Louie's not a bad guy."

"How about we write a letter and just put it under his door?"

"Okay, but we have to make sure no one can trace the letter," Jim says with an aura of paranoia, "like a handwriting expert or something."

"We could cut letters out of a magazine like a ransom note."

"Not a bad idea," Jim says, grabbing a couple of *Time* magazines off the desk.

Over the next couple of hours, we carefully cut-and-paste—or I should say "tape?" the following letters onto a piece of typing paper. It reads:

> Dear Father Louis We are sorry to tell you the crucifix you found was planted there by immoral students as a joke. We have to hide our identity or face severe repercussions from the guilty ones. Signed, Just trying to help.

"Perfect," I say. If we get caught, we can say we were just telling on the ones who really did it."

"It's a brilliant plan, I must say," adds Jim. "When can we put it under his door?"

"Tomorrow morning when he's saying Mass. There's lots of people who don't go to Mass, so it will be hard to suspect us."

"Okay, tomorrow morning we can sneak over to his office."

Early Sunday morning, Jim and I walk to the cafeteria as if going to breakfast. Once inside the main building, we make our way to Fr. Louis's office and slip the note under his door along with some of our guilt.

"Let's get outta here before someone comes," Jim says.

We scurry back to the cafeteria, where we hang out, waiting for the seminarians to come from Mass. They soon file in looking half asleep from getting up early. Most of the students from the college are still sleeping. We are hoping to get some new tidbits by eavesdropping on the archaeology table, but there is no new news, so we head back to the dorm to nap.

Around ten o'clock, a knock at the door awakens us. It is Keith, one of the seminarians. He announces, "There is a meeting of all seminarians at eleven this morning. Fr. Louis wants you to come." He then leaves Jim and me standing there in our underwear.

"Oh shit, he must be onto us," I say.

"Do you suppose he suspects us?"

"I dunno, we'll find out."

We arrive at the seminarian study hall and wait with the other seminarians for Fr. Louie. We are nervously sitting in the back of the room when Fr. Louis comes in. We can see he has the "ransom" note in his hand.

He towers in the front of the room and says, "Yesterday we thought we had found evidence of Fr. De Smet traveling through North Dakota, but now I have evidence this was a prank." The room becomes quieter.

He reads the note out loud over my thumping heart. "It's important we find out who did this," he says. "I'll need your help. Keep an eye out for who did this."

Jim and I sit in the back of the room thinking about the irony of this. We are being asked to help find us, the culprits, ourselves. Over the next few weeks, talk about the incident dies down, and Jim and I gradually relax. We become tough guys again. "Those dumb asses, they believed that shit," we say to each other in so many words.

Over time, our memories of the incident embolden us, and we turn ourselves into local heroes who duped Fr. Louis. But inside, my feelings of guilt about using the bishop, the church, my parent's reputation, Fr. Louis and the whole seminary thing for my own selfish avoidance of the draft gnaws away at me. Years later, I suspect, I will have to make amends with myself and many others.

Chapter 29

Another Round of Steaks on the House

The school year ends with what seems like nine long months of detention. Finals week finds us cramming for exams in Latin, Philosophy, American History, Theology and English, all those subjects that will get you a great job as CEO of Philosophy, Inc. or Priests-R-Us. We cram in groups of three or four, usually in the day room of the dorm, pulling all-nighters and staggering into finals to dump our short-lived knowledge on a piece of paper and then head to the dorm to sleep until the next cram session.

Tuesday night, Malley, Jim, Driscol and I cram, trying to inject coffee, potato chips and the Spanish-American War directly into our veins. Around one in the morning, Malley says, "Hey guys, I'm hungry, let's go fry up some steaks." Malley had stolen a key for the kitchen from one of the other students who works there, made a copy and then returned the original before anyone noticed. We all quietly steal out of the dorm and head over to the cafeteria under cover of darkness.

"Quiet, yous guys," Driscol whispers in perfect New Jerseyspeak, "Yous never know if da black robes are around. Eh, stay low an' keep movin."

I trust Driscol. Being from Jersey, he probably has had on-the-job-training in night maneuvers from the Mafia. We find our way to the cafeteria, where Malley unlocks the main door with the skill of the cat burglar while Driscol covers our backs. Inside, we make our way to the kitchen, turn on a dim light and fire up the grill.

Malley digs through the refrigerator and says, "Okay, you have a choice—top sirloin or T-bone." These special cuts are reserved for the priests, who are served in a separate dining room. This isn't the first time we've had a "snack" in the middle of the night courtesy of Malley. When the priests have extra guests, the steak inventory goes up, and a few missing steaks are not noticed. We get by with this trick a couple of times a month.

"I'll have the T-bone," Driscol pipes up. We all put in our orders, and Malley soon has two T-bones and three top sirloins sizzling on the grill. He has it down to a science.

"Okay, Dris, one rare T-bone coming up," Malley says, flopping the steak on a plate. We all tear into our steaks with the enthusiasm of wolves without the howling. A half-hour later finds us sneaking back to the dorm.

I get my final grades—Latin, B; Philosophy, C; American History, C; Theology, C; and English, C. As I look at my grades, the voice of my eighth-grade teacher, Sister Mary Phillips, rings in my head, "If you would only apply yourself, you could get straight As." Well, a 2.2 GPA is enough to keep me out of the draft, so I quickly push Sister Phillips' admonishment out of my head and continue underachieving.

Chapter 30

Sentence Served, Heading Home to the Draft Board

Finally, the school year is over. On our last Friday morning, everyone is moving out of the dorm and heading home. Some load their luggage in cars and others catch a ride down to the train station. Malley and Driscol load up Malley's black 1964 Pontiac Bonneville for their trip back to the East Coast.

"Yous guys stay out of trouble," Driscol says.

"Yeah, good times with you boys from Montaaaaana," Malley says, mocking us like the bleating of a sheep.

I shoot back, "Yeah, you guys turned out to be okay for city slickers. If your car gets low on oil, just wring some out of your hair."

Malley revs up the 389 cubic inch engine in the Bonneville, pops the clutch and yells out the window, "See ya, suckers!" He proceeds to spin a half-dozen brodies in the parking lot, throwing dust and gravel in a wide circle. The car fishtails out of the lot, its spinning rear tires squealing as they hit the pavement. I think of Glenn spinning brodies in the Four Lights parking lot.

Jim, Lucky, Layne and I load up the Eyeball for our trip home to Great Falls. We jump on the roof to cave it into a depression to better carry luggage. Then we tie the luggage down, add a quart of oil, pump up one half-deflated tire, fire up the engine and head down Highway 10 toward Beach, North Dakota. The Eyeball senses we are going home—it backfires and blows smoke out the muffler as if saying, "I'm done with this bullshit, let's roll."

Eyeball ready to roll

Spring has sprouted through the landscape as a green wave washing across the prairie over scattered skeletons of livestock who succumbed to the Blizzard of '65–66. Life has returned to the land; birds flit, cows graze, grasses wave and antelope romp. We ignore the carnage, whistle with the birds and dream of being home.

"Finally getting out of this shithole," Lucky says.

"Yeah, you actually look happy."

"Whatever."

I'm trying to figure out how to tell the bishop that I've "lost my vocation." He's footed the bill for my last year of college. I feel a bit guilty for taking advantage of him, but it quickly goes away when I consider how the Catholic Church weighed me down with unnecessary guilt. We were taught that we all suffer from "original sin" and are therefore flawed in some way and need to be saved. I always wondered how babies could be flawed by original sin as if it were their fault that Adam and Eve had decided to think for themselves. I should say Eve did—Adam just followed along like a typical guy.

Eve got the bad rap for tasting the fruit of the Tree of Good and Evil, but I've always looked at it differently. That first couple could have stayed in the Garden of Eden and frittered away their lives in luxury, never doing anything to grow mentally, emotionally or spiritually. In a sense, the Garden of Eden was like a form of denial, just maintaining the status quo. Eve, like most women, wanted to grow and expand herself. I think this is why women like to go to counseling and men would rather watch sports on TV.

So, Eve took a bite out of the fruit and moved from denial into recovery or a state of growth. Adam, unable to see the benefits of recovery and growth, went along for the ride, and thus the human race entered into recovery. And this is the way it is today— some folks live their lives in denial, and some have moved into recovery. Eve never got credit for having the guts to move into new territory and is blamed for ruining Adam's addiction to watching sports on TV.

The miles and cans of Hamm's Beer click by quickly as we roar through familiar small towns and dots in the road.

We stop at the Speedway Café in Forsyth and find our favorite waitress standing behind the counter. "What brings you boys back?" she asks.

We don't have the nerve to answer honestly, "Your perfume and half-open white blouse," so we just mutter, "Coffee and french fries."

Refreshed from our visit, the miles go by fast as we speculate about an "older woman," in other words, anyone over twenty-five.

Once again, the Big Stack of the Anaconda smelter signals us across the prairie, and Great Falls appears on the horizon—we are almost home. The speedometer on the Eyeball bounces off seventy as if it doesn't give a shit. I'm free from North Dakota, but now I must face the bishop and Tollefsrud at the draft board.

Jim and I roll into town, stop by our parents for a visit and then head for the Stein Haus. "The priests are back," Art says. "Should we bow, kneel or genuflect?"

"At ease. We lost our vocation, so you can get up off your knees," Jim says.

"Sure, anything you say, Father." Art clunks two bottles of Hamm's on the bar.

It's the summer of 1966, and I have a mission. First, to beat the draft. Second, to tell the bishop that I lost my vocation. And third, to find a girlfriend.

The following Tuesday, I nervously wait outside the bishop's office to see him. His secretary finally ushers me into his office, where the large photograph of the Pope stares at me and says, "I know what you did. You're going to hell."

"So, how was the semester?" the bishop asks.

"Good. I had a lot of time to do some soul searching and came to realize I'm not sure of my vocation and need some time to pray about it," I say as if I'm reading off a cue card.

"It sounds like you have some doubts about it, my son." He calls everyone with a vocation "son."

I continue to read from the cue card the Pope seems to be holding for me. "Yes, I'm not sure I'm worthy to be a priest and need to do more introspection." I'm slowly weaseling my way out of the seminary. "Maybe by the end of the summer, I'll have resolved this feeling of not feeling worthy." With these words, the Pope tosses the cue card in the wastebasket. In my mind, my speech is perfectly logical. After a less-than-unworthy year in North Dakota, I'm technically not "worthy."

"Well, pray over it, and I'll pray for you."

"Okay, I'll let you know how I'm doing at the end of the summer," I say goodbye. The Eyeball waiting around the corner mutters, "Talked yourself out of another one." But like a loyal dog, he fires up and delivers me to the office of the draft board downtown, where I find Lars Tollefsrud still sitting behind his desk. Lars doesn't seem to have moved or changed clothes since I saw him nine months ago. He isn't too happy to see me and comments, "Are you still doing that priest thing?"

"Yes sir, I still want to be a priest and plan to return next year to the seminary." Little does he know I have put the bishop on notice but am keeping the door open until the end of the summer.

"You better be going back to the seminary," he says. "In the meantime, we're sending you for a physical in Butte just in case you don't return. You'll get your seminary deferment status back when you return to school," he tells me with joy in his voice.

Now I'm a pawn caught between the bishop and the draft board.

Check.

Chapter 31

U.S. Army Closing In

A chartered Greyhound bus strains over Elk Park Pass at 6,300 feet above sea level and coasts the steep four miles into the Butte bus station before grinding to a stop. A waiting army sergeant barks, "Okay, everybody outa the bus. Check into your room at the Finlen and report to the induction center on Granite Street at eight a.m. sharp."

"If this is army life, I don't like it already," I comment to Willie, my seat mate.

"Yeah, I already don't like it," he says.

"Let's get to the Finlen and get a room ahead of these guys."

Willie and I highball it to the Finlen and check into a room with two single beds, a sink, two chairs and a small table. The bathroom is down the hall. We throw our small bags on the bed and head out.

"Let's hit the M&M first," Willie says.

"Yeah, that's where most everyone is gonna meet up."

We had just arrived with thirty other guys to get the US Army physical, which basically checks for hernias, hemorrhoids, flat feet—and to see if you have an IQ over eighty.

At the M&M, beer is cheap, as with every other bar in Butte. Soon a dozen inductees are chattering at the bar.

"Fuck the draft, what a bunch of bullshit."

"I hope the X-rays of my feet get me a deferment. Some guys get out with flat feet."

"Yeah, I heard that."

"When they going to ship us off?"

"Dunno, maybe in a few weeks."

"Buddy of mine got killed in Nam, Glenn Black."

"Yeah, saw that in the *Tribune*. Only lasted for three weeks."

"I heard one guy got killed his first day."

"Bunch of 'em got killed the first day."

"Better than getting killed on your last day."

"Hey, let's get the hell outta here and head to the Alcoma."

"Yeah, heard there are some gals hanging out there."

With this, we begin checking off a long list of bars on our rounds of the town— the Alcoma Lounge, Club 13, the Corner Bar, the Helsinki, Maloney's and a half-dozen others lost in a fog of beer. Fortunately, or unfortunately, in Butte, one can always find bars that are open after the legal closing time of two o'clock. At four, we find ourselves back at the M&M devouring rib-eye steaks, eggs, toast and hash browns smothered with Heinz ketchup. After breakfast, we nurse a "red-eye" to ward off a worse hangover, and with little time to spare, rush to our eight o'clock appointment for physicals.

Thirty of us stagger into the exam room. There is nothing worse than to see thirty hungover, smelly, farting, belching, dry heaving guys standing single file in their shorts, scratching their asses and nuts. The physical is quick—turn your head and cough as the doctor sticks his fingers up your scrotum looking for a hernia. Then drop your shorts, bend over, spread your cheeks as the doc checks for hemorrhoids. Basically, if you can walk and chew gum at the same time, you pass the physical. Many of the recruits carry X-rays and doctor reports as evidence that they should be excluded from the draft, but it's usually is a futile argument with the bored doctors who are probably paying off medical school bills by serving in the military service.

I pass the physical—no surprise—and head home hungover, depressed and thinking of Glenn taking the same physical.

The following week I get a letter saying I am draft status 1-A. I'm told to make sure the draft board knows of my whereabouts during the summer. Basically, I'm a suspect being told not to leave town. My 2S student deferment will be reinstated if I return to the seminary in the fall.

A week later, I sit patiently in the recruitment office of the Montana Air National Guard at Gore Hill. I'm here to enlist in the National Guard. A couple dozen "draft dodgers" are also waiting in the reception area to sign up. The competition is stiff. It's either get into the Guard, go to Canada, become a conscientious objector or a priest, or end up in the army. For me, there is one glitch—if a person has already been drafted, you can't join a guard or reserve unit.

I fill out the application paperwork and conveniently forget to mention that I've been drafted, hoping they won't check. I'm given an aptitude test, which I pass with four scores of 100 percent. The voice of my eighth-grade teacher whispers in my ear, "See, I told you that if you applied yourself, you could do well."

The National Guard recruiter is impressed and sends me to speak with Captain Earl.

"You aced all your tests," he tells me. "Would you be interested in going into crypto?"

I'm not exactly sure what crypto is, but I show interest in anything that will keep me out of the draft. "That sounds very interesting," I tell him, hoping he will explain what it is.

"Crypto requires a top-secret clearance by the FBI and entails deciphering top-secret messages and operating the military's communication network. Do you have anything in your past that might keep you from getting a top-secret clearance?" he asks me.

At this moment, every questionable thing I have done in my life flashes before my eyes. While I've pulled some pranks, I hope they aren't serious enough to keep me from getting a security clearance.

Would the fact that I confessed those things make me look better with the FBI?

"Do you have any criminal record?" he asks.

This time I can answer truthfully, unless getting into someone's bra, lying to the bishop or getting served with phony IDs is criminal. "No, I can't think of anything criminal. I've never been arrested for anything."

"Great, we'll process the paperwork and swear you in a month or so after the FBI does a background check," he says.

During the next month, several of my friends ask if I'm in trouble. An FBI agent has been asking around town about my background. I see my roommate Larry at work, and he says excitedly, "An FBI agent was in the store today asking about you. He wanted to know how much you drink."

"What'd you tell him?"

"That you didn't drink no more than anyone else. Oh, but I didn't tell him how much everybody else drinks. You in trouble?"

"No, just a background check for the Guard. I gotta get in the Guard or I'm off to Nam. My grades aren't that great, so I don't know if I'll get a deferment."

"Yeah, I'm trying to study and keep my grades up," Larry says. He's a farm/ranch boy from the Judith Mountains south of Great Falls—a good guy with a great heart. I would trust him with anything. Physically, he's a big guy, and a couple times being with him in a rough bar was enough to keep drunk cowboys from bothering us.

After a long wait, I am accepted into the Guard. The swearing-in ceremony is short, and with three other guys, I pledge allegiance to the constitution of the United States of America. After the ceremony, I'm handed papers showing I'm in the National Guard and head down to see Lars at the draft board. I'm on my best behavior, being my usual Eddie Haskell lookalike. I carefully explain to Lars that there must be a mistake because I'm a member of the National Guard and shouldn't be 1A draft status.

"So, you're not gonna be a priest?"

"No, I decided to go into the National Guard," hoping he likes this better than being a priest.

"Well, if you're in the Guard, we'll have to change your draft card." He once again begins the long and painful process of processing my file. After what seems like two weeks, he pulls completed forms out of his Underwood, lays them on his desk side by side and reaches for his stamp buried somewhere in the cluttered cardboard box on his desk. He slams the stamp on the ink pad and then onto the forms, signs the forms and hands me a copy.

For some reason, he doesn't check the date on my military letter which would have informed him that my acceptance into the Guard came after I was classified 1A. I sit quietly during this process and try not to drip sweat all over the floor. For the past ten minutes, I have experienced what hell must be like.

With papers in hand and free from the draft, I fire up the Eyeball and head for the Stein Haus. As I walk in, Art says, "It's the priest, what's up?"

"I just beat the draft," I say, showing him my papers. "No priest, no draft, a round of beer for everyone. Screw the draft." I write a ten-dollar hold check dated for next week, and Art puts it in a cigar box behind the bar and hands me ten bucks in cash until I can make the check good on payday.

"Glad you beat the draft," Art says, "but I think you would have made a good priest."

"Yeah, uhh—thanks."

Chapter 32

Everyone Needs a Date Who Loses Her Panties

"I called Lucky. He says to come up, and we can party," I tell Sig.

"Cool."

"He said he can line us up and get us served."

"Good for Lucky, I'm glad he's not still pissed about freezing his feet driving home with you guys."

"Yeah, he got over it."

With this exchange, Sig and I plan a trip to Glacier National Park. It's 140 miles north of Great Falls. We wash the sheets on the Eyeball seats, pour in a quart of oil and fill the gas tank at the Maverick Station, where gas sells for thirty-one cents a gallon. The pump has a coin slot that takes silver dollars. We drop five of them into the slot, enough to fill the twenty-gallon tank. In 1966, silver dollars are still the preferred currency in Montana. Paper dollars just can't be trusted.

The next stop is Buttrey's for a case of Hamm's Beer for $2.69, which we put on ice in a Styrofoam cooler. We throw in a large bag of peanuts in the shell, two bags of potato chips, a container of french onion chip dip, two big cans of tomato juice, a box of Ritz crackers with two pounds of cheese, a dozen Hershey bars, six packs of Marlboros for me and six of Lucky Strikes for Sig. We head north out of Great Falls through the tiny communities of Vaughn, Dutton, Conrad and Valier, making pit stops on the side of the highway to the chagrin of passing motorists. At Browning, we restock our beer supply with six 40-ounce bottles of A1 beer, paying thirty-nine cents for each one.

"Boy, Browning is a tough-looking town," Sig says.

"Yeah, some hard times here."

"It's sad what happened to the Indians."

"My aunt taught school here in the forties. She loved it. Thought the Indians were great."

"It must have changed a lot since then."

Browning is the tribal seat for the Blackfeet Nation. It's a small town of fewer than 2,000 people, 95 percent of whom are Blackfeet. It's a mixed community of native pride and culture but with an unemployment rate of 69 percent and a high incidence of alcoholism. Indian reservations are a sad commentary on how, over 400 years, the U.S. government managed to eliminate half the Native American tribes—from 1,000 when Columbus landed to just five hundred today. But the elimination went further—it also eliminated language, religion, custom and identity. It separated families, too, using the system of boarding schools. The Christian boarding schools were notorious for the physical and sexual abuse of young Indian children taken from their parents' arms.

In the 1960s, many of the natives remain lost between the white man's world and isolation on reservations. Browning is no different. It's a tough place. The bars are rowdy, so we buy our beer at a local grocery store.

Browning holds the world record for the fastest temperature change in a twenty-four-hour period. In 1916, from noon on January 23 to noon on January 24, the temperature dropped 100 degrees—from plus forty-four degrees F to minus fifty-six degrees F. Things happen fast out on the western plains, and people can get in trouble in many ways.

Today, our goal is to find Lucky Black, a classmate from the seminary in North Dakota. He lives in the small village of St. Mary's twenty-three miles up a reservation road on the edge of Glacier National Park.

We find Lucky at the park's summer employee dormitory. There are two dorms, one for men and one for women. St. Mary's is a small community of fifty locals and a couple hundred seasonal workers who provide services for tourists in the park. Lucky's dad owns the hotel and restaurant along with the dorms where the seasonal park employees live.

"Good to see you," Lucky says. "I see the Eyeball is still running. Gotta hand it to her, she got us outta North Dakota."

"Yeah, old reliable."

"Surviving the draft?

"Yeah, got into the Guard."

"So, you not goin' back to the sem?"

"Nope, lost my vocation."

"Me too," he tells us. "Don't know if I had one in the first place, but it kept me out of the army. I'm trying to keep my 2S and go back to college this fall."

"So, where are the girls?" Sig asks.

"Over at the girl's dorm waiting for you guys to get here. I've got you all lined up for the night. We'll go up to Babb where we can get served."

A tiny town of less than a couple dozen people, Babb is nine miles north near the Canadian border in the middle of the Blackfeet Reservation. I have a feeling we will be the only white guys there tonight. Lucky seems to know his way around here, so I trust he'll take care of us.

We walk into the foyer of the dorm and see three girls sitting on a wooden bench carved out of a big log. "Who's got who?" Sig whispers to Lucky.

"Patty's mine," Lucky explains. "You and Dan decide between Jill and Rhonda." He doesn't seem to realize the girls might have something to say about it.

We walk up to the girls, who are as friendly and nervous as we are.

"Hi, this is Sig and Dan," Lucky says, then points to each girl in turn. "This is Patty, Jill and Rhonda."

I quickly do some figuring on who I should hustle, Jill or Rhonda. Jill is slimmer, but Rhonda has a nice smile.

"Hi, glad to meet you," I say, shaking each of the girls' hands. Sig does the same.

Patty is the first girl to speak. "Lucky tells us you all were in the seminary together. Looks like it didn't take."

"Yeah, we kinda lost our vocations," I say, not sure if they would know what that means.

"Yeah, my brother lost his vocation too, but he was never very serious about it," Rhonda says. With this, I figure Rhonda is Catholic too, so we have something in common.

Lucky interrupts by saying, "Well, shall we head up to Babb?"

We walk out to the Eyeball. "Hope you don't like us just for our car," I say.

The three girls look a little surprised by the appearance of the Eyeball, but they laugh.

Rhonda says, "Yeah, I always wanted to go on a date in a car with an eyeball painted on the front and bullet holes in the door."

As we get in, I quickly say to Rhonda, "Wanna ride up front with me?"

"Sure."

Lucky, Patty and Jill get into the back seat, leaving Rhonda sitting in the front between Sig and me. It's not the best situation as things are still awkward—it's the beginning of a date. We fire up the Eyeball and rumble north toward Babb. Rhonda settles in next to me and warms up against me. I try to look into her eyes when talking to her, but it's hard not to notice her soft cleavage. She is working here as a waitress for the summer between her freshman and sophomore years at the University of Colorado.

The drive is dark and crooked through the Blackfeet Indian Reservation. To the west, the craggy peaks of the Rocky Mountains, which split Montana in half, are like shadows in the moonlight. To the east, the rolling grasslands flow for an eternity. Overhead, the black sky is salted with stars. The Eyeball feels like a spaceship traveling through warped time with mystery as our destination. The eyes of invisible deer, bobcats and other critters glow in our headlights, looking like meteorites flying by. Above, real meteorites zip across the sky. As we plow through black space, distant stars ahead finally morph into the yard lights of a half-dozen houses along the main street of tiny Babb. One of these stars is the Babb Bar. On our thirty-minute journey, we hadn't encountered any other space travelers on the road.

Lucky points at the bar. "Pull in here."

A dozen tired-looking pickups and a few cars are scattered willy-nilly in front. I park at the end of the pothole-filled parking lot, and we all head into the bar. It is obvious this is an "Indian bar." I estimate about thirty Indians and a couple of white guys in the place. With our three dates, we have just tripled the number of white girls here. Fortunately, I've been in tough bars before and learned to make a few friends just in case things get rough.

A drunk Indian comes over and slaps Lucky on the back. "Hey, Lucky!" He has a can of Schmidt beer in his hand. All the beer is in cans, which can't be broken over someone's head like a bottle.

"Hey, Frank, how you doin'?" Lucky says.

"Good—you come to party with us?"

"Yeah, good to see my buddies. Meet Dan."

"Hey, Frank," I say, "good to meet you." I shake hands but divert my eyes downward in respect of how Natives shake hands.

"Aho."

A couple of Lucky's friends bounce off each other as they walk over. He knows almost half the patrons here. "These are my friends from the seminary," he explains, introducing Sig and me, even though Sig was never in the seminary.

One of his friends says, "Oh, priests. We better be good." And they all give out the loud, genuine laughs Indians are so famous for. Most of the Indians on the reservation mix Catholicism and native religion, so I'm thinking it's good they see us as priests. Maybe this will bring us some respect in case things get rough. Prejudice between Natives and whites is endemic in Montana culture for good reason. Natives have been traumatized by whites over hundreds of years. I'm sure the trauma and mistrust reside deep in their injured spirits.

The six of us saddle up to the bar putting the three girls between us for protection.

As the first fight of the evening breaks out at the far end of the bar, the wide-eyed girls look more frightened than Sig and I do.

The bartender doesn't blink when Lucky orders up drinks for the six of us. I have a fake ID in my wallet that says I work for Circle K Construction, but I'm not asked to pull it out. The Indian bartender wears an immaculately starched white shirt with the sleeves rolled up just one turn of the cuff. He brings us six cans of Hamm's Beer and six shots of peppermint schnapps.

"It's a long way up here just to get your dates served," he says with a wink.

"Yeah, we wanted to impress them," I say.

"Watch yourself."

"Okay."

About twenty minutes later, another round is set in front of us courtesy of Lucky. "Let me buy some rounds," he explains. "You guys drove all the way here from Great Falls."

A second fight starts outside, and we can watch the action through the open door. Soon the winner comes back in, but the bartender yells at him, "Get out, you're 86ed for the night."

"I don't care, I'm goin' down to Browning!" the winner yells before leaving. Glenn would have loved this bar.

At one point, two staggering guys come up and insist Patty and Jill dance with them, but before we have to defend their honor, Frank shoves one guy and says, "Leave 'em alone, they're priests."

The two guys stagger off, muttering, "What they doin' with women?"

After three or four rounds of beer and peppermint schnapps, we are on our way to getting hammered, greased, loaded and sloshed. We decide we best head back to St. Mary's. For the past half-hour, Rhonda has been complaining about her back. As we get into the car, the back pain becomes worse, and she's becoming delirious. I begin driving back to St. Mary's.

"Is it your back or your kidneys?" I ask, but she doesn't answer. "Do you have to pee?"

I turn onto a small side road that ends in a garbage dump and let her out of the car to pee. It's dark, and I leave her behind the car and get back in. When she doesn't get back in after a few minutes, I go back and find her standing naked behind the car. Then she takes off running. I grab a sheet off the car seat and run her down, wrap her in the sheet and put her in the backseat with Jill and Patty. I gather her clothes off the ground and toss them in.

"Get her dressed," I shout. "We need to go to the hospital."

The return trip seems darker and even more crooked. Somewhere ahead in the darkness is Browning and a hospital. I trust the Eyeball will get us there, but just outside Browning, we run out of gas. I coast into a small gas station consisting of one pump and a house where the owner lives. I park next to the pump and knock on the door. It's three in the morning. A disturbed and grouchy owner appears at the door.

"We have an emergency," I blurt out before he can say anything. "The girl in the back seat is sick, and we need to get her to the hospital, but we're out of gas."

"Okay," the man says, "you can have gas, but I need cash first."

I give him three silver dollars, which is almost enough to fill the tank. He puts in the gas, and we head out again, but suddenly Rhonda seems just fine. The pain in her back is gone, and she is coherent.

"Jill, Patty—make sure she's dressed. We gotta get you guys home." Any romantic notions are suddenly gone. Like a stealth spaceship, we quietly coast down a long hill into St. Mary's with the headlights and engine turned off, hoping to escape the attention of the local sheriff who has been keeping an eye on us since we arrived.

We drop the girls off at the girl's dorm, and Lucky walks over to the men's dorm. Hoping to avoid the sheriff, Sig and I decide it's time to get out of town. Again, we head down the dark and crooked road to the entrance of Glacier National Park. The blackness begins to retreat as the sky softens to a bluish-black, and a then tinge of rose appears.

Near the entrance, we park in a grove of aspen trees and stretch out. Exhausted, we both take a coma. A few hours later, we wake to a blaring sun, hungover, stiff, cold and hungry. We head down the road, and Sig leans over to see if there are any empty beer cans to clean out before we get to the entrance.

"Look what I found," he says, dangling Rhonda's panties on one finger. "She left them in the back seat. Her loss, our gain."

"Put 'em in a place of honor," I say as Sig hangs them on the rear-view mirror. "Now we have something to look forward to."

We pull up to the entrance to pay the fee, but a park ranger motions for us to pull over. He is wearing a wide brim ranger hat like the one Smokey the Bear wears. "Where you boys from?"

"Great Falls."

"Where you going?"

"Through the park for the weekend."

"So, how did you get these bullet holes in your car?" he asks.

"Just having fun with some target practice."

He is not amused. "Okay, open up the trunk." He searches the trunk, back seat and under the front seat for contraband, which in our case would be beer, but he finds nothing. He glances at the panties hanging on the rearview mirror but makes no comment.

"I don't like the looks of this car or you," the ranger says. "We'll be keeping an eye on you. Do anything wrong, you'll answer for it. Now pay your two dollars and get going."

"Thanks—like your hat," I say.

We drive through the entrance. “Whew, that guy didn't like us,” Sig says.

“No shit, Sherlock. At least he didn't confiscate the panties.” We both admire our trophy. It's the closest we will come to any intimacy with girls on this trip.

For the next three days, we cruise around the park, hiking on the crystal glaciers, being intimidated by grizzly bears, cooling beer in ice-cold streams, cooking hamburgers on open fires, waving at girls on vacation with their suspicious parents, and waking up stiff each morning from sleeping on the ground.

We are forced to return to Great Falls tired, broke, hungover, hungry and almost out of gas again, but still laughing up the adventure at the Babb Bar. In Fairfield, our tank is empty, we're broke, and we still have twenty-three miles to Great Falls. At a local gas station, I convince the owner to give me a dollar's worth of gas—about three gallons—for an extra headlamp I have in my trunk. We are on the road again.

I think back to the bar in Babb and wonder what happened to those proud Indians, the foundation of our country, and how my prejudice toward them came to be. I have a few Indian friends, but they are not close friends. It will take me years to realize how subtle my racial prejudice is and to realize how our white, Christian-based government killed one million Native Americans in the name of Manifest Destiny.

When Columbus arrived on the North American continent, there were a thousand native tribes, but half of them were exterminated in what Hitler described as the best example of genocide the world had witnessed. It is estimated fifty-six million Indians were exterminated on the North and South American continents between 1492 and 1900.

Chapter 33

Leaving the Blackfeet Reservation, But Not the Memories of My Aunt Cecilia

"Here, sit up here so you can play the song with me," my Aunt Cecilia told me.

It was my second birthday, and I was sitting on my aunt's lap at the piano keyboard. She guided my tiny fingers over the keyboard as we plunked out the song, "Happy Birthday."

"I do it."

"Yes, you do," she said. "Now sing. Happy birthday to you, happy birthday to you, happy birthday dear Danny, happy birthday to you."

* * *

Our drive home from the reservation brings back that memory of my favorite aunt Cecilia, my mother's sister. In 1944, at the age of twenty, with the ink still wet on her teaching degree, she moved to Browning to teach school. She was a young German girl on a big adventure to a very remote place in the world. She died at twenty-three of an obscure kidney disease or ear infection—no one really knows which. In letters she wrote to my mother during that time, she described a wondrous time and a love of the native people. Years later, I found one of the letters with a postscript after her signature: "Give my love to everyone, especially Danny."

Many Indians still lived in tepees at that time, and much of their culture was still intact. Cecilia was a beautiful woman, and I still admire her courage and acceptance of people. A picture of her still sits on my desk, reminding me to take chances and not pass up opportunities for adventure.

Sitting at the keyboard with Aunt Cecilia is my first memory and one that has comforted me over the years. I remember looking at her in an open casket in my grandparents' living room. It was customary for the deceased to lie in state for a day or two so family and friends could grieve. She looked like a sleeping princess in that box, but I remember touching her cold hand and thinking it was different than when her warm fingers had glided mine across the keys. I barely understood that she would not wake up. I had lost my one real connection to my extended family.

As I was growing up, our family was stranded on an island of its own, surrounded by a huge extended family that didn't have any real interest in us. I had four grandparents and nineteen aunts and uncles.

My father's parents were stoic Germans, and I can't recall having a conversation with them or being acknowledged by them, but I recognized that Grandpa liked his wine. I asked my father how it was growing up as a child. His simple answer was, "Your Uncle Tony and I were orphan slaves. We had to leave our home when I was fourteen and Tony was sixteen. We found work with a farmer and a place to sleep and food to eat."

My mother's parents were there, but I didn't really know either of them. My grandfather was probably an alcoholic and emotionally disconnected. I remember him recognizing me one time when I was about seven. My brothers had run off and left me at my grandparents' house. I was crying, and my grandfather said, "Did you get left behind?"

I had never spent any one-on-one time with her. My grandmother and I got to know each other later when I was about twenty. I drove my '49 Ford, the Eyeball, from Great Falls to Bridger to visit her. My grandfather had died, and she was alone in their small house. It was summer, and I helped with her garden before we had lunch. Over lunch, she told me this story:

"We sailed from Bruges, Belgium, the summer of 1900," she said. "I was sixteen. Our port was Galveston, but as we got closer, our destination changed to Corpus Christi. We docked there in a very bad storm and later found out Galveston was destroyed by a hurricane. Ten thousand people were killed. We were lucky. If we had gone there, we would have died.

"The trip took ten weeks. I met the captain of the ship, and we fell in love. His name was Robert, and he spoke German. He was tall with dark hair and a nice mustache. He was very handsome in his black wool uniform and his cap with gold embroidery on the bill. When his assistant was running the ship, we would visit for hours and hours. My parents didn't like this idea because they had arranged for me to marry Grandpa when we landed in Texas. I had never met Grandpa and was very nervous about meeting him.

The captain was kind. We made plans to meet later in Texas, but things changed. I was sent to Navasota, Texas, where Grandpa was waiting for me. We were married a few weeks later, but I couldn't stop thinking about the ship captain. I was only sixteen and didn't have any say about it. A month later, the captain found me, but it was too late. I was already married to Grandpa."

A long tear ran down her cheek, and she wiped it away with the corner of her apron.

"Have you told this story to anyone else?" I asked.

"No—no one would understand. It would make Grandpa look bad."

I watched as she longed for her true love, a man long lost but still in her heart. "I'm sorry, Grandma, it wasn't fair."

"Life is like that. Sometimes we don't get what we want. That's just the way it is. If I knew what I know now, I would have stood up for myself. Don't forget this lesson."

"I won't, Grandma."

"So, let's make some apple strudel. You can help."

As we rolled out a ball of dough and began stretching it to the size of the kitchen table, she said, "It needs to be thinner than paper. You can tell when it is thin enough because you can spit through it." She laughed, "But we won't be doing that today."

When I left her that day, I wondered if I would have another chance to visit her. She had shared with me the most important thing in her life, and this one visit would keep Grandma in my heart for the rest of my life. As I drove off, I thought about how she had made a life for herself, and I remembered her encouraging words, "Stand up for yourself." I also thought she was lucky to find love even if she didn't get to share it with the one she loved.

I wondered if I'd ever find love like that.

Chapter 33

End of Summer, Dating Uncle Sam

With the end of summer coming, I'm getting ready to go to Lackland Air Force Base in San Antonio, Texas, for basic training. While I've beaten the draft, it still feels like my life is hanging on a thin wire of uncertainty. I've got six years of National Guard duty ahead of me, a couple years of college, and the continuing sadness of Glenn being killed in a war that makes no sense to me.

I guess Glenn represents the tens of thousands of young men who have been killed in the war, but I don't know personally. He is the only real face I can put on the Vietnam War other than the TV footage of bodies that are returned daily in flag-covered coffins. The war is escalating, with a body count every day in the news. Some days it is a dozen killed, some days, it is several dozen and into the hundreds. One day, 273 young Americans lost their lives. The news is mind-numbing, and the numbers are getting harder and harder to digest. But the young people in the country are beginning to stir, and soon they will fill the streets with antiwar protests.

For now, I'm not active in the protest movement because I've been ordered to report to the Montana Air National Guard headquarters on Friday morning for a flight to Lackland AFB. There, I'll begin six weeks of learning how to be a soldier or airman. After that, I'll get another six weeks of training at Shephard Air Force Base in Wichita, Texas, where I will study encrypted communication. This is my last weekend at home so I'm spending more time with my parents and a few friends.

Tonight is my last Saturday night at the Stein Haus with the guys and Shirley, my girlfriend for the last few months. I think I've fallen in love with her, but I don't think she knows it. I'll be gone for three months, and that seems like a long time to be away from her. I wonder if we will still be dating when I return in June.

I take her home, and outside her house, I mumble, "So—see you when I get back."

"Sure, take care of yourself down in Texas."

I give her a kiss goodbye. Her lips are as soft as her blond hair.

"You're a good kisser," she says.

"Yes, you, too. Take care."

I walk back to my car, wondering if that last kiss will last for three months. Shirley is beautiful, bright and fun—just a great gal. I'm sure there will be lots of guys after her the minute my plane leaves the ground.

Sunday morning, I board a C-130 military transport plane for Lackland. My only possessions are the clothes I'm wearing and a shoebox containing a toothbrush, comb and razor. The plane is designed for hauling cargo and paratroopers, so there are no amenities. Everyone is quiet, wondering what we are in for. I know almost everyone on the plane because they are fellow draft dodgers and classmates from college or work. There is Pete, whose dad owns the Cadillac dealership; Rhino; Hippo; Don the bronco rider from Cascade; and a few other guys I just know by first name. Jim is from Cheyenne and was on the plane when it landed in Great Falls along with a few other guys from Wyoming.

We land, and when the rear cargo door opens, the first thing I notice is the heat and humidity. We had left the coolness of Montana and had flown into the heat of Texas. We scramble off the plane to be greeted by our drill instructor, Sergeant Jones. He is an African-American in his twenties with a finely trimmed mustache and short military-style haircut. He wears reflective sunglasses that hide his eyes. His uniform is impeccable—not one wrinkle. His shoes and the bill on his cap are shined to a mirror finish.

"Fall in!" he shouts. "Make two lines of ten facing me."

We do our best to scrunch together in a line and probably look ridiculous.

"Face to the right," he commands, "ready to march—left foot first. Ready—march!"

We awkwardly shuffle off in something resembling a group. Sgt. Jones marches beside us, calling "Left, right, left, right," as we struggle to march in the same step. After a couple of blocks, we stop at the barbershop where our heads are quickly shaved, all vanity falling on the floor with our shorn locks.

Next, we march to the quartermasters where we are issued uniforms and shoes that don't quite fit, and then on to our barracks, a two-story open structure with twenty beds on each floor. The latrine is also an open design with six stools lined up against one wall and ten sinks on the other. At one end is an open shower with ten shower heads. Privacy is nonexistent here.

On the first day, we learn how to dress, shine shoes and make sure our clothes are properly folded. Most importantly, we learn what constitutes dirt. Everything is dirt if it is out of place and not part of a usable article. For example, shoe polish on the inside of the lid of the polish tin is considered dirt. Any traces of dirt on anything counts as a demerit, and too many demerits mean failure, getting shipped home and being placed back into the draft.

At six o'clock sharp each morning, we "fall out" in front of the barrack in military formation for personal inspection and calisthenics. Then we march to breakfast and continue the day doing military maneuvers, rifle range, obstacle courses and classes on military bearing, survival and first aid. Sunday is a free day. Every other day is crammed full, and there is always a threat that we'll be sent home to the draft if we don't perform to military standards.

Sgt. Jones is tough but seems somehow out of place in the military. While he plays the part of a tough guy, he seems too nice to be in this business. The first day, he picks one of us to be dorm chief, the person responsible for the dorm when he is absent, which is mostly at night. He picks my new buddy from Cheyenne, Jim, because he looks older than the rest of us even though we are all in our early twenties.

At first, Jim is bummed about getting this responsibility, but we soon realize the job has its perks. On the weekends, we have extra duties cleaning and policing the area for rubbish. After Jim sends everyone off for duty, he and I sneak over to the enlisted men's club and drink beer. This continues for the next six weeks as we make friends with some of the guys at the club.

One weekend we even manage to sneak over to the golf course with two buddies from Great Falls, Pete and Bob. Here, Pete gets behind the wheel of a golf cart and thinks he is driving one of his father's Cadillacs.

"Pete, careful, you're going to roll this thing," I say as we scream around a corner on two wheels.

"Don't sweat it. I've got everything in control."

Instead, we head right into a pond. Three of us dive off the cart as Pete plows into the water, soon followed by a gurgling of bubbles coming up from the submerged cart.

"Holy crap, let's get out of here," Rhino yells as we hot-foot it across the fairway and over the fence.

Pete is right behind us, dripping wet and laughing hysterically. We make it back to the barracks undetected and sweat it out for the next few days, wondering if we will be caught. Nothing comes of this incident, but until our plane lifts off the runway heading to Wichita, I worry about being caught and sent home to Lars and the draft.

In Wichita, we are assigned to Shephard Air Force Base and six weeks of technical school learning crypto, a way of coding messages. The course is easy, and Jim and I have no trouble getting good grades and avoiding extra work. Once again, he is appointed dorm chief.

Classes are from eight to noon. Afternoons are reserved for students to clean specific buildings. After lunch, Jim lines up the troops and marches them to their duty area, leaving himself and me until last.

Ben, one of Jim's classmates from the University of Wyoming, has finished Officer Training School and has been assigned to duty here. Jim arranges to meet him at the officer's club. Once everyone has been assigned to work duty, Jim and I change into civilian clothes and head for the club to meet Ben and drink beer.

After six weeks of technical school, I say goodbye to Jim and head for the airport for my flight to Montana. As I board the Western Airlines flight to Great Falls, I realize I have suddenly returned to civilian life when the stewardess, wearing a lime green uniform with hot pants, asks me, "What can I get you to drink, soldier?"

Chapter 34

End of Basic Training, What a Riot

Back home in Great Falls, life is easier now that I don't have to worry about the draft.

I call Shirley, the girlfriend I left behind. "Hey, I'm back," I announce.

"Oh, great. Glad you survived."

"Wanna go out tonight?"

"Well, I'm kinda busy."

"How about tomorrow?"

"Well, pretty busy."

I'm smart enough not to ask her out for the third time. "Okay, maybe catch up with you later."

"Sure."

I know I won't be catching up with her later. That last kiss didn't last the whole three months. Shirley has moved on, and while I'm heartbroken, I get over it. I'm beginning to think I should return to college for an education and a way to better myself. Life in the 1960s is colorful, to say the least, with student gatherings at funky coffee houses listening to folk music and poetry. Life seems like a huge overlapping patchwork of long hair, the Beatles, Bob Dylan, tie-dyed shirts, hippie counterculture, hot pants, psychedelic drugs, vegetarians, James Bond, *The Graduate*, bell-bottom paisley pants, polyester leisure suits, segregation, the Ku Klux Klan, Ray Charles, Los Angles race riots, acid, JFK, a man on the moon, muscle cars, backyard bomb shelters, The Pill, and the still-raging war in Vietnam.

The '60s are more than just rock and roll and drugs, but a major cultural shift, not only in the US but around the world. In Africa, for example, thirty-two countries gain independence from their European colonial rulers. This counterculture movement questions and changes social norms regarding racism, sexism, clothing, education, drugs and music. Benchmark legislation is passed to enforce equality, opportunity and recognize persons with disabilities. New laws allow homosexuals to meet in groups without being arrested. A dozen major cities experience major anti-war and race riots.

Every day, something new is happening, and while this explosion of change proves painful, it is mostly for the better. With so much happening, life is a blur at times. Cruising the drag, I listen to Kenny Rogers and the First Edition sing, "Just Dropped In." It was written to relate to those tripping on LSD, but the words relate to most of us trying to make sense out of life.

I woke up this mornin' with the sundown shinin' in
I found my mind in a brown paper bag within
I tripped on a cloud and fell eight miles high
I tore my mind on a jagged sky
I just dropped in to see what condition my condition was in
(Yeah, yeah, oh-yeah, what condition my condition was in)

I pushed my soul in a deep dark hole and then I followed it in
I watched myself crawlin' out as I was a-crawlin' in
I got up so tight I couldn't unwind
I saw so much I broke my mind
I just dropped in to see what condition my condition was in
(Yeah, yeah, oh-yeah, what condition my condition was in)

Someone painted "April Fool" in big black letters on a "Dead End" sign

I had my foot on the gas as I left the road and blew out my mind
Eight miles outta Memphis and I got no spare
Eight miles straight up downtown somewhere
I just dropped in to see what condition my condition was in
I said I just dropped in to see what condition my condition was in

Yeah, yeah oh-yeah

I began the spring semester at the College of Great Falls determined to study and get good grades. With so much happening around me, I feel distracted from finding my way in life. Even at this small private college, there is unrest. Life on college campuses is in upheaval. Students are becoming more socially conscious, and a great majority of them are against the war in Vietnam and becoming very vocal about it. Thousands of our soldiers are dying in Vietnam in what seems like an unwinnable war. Peaceful demonstrations are erupting into violent confrontations between students and police, and eventually, the Army National Guard is called out by different state governors to patrol college campuses.

On May 4, Ohio National Guardsmen fired sixty-seven rounds into a group of unarmed student protesters at Kent State University, killing four and wounding nine others, including innocent bystanders. The nation is shocked, and students and citizens everywhere are angry. State governors react to this by shoring up the National Guard in case of further unrest on college campuses.

It is no different in Montana. Governor Tim Babcock issues orders to National Guard Units to prepare for possible riots on college campuses.

One weekend a month, I report for military duty at the Montana Air National Guard in Great Falls. I have quickly become bored with crypto and sign up to go to fighter pilot school for eighteen months. For some reason, I think being a pilot is a good idea.

Before leaving for flight school, I begin training in an F89 trainer. After one of the training missions, we land back at our home base in Great Falls, and I suddenly realize I don't want to become a pilot. Flying in a fighter jet is the most thrilling thing I have ever done. I love it, but I have a feeling that the high-speed thrill will be the cause of my death. Also, the thought of killing unseen people from a plane seems too far removed from the reality of death.

I climb out of the cockpit and, still wearing my flight suit, walk to headquarters and report to Major Earl. "I love flying, but I can't do it," I tell him. "I'll either kill myself or someone else. I'm resigning from the flight school."

The Major is disappointed but can see I'm serious, so he changes my orders. It is hard to walk away from the dream of being a fighter jet pilot. But this is one of the few times in my life I know I should listen to my heart rather than my head. The whole episode also brings back Glenn's plight—defending the country but sacrificing his life.

Maybe I'm just being selfish.

The day I resigned from flight school.

Since I had found crypto boring, I ask for a transfer to the photo lab. Photography had been a hobby since I was a child, and my mother would let me snap pictures with the family box camera. I found the photo lab interesting, especially the eight-gallon keg of beer we kept hidden in the darkroom refrigerator. "Get your work done and have a beer," was the management style of my new boss, Sgt. Carte, a hard worker and hard drinker. "Don't get me into any trouble, and I'll let you play when the work is done," he would say.

One Saturday morning, I arrive for weekend duty hungover from partying at the Cartwheel Bar the night before. I walk into the photo lab, looking for a place to hide and sleep off my headache, when Sgt. Carte greets me.

"You're supposed to report to headquarters at 09:00 hours (nine in the morning)," he says. "Something about riot control training."

"What? Riot control training? What's that—and why me?"

"They're training a squad for riot control in case student riots break out over at Missoula. You were picked because someone wants to get even with you," he says with a laugh.

Missoula is where the University of Montana is located, the liberal nest of Montana and a place full of hippies, drugs and social unrest.

"What did I do?" I complain.

"Actually, I can think of a lot of things," Sgt Carte says. "Maybe someone has it out for you. At any rate, make sure you're there, or you'll be in bigger trouble."

At 0900 hours, I enter Headquarters and see about thirty guys all waiting to find out about this riot control training. About half of them are cohorts with me in practical jokes, a way we pass the time while on duty. I begin to see that this is a platoon of military misfits. Most everyone here was picked as a form of punishment.

The trainer, Sgt. Blare, walks into the room and yells, "Fall outside and form two ranks." Then he barks, "Attention!" and we all line up and stand at attention.

Blare then briefs us: "You have been chosen to be trained as a crack riot control squad. You will be under my command for the rest of the weekend and do what I say. Understood?"

"Yes, Sergeant."

"I can't hear you."

"Yes, Sergeant!"

"I still can't hear you."

"Yes, Sergeant!!!"

I'm thinking, oh crap—a weekend of this on top of a hangover. What can we do to cool this guy down? Sgt. Blare has just returned from Vietnam and transferred from active Army to Air National Guard. He is gung-ho and doesn't seem to like us draft dodgers. He's tough, but we are tougher when it comes to slacking off. In the rank ahead of me are Rhino, Hippo, the Little Professor and other screw-off buddies. Blare just bit off more than he can chew.

He marches us over to supply, where we are issued helmets, rifles, gas masks and bullets. Yes, real bullets. He seems to have forgotten that we didn't join the Army but the Air Force, the technical branch of the armed services. Air Force guys rarely see a rifle, let alone use one. The USAF provides all the communications for the military and drops bombs on things miles below. Rifles—who needs them, and more importantly, who wants them?

With our new equipment, we march out to the parade field, where we practice wedge formations to split a crowd and provide a "show of force," a military term that means looking tough. I'm thinking, what if there is a demonstration at the University in Missoula? Will I go over there and do a "show of force" to my friends who are demonstrating? As the day wears on, the hangovers wear off. At 1400 hours (two that afternoon), Blare announces, "Okay, you have the rest of the afternoon off. Report back here at 1900 hours (seven o'clock) for night maneuvers. Fall out."

We walk to the parking lot, and six of us pile into my '63 Chevy Impala. I bought this to replace the defunct Eyeball and the '53 Oldsmobile my brother had wrecked. We head down to the Cartwheel Bar just in time for the Saturday afternoon shift. Wearing battle fatigue uniforms and attitudes, we promptly order up rounds of Great Falls Select beer in the can.

As the afternoon progresses, the conversation becomes louder and dumber. We're tough guys—riot control, whatever. In the Sixties, it is not permissible for military members to wear battle fatigue uniforms in public unless one is working on something that requires informal dress, such as mechanics.

An officer from Malmstrom Air Force Base, the *real* Air Force as compared to the Air National Guard, reprimands us for wearing battle fatigue uniforms in a public place. He is not sure if we are regular Air Force or National Guard, and we aren't about to tell him. But not to worry—Rhino steps into this guy's face and says, "Hey, buddy, why don't you go screw yourself."

"You can't talk to me like that. I'm an officer."

"That's your problem. Buzz off, Jet Butt," Rhino replies.

At that, the officer walks over to a pay telephone makes a call. In my infinite wisdom, I realize he is calling the military police from Malmstrom.

"Hey guys," I say, "that officer's calling the air police from the base. We gotta get out of here."

Before leaving, we each get a six-pack of Great Falls Select in cans, then head out the door, jump in my car, and with tires squealing, head for the Guard base at the airport, which luckily is in the opposite direction as the AFB. In my rearview mirror, I see four blue Air Force pickups screaming into the Cartwheel parking lot with sirens blaring and red lights blinking.

We pull into the parking lot at about six-thirty, or 1830 hours if you're military, and park the car. Opening a can of beer each, we wait for night maneuvers to begin. Quickly, we figure out that a six-pack fits neatly into our gas mask bags, so we leave the gas masks in the car. We fall into formation, each armed to the teeth with a rifle, a helmet and a gas mask bag full of beer.

The rest of the night is spent dodging Sgt. Blare and becoming highly trained killers by knocking off an occasional twelve-ounce can of Great Falls Select. During the coming years, there is never a need for the governor to call out the riot control squad, and any notion of a pending riot or violent demonstration in Montana fades.

Riot Control Expert

A few months later, I find myself marching down Central Avenue with a couple of priests, about a hundred college students and other Great Falls citizens in a peaceful march against the Vietnam War. This time I'm not wearing a uniform or carrying a rifle or a beer in my gas mask bag. The streets are lined with people. A few of them support the war, but most don't. The parade is uneventful, and while it makes the newspaper, it is just one of many demonstrations happening around the country. The tide is turning against the war. Protesters and others are beginning to make a difference. So here I am opposing an unwinnable war that Glenn sacrificed his life for.

Was it a waste for him? Is it a waste of time for me?

Somehow, I manage to plow through my studies at the College of Great Falls, a small Catholic college. I feel as if I'm still being watched by the bishop, but now I'm paying my own tuition, which is triple that of the state schools like the University of Montana at Missoula. But I don't have the confidence to move to Missoula, so I continue to take out college loans, work forty hours a week at Buttrey's Food Store and another twenty hours at the Stein Haus. I carry 12 to 15 credits with a stunning 2.0 GPA earned by glancing through the textbooks and cramming for tests assisted by diet pills "borrowed" from my friend Gunner's mother's medicine cabinet.

I'm still studying theology, philosophy, psychology and Latin with no clue of what I want to do in life. I'm hearing the same things from my teachers as I heard in high school. Occasionally, they will call me into their offices, but the gist of their speeches is the same: "You know, Dan, you have a knack for life, people and studies. You have a lot of talent that is going unused. If you would apply yourself more, you could do anything you put your mind to." Apparently, I'm sabotaging myself but don't realize it or know why.

During this period, Bob and I head over to the Cartwheel Bar with some friends one evening. We're looking for girls, of course. It's September, and the local schools have just begun for the year. The Great Falls School District always hires new teachers this time of the year, so we are on the lookout for new dancing and dating prospects. Our main competition is the local airmen from Malmstrom. As we walk in, the Wheel, a local band, belts out "Louis Louis" by the Kingsmen. About twenty couples are showcasing their dance moves by doing the The Frug, Mashed Potato and The Watusi. We spy four gals sitting at a table.

"Gotta be teachers," I say.

"Yeah, probably from Montana State."

We head over to the table. "Hi, would you like to dance?" I ask the first gal that catches my eye. "I'm in the United States Air Force," I add jokingly.

"Air Force, really?"

"Yeah, Airman First Class."

"Right, first class, I bet," she says, getting my joke of ridiculing the airmen in the bar.

"What's your name?"

"C. A."

"I'm D. J."

She has a great sense of humor as we groove it out on the dance floor. I walk her back to her table and sit with her friends for a while. They are all teachers who just graduated from Montana State. It's their first teaching job, and they're new to Great Falls.

At two in the morning, the bartender blinks the light in the bar to signal closing time.

"Hey C.A., can I get your phone number?"

"Sure." She writes it on the back of a deposit slip.

"Thanks, I'll give you a call."

She heads out the door with her girlfriends. The next day, Bob asks me, "Did you call her yet?"

"No, don't want to seem too eager. Maybe tomorrow."

"Don't wait too long. She might be snatched up by the competition."

I call her the next day, and within a week we are going out and discover we have a lot of mutual friends. We see a lot of each other for the next six months. We're young and in love. We enjoy skiing, partying with our friends and quiet evenings making dinner. I'm thinking of asking her to marry me. We are both twenty-six years old, and many of our friends are married or getting married. Maybe it's time to settle down. I invite her over to my apartment for dinner.

I'm nervous and have been planning to ask her to marry me for weeks now.

"So, I was thinking maybe we should think about the future," I stammer.

"What do you mean?"

"Well, you know, maybe getting married," I say as I inch closer to asking her. "Would you like to get married?"

"I was thinking of the same thing and wondering when you'd ask me."

"So, you'll marry me?"

"Of course."

I'm happy, scared and anxious. Marriage—I can't believe it. I think we are both relieved that the question has finally been asked. I'm not sure we understand all the implications.

I still haven't finished college and have one semester left. A typical four-year degree, in my case, stretches into six years with interruptions for military service, a partial credit load from working full time, and failed courses that need to be retaken. Upon beginning my final semester, I realize my overall GPA of 2.00, less than the 2.25 needed for graduation. That means I will need to carry a 3.00 GPA my final semester. For me, getting a B average for a semester is unheard of, so I'll need to do things differently this semester, such as actually read the textbooks.

To my utter surprise, I pass all my courses with As and Bs, earning an overall GPA of 2.25 that allows me to graduate.

My parents come to graduation day, but it is a foreign experience for them to have a child graduate from college. They don't know how to congratulate me. Their focus was always on my brothers and how they were having such a hard time in life. For my parents, it must seem unfair that I got a degree and they didn't. I was always the model child who tried not to create any problems, and while this may have made their lives easier, they never acknowledged it and continue to ask me to help my brothers.

So, in June of 1969, I graduate from the College of Great Falls with a degree in philosophy and prepared for life—philosophically, that is. My girlfriend, C. A., and I get married in August. That fall, C. A. gets a teaching contract, and I'm accepted to graduate school at Eastern Montana College in Billings. It's a two-year program with a curriculum based on counseling psychology. C. A. and I rent a small house in Billings while I'm attending school. We make new friends, and I reconnect with some old friends from high school. It's a fun year. C. A. enjoys her job teaching fourth grade, and I have a new confidence as a graduate student. My curriculum in counseling psychology and rehabilitation fits me well.

At the completion of graduate school, C. A. and I have saved enough money to travel to Europe. With a Eurail pass, we skirt around Great Britain and a dozen countries in Europe. We're on an adventure—meeting new people, eating new food, experiencing new languages and enjoying different cultures. C. A. is a great travel companion, and it's like a second honeymoon. We return to Billings, and I begin my first real job as a rehabilitation counselor. C. A. and I buy our first home and spend the next year fixing it up. Our first daughter Marie is born the following year. Our second daughter Keri is born twenty months later.

They are my life. I'm a doting father who loves to spend every moment watching them grow up. I continually brag about them, spending many evenings on the living room floor playing games and letting them climb all over me, sitting on the couch while they fall asleep on my chest, and gently tucking them into bed. Perhaps I spend too much time with them and not enough with their mother. At one point, C. A. complains that we spend a lot of time talking about our girls but not much time talking about ourselves. I know she's right, but I don't have the courage to tell her how I feel. I'm struggling to stay connected with her, and for now, I will try to keep that a secret within myself.

I watch the girls grow up and think about separating from C. A., but they are at such a tender age I can't imagine leaving them. I fall into depression and anger but try to hide it. The emotions build, and finally, when the girls are six and four, I tell C. A. I need to leave. I move out, heartbroken and missing my daughters. Our divorce was finalized in 1981. After these last dozen years together, I'm confused, angry and perhaps leaving my marriage for reasons both right and wrong. A lot of it is my immaturity and co-dependency, but I won't realize this for several years. I leave and try to be a part-time parent, having the girls every other weekend and Wednesday nights. It is hard on me, my daughters and their mother. I can tell they are struggling with me moving out of the house. We make the best of it, but our family is separated both physically and emotionally.

I try to stage a second home for my daughters in my duplex. We cook meals together, do homework, play games and go camping. I buy a hot tub as another toy, but my place isn't the same as home for them. It's still dad's place and not theirs. They continue to live in our original home, which I gave up for their stability.

As my daughters approach middle school age, I can tell their interests are more focused on their friends, so we spend less time together. Then, suddenly their mother decides to move to Washington State.

I check my divorce papers and, for the first time, realize I don't have joint custody. We were using a mutual friend as a lawyer, and I had thought he was representing the interests of both of us, but in retrospect, he was not. The children's mother has full custody, and I can't do anything about her taking them out of state.

I'm heartbroken for the next two years while they are in Washington. I make a few visits, but the gap between us seems to yawn even wider.

Chapter 35

The Spring of '82, Joyce

In the spring of 1982, I meet Joyce while skiing at Red Lodge Mountain. She is six years younger and bright, perky and beautiful. We begin dating and marry three years later in 1985. Her relationship with my children is off and on, but she tries to be a good stepmother. This marriage is one of adventure and travel.

"Don't move, I think it's starting to slide," I say to Joyce, who is halfway across a screed slide on the side of an unnamed mountain in the Beartooth Wilderness.

"Okay," comes the hushed reply.

The mountain is beginning to move, and we are on it.

"Just sit down and ride it out," I yell as I watch her ride an avalanche of screed down the steep slope to the valley floor. She doesn't answer and appears frozen.

Now it's my turn as the rock under my feet begins to move. After about thirty seconds, we find ourselves on the banks of Rock Creek, just a few feet from dropping into the white water. The slide has stopped with us skimming along on top of it to the bottom.

"Are you okay?" I ask.

"Yeah—shook up. Boy, that was scary."

We sit and laugh nervously at our unexpected trip off the mountain. We had left earlier that morning to climb the "Spires," a series of five sharp pyramids thrust out of the ancient granite of the Beartooth Plateau. Our favorite camping spot is at the base of these spires on the bank of Rock Creek, a whitewater gusher that jets itself from the top of the 12,000-foot-high plateau.

"Well, at least we didn't have to walk back to the camp," she quips.

We return to camp and pop a bottle of champagne, calm our nerves, and then pop another bottle.

We are good friends and enjoy doing things together. Life seems good. But in the back of my mind, there is a haunting sense that I'm drinking too much.

The next few years, we often travel, finding adventures, meeting people, making friends and continuing to party. I admire Joyce for her independence and confidence. She is a woman who can hold her own in a room full of men with a dignified and strong presence.

Somehow, I rationalize my drinking by telling myself that I have a successful career, have never been in big trouble and can handle how much I drink. Later, I will realize this is classic denial for many alcoholics, but for now, I just keep going.

The years continue, but there is an emptiness inside me that I work very hard to hide. Occasionally, a friend will hint that I'm hiding my own struggles with self-esteem. At a professional conference for the Montana Association of Rehabilitation in Missoula, two of my friends, Georgina and Suzie, joke with me.

"Here comes pretty boy in plastic," Georgina says, laughing.

I know she is joking, but I don't want to think of what this might mean.

"You giving me a bad time?"

"No, we just wonder how you always manage to look so good, Mr. Smooth," Suzie answers.

I laugh and put on a great façade, but inside I'm scared, faking it. I'm looking for a deeper meaning in life, but I'm not sure where to look. I'm intrigued by religion but have difficulty understanding why it has been one of the main causes of strife and war in the history of the world. Not only do religions have difficulty agreeing with one another, they can't agree within themselves.

I start to read about various religions again and visit different churches but never join any of them. I always find something that doesn't seem logical. Lots of religions are steeped in ritual that doesn't make sense to me. Many don't address major issues such as the equality of women, yet all proclaim they are the one true religion. With over 30,000 sects of Christianity alone, I find it hard to believe each is the one true church as they all proclaim. My search is a continuing project. Joyce isn't interested in my search for religion and has her own spiritual connection to the universe. She is an intuit and has often connected with lost spirits. During these times, I can sense their presence but have no real connection.

In the 1980s, my career blossoms. Joyce and I travel to Communist China and the USSR (Russia) shortly after they open to study groups but still frown on tourists. Through all of this, the Vietnam War and Glenn's death still haunts me. The war ended badly in 1975, with the United States making a hasty retreat and leaving hundreds of thousands of South Vietnamese allies at the mercy of the advancing Viet Cong. After twenty-four years of fighting, with some three million people dying, including 58,000 Americans, one of which was Glenn, the "good guys" lost trying to mold politics in a country far, far away.

Chapter 36

The Wall is Calling, Vietnam Memorial

It's November of 1982, and my plane bounces on the runway as the pilot jams on the brakes with just enough time to turn and taxi to the American Airlines terminal at Boston Logan Airport. I'm here to attend a conference for the National Rehabilitation Association, my professional organization. It's my first time in Boston, and I look forward to seeing old friends. We are friends, though, only through this organization and see each other once a year at national conferences. I take a taxi to the hotel, unpack and sit in the lobby looking for familiar faces. I have four days here with a little business to conduct, some educational workshops and some fun.

Sitting in the lobby, I browse through the *Boston Herald* and read an article about the new Vietnam Memorial that recently opened on the National Mall in Washington, DC. The same undertow that washed through me in Great Falls nineteen years ago washes through me again as I read the article. I think of Glenn.

The conference is usually fun, but I'm not enjoying it and feel depressed. On day three, I wake early and lie in bed thinking about Glenn and others I knew who were killed in Vietnam. I get up, shower and go down to the lobby where a small travel agency has its office. I ask the agent, "Can I get a round trip ticket to DC today?"

"Let me check," she says, then scans through flights on a desktop monitor. "Yes, Republic has a flight in a couple of hours and returns at seven tonight. There is a seat available."

"That would be great. Get me a ticket."

I hand her my credit card. Twenty minutes later, I'm on a hotel shuttle to the airport, still clutching the ticket. At 10:10 that morning, I'm sitting in seat 21A, waiting for the short flight to take off. By noon, I'm flagging down a taxi outside the DC airport.

"Take me to the Vietnam Memorial," I tell the driver.

My hands are sweating, and my heart is beating rapidly. Suddenly, I feel the same kind of anxiety I had experienced when Lars Tollefsrud was scrutinizing my draft records. It was the same anxiety I felt when Mr. O'Conner opened Glenn's casket. It was the same anxiety I had when I went to confession as a child. But today, the anxiety has an undertow of guilt—the guilt I have tried to discount for the past twenty years.

The taxi driver can see my stress in his rearview mirror. "You okay?" he asks.

"I dunno, nervous about going to the memorial. You seen it?"

"Yeah, quite a deal."

"What's it like?"

"You'll see—hard to explain."

He drops me off a block from the memorial. Late autumn has yellowed and reddened the trees and bushes that line the mall. A few flowers have survived light frosts, but most are in their last throes. The autumn sun burns through my light jacket, but not the guilt. My anxiety continues to grow, almost as if I were soon to meet my maker. A small sign directs me to the memorial, but I seem to have walked past it. Then I realize the wall sits below ground level, hidden from passersby.

I turn down a long walkway the length of a football field that gradually descends about ten feet. The top of the wall is at ground level while the bottom gradually slopes into the ground, creating an open but underground sanctuary. I descend into an eerie but comforting calm, dropping into mother earth but still seeing the sky here and there, being hidden but still seen. I feel my heart rate calming and the anxiety dissolving away, like coming home after sailing on tormented seas.

There are less than a dozen people standing here quietly, some sobbing, some kneeling, some bowed, some looking toward the heavens, none of them talking, all of them glued to the 58,000 names inscribed on the Wall— the names of US men and women who died in the war. The wall is black granite, black as death, with the names of each soldier etched in chronological order by the date of death.

I find a two-inch-thick book the size of a city phone book. A phone book lists the living, but this book lists the dead. Scanning through the ghostly names of real people, my finger screeches to a halt on Glenn's name, which lists its location on the wall. I quietly move to Section 10, let my squinting eyes slide down row after row of names and suddenly there it is—Glenn Charles Black.

Just as the undertow of grief had washed through me when Glenn had died in 1965, my guilt, fears and denial of the war wash away from me, leaving me standing there limp, weeping and torn open. I stagger over to a tree and lie down on the grass beside it, weeping profusely—tears for Glenn, tears for *all* those whose names are on the wall, tears for myself, tears for lost loves, tears and more tears.

A quiet voice standing over me says, "Been a long time, son?"

Squinting through swollen eyes, I see an elderly Afro-American man with a smile of compassion. "Yes, too long," I manage to reply.

"It'll be all right now. The worst is over, son." He reaches down and touches my shoulder to comfort me, then slowly walks away, looking back once in reassurance.

He's right, I think. The worst is over— the worst being my own fear and guilt.

Glenn's okay. I'm okay. The world is okay.

Chapter 37

Back to Montana, Putting Some Pieces of the Puzzle Together

On the last leg of my return trip to Billings, I board a Western Airlines flight out of Minneapolis, dragging the memories of the memorial with me. As we head west, we fly over the vast expanse of North Dakota and Eastern Montana—endless rolling plains, squiggly sandstone ridges dotted with pine trees, snaking rivers, rectangle swathes of farmland and lost horizons. I peer down on North Dakota and see "nowhere" below, a place removed by twenty years and thousands of memories.

The past years seem short now, like yesterday, and most of those memories of the Abbey have morphed into sweet remembrances of good times: Fr. Louie, Driscol, Malley, Don, Jim, Lucky, Rick, Bob, The Flying Bloodshot Eyeball, Sherry, Sally and the confessional, snow, ice, wind, cold, beer, nerd seminarians, Everclear.

Back in Billings, I can't stop thinking about Glenn's parents in Great Falls. After a few days, I decide to visit them. They are still living in Great Falls. The drive from Billings to Great Falls takes me over a familiar road—220 miles of open plains. It's the same road on which I drove the Eyeball in 1965 on my way to Richardton. In the distance, Great Falls and lots of memories rise out of the plain.

Missing today, however, is the Big Stack of the Anaconda Smelter. Twenty years ago, Glenn's dad, Charlie, worked in its shadow, eking out a living for his family. It dominated the skyline in Great Falls for seventy years but was demolished in 1982 with dynamite. Two years earlier, in October of 1980, "The Company" (Anaconda Copper) announced that the doors of the smelter were closing. Over 500 employees of a workforce, once numbering 2,000, were suddenly without a job. Times became tough in Great Falls. The Great Northern Railroad offices moved to the Hi Line—the extreme top section of Montana spanning the entire state from west to east. The Great Falls Select Brewery closed and left another hole in the economy.

As I drive down Central Avenue past the bishop's residence, O'Conner Mortuary, Sandy's Drive Inn, All Sports and Tracy's Restaurant, I notice several vacant lots where downtown businesses have been demolished. The once-vibrant downtown is now quiet and resembles a large parking lot. The Ebony Club, gone; cruisin' the drag, gone; peace marches, gone; busy streets, gone; cat houses, gone; energy, gone. I turn around at the Civic Center and drive back up Central Avenue, turn left over to First Avenue North and park in front of the Stein Haus. Inside, I don't see anyone I know. Art is gone, peanuts shells, gone; Red Ball, gone; woks of popcorn, gone; pastrami, gone; Great Falls Select, gone; friends, gone; cleavage on bar stools, gone; sweet young girls, gone; innocence, gone; glory, gone.

"Where's Art?" I inquire.

The bartender, friendly but worn with twice-bleached hair, tells me, "Moved down to the Club Cigar, couple years now. Sold this place, just bartends part-time. Kinda retired."

I figure Art is in his late sixties now and probably on Social Security.

"Okay, thanks, I'll find him over there."

"Can I get you a beer?" she says, looking for a customer and perhaps someone to visit with.

"No thanks, gotta go."

I lumber out of the Steiner, hands in my pockets and trying to pull those good memories out the door with me, but the era is over. No one will ever be able to put together a family of friends like that again. It truly was a family in that we looked out for each other between arguments over sports or girlfriends. But you could always count on the Stein Haus crew to cover your back, just as you would do for them. It was a time of growing up and putting together the bits and pieces of who we were then and what we might become.

I walk over to the Club Cigar just a couple blocks away. I guess I'm looking for more than just Art. I'm looking for what used to be. It was a family of sorts, and Art was the dad. I find him behind the bar, wearing a crisp white shirt with the sleeves rolled up one turn. His wavy hair is still parted in the middle, but now it's mostly tarnished silver. He is in his sixties now but still moves with the agility of a boxer behind the bar. He's washing glasses, two in each hand, pushing them up and down over two brushes sticking up out of a sink of hot soapy water. He then dips them through two rinse baths and sets them on a perforated rubber mat next to the sink to dry.

"Hey Art, how many glasses have you washed in the last forty years?"

"What the hey! It's the priest."

"Yeah, I'm back for a couple of days to see Glenn's parents. What happened to the Stein Haus?"

"I got tired of running the place. Too many hours. So, now I just work part-time and take it easy."

"Good for you. It doesn't look the same."

"No, things change—we all do. You're looking good."

"Yeah, just got back from the Vietnam Memorial. Saw Glenn's name on the Wall."

"I heard it's quite a deal."

"Kinda hard to see, but made me feel better about the whole thing."

"Nam's been hard on a lot of folks. Still is."

"Those were good days back at the Stein Haus. I'll always remember them, and you, for keeping an eye on us."

"You were good kids, just got a little crazy now and then. Most finished college or found good jobs. I didn't want any of you to end up as bartenders. I figured you had a chance of somethin' better. So, what you doing now?"

"Been working as a counselor with disabled people for the past fifteen years. Been a good job. I like the people."

"Good for you. Kinda like being a priest."

"Yeah, in some ways. I'm heading up to Glenn's parents' place to show them these pictures of the Memorial with Glenn's name on it."

Art looks over the pictures. With a sigh, he says, "It's just too bad. He had a little daughter when he was killed. Never heard anything of her."

"Me neither. Don't know where she is. Well, I'm off. Good seeing you, Art."

"Hey, wait a minute." Art comes around the bar and gives me a hug. "Don't be bringing any underage girls in here. And no monkey business."

"You got it."

I leave and think, "some things don't change." Art is the same.

Chapter 38

Shot Gun Talking to Us Better Listen, Ebony Club

I leave Art and drive a few blocks over to the former location of the Ebony Club at 217 First Avenue South, but it has been demolished for a now-vacant parking lot, which is where I park. I remember the Ebony, a haven for jazz, rock and roll and the blues, and a late-night hang-out for Afro-Americans, or black people as we called them then, from Malmstrom Air Force Base.

Diversity in Great Falls was simple back then—a big majority of white folks, a few Native Americans living in a rundown development on the edge of town known as Hill 57, and a few black servicemen serving at the airbase.

The first time I went into the Ebony was with Glenn. I remember it like it was today.

Glenn is my only chance of getting served there with his heavy beard overshadowing my baby face. I'm eighteen but look twelve. We have just graduated from high school.

As we park the car, he says, "Just do what I do and don't do anything stupid."

"Yeah, yeah, as if you're not stupid."

"Don't be a smart ass, or I won't get you in there."

"Okay, you're not stupid—not now anyway."

"I'll do the talking. If we can get past the bouncer, we'll have it made."

The bouncer, a six-foot-three black man, weighing 250 pounds in a shiny, black silk suit, is really intimidating. We're little and scared.

"What you two white boys want in a place like this?"

Glenn smiles, "Remember me? I was here last night. We came to hear the music, best music in town. Our buddy, Greg, plays in the band."

"Yeah, Greg, that skinny white boy who's tryin' to play black music. He knows how to play the keyboard—gotta give him credit for tryin'. We got the only music in town that has soul, man. Who's your buddy?"

"My army buddy, Dan. We're going to Nam together," Glenn is trying to make it seem like we are older.

"Too bad, tha's why I got in the Air Force. Less chance of gettin' shot. Okay, you boys enjoy the music, but cause any trouble, an' I'll throw yur azzes out."

"No worry, we'll behave," Glenn says, and we walk through the door and into a mysterious realm of blue cigarette smoke, dim lights, red fabric, haunting music, flowing gin and people moving their bodies to the music in ways we can only imagine. White people are shadows, and black people are almost invisible.

There are three white folks in the bar besides us. One is Greg, who's playing the piano with a quartet that floats lonesome blues across the room. The other two are high school classmates Mick and John, who sit at the bar acting like they are twenty-one and trying to cool it. I try to cool it too. The bartender asks, "What'll you have?"

"Couple a Luckies."

The bartender sets two Lucky Lager's on the bar, picks up the silver dollar I plunk down, pushes the one-dollar button on the cash register, pulls back the handle with the familiar ring of a bell as the drawer slides open, tosses it in the dollar tray, and rings up the sale—two beers for a buck. I've got another four silver dollars sitting heavy in my pocket. I have to give Glenn credit—he's gotten me served in the Ebony. It makes all the bullshit I put up with from him worth it, but I wouldn't trade the bullshit for anything.

As my eyes adjust to the dim light, I look around. About thirty black folks sit at tables and the bar. The band is playing at the back of the room. Everyone is dressed up. Most of the men are wearing neckties, sports jackets, big gold watches and gold chain bracelets. One guy has a big gold chain necklace with a cross over the top of his tie. A couple of guys have expensive suits that look like silk. The women shine with gold and silver jewelry. They smell good and move around with slinky dresses accentuating their curvaceous bodies. Everyone is smiling. This could be a jazz club in Chicago instead of Great Falls, Montana. I've never seen people who are so classy and elegant, not even in church.

The band plays a mix of blues, jazz and an occasional rock number. We hear "Louie, Louie" by the Kingsmen, "Heat Wave" by Martha and the Vandellas, "Busted" by Ray Charles and "Shoutin" by Stanley Turrentine. A bass saxophone wails the blues across the dance floor as black folks shake their booties with moves not seen before by these four country boys sitting at the bar. The place is funky, jivin' and getting down.

Lots of musicians travel through Great Falls and perform at the Ebony Club on the Great Northern train circuit from Chicago to the West Coast. They have names like drummers Ernst and Israel, a guitar player from Mississippi named Ernie, Johnny Copeland from St. Louis, Aaron MacNeil from Houston and Benny Sharpe from St. Louis. Over the years, most of the big names in blues and jazz have walked through the door of the Ozark and Ebony Club.

The music moves into a bump and grind song and a curvy, big breasted coffee-and-cream-colored gal appears on a small corner stage. A chrome pole runs from the middle of the stage to the ceiling. She begins swinging around the pole and slowly removing her clothes. I'd heard of strippers, but this is a first for me. Now our group is definitely on alert—DEFCON 1, cocked and loaded. It's so dark in the bar, the stripper is almost invisible. We strain our eyes to see more, but our overactive imaginations and hormones fill in the gaps. After about three songs, she picks up her clothes and disappears through a door behind the stage. We all sit there sweating and silent, then someone blurts, "Oh man, did you see that?"

"Yeah, I can't believe it, I mean, she was built!"

"No shit."

A few minutes later, she comes out into the crowd wearing what looks like a negligee and six-inch high heels. She proceeds to circulate through the bar. At last, she comes by us and says, "You boys care to buy a poor girl a drink?"

"Well, err, ah, um—sure."

"You look a little nervous. Don't worry, I won't hurt you."

The bartender sets a "screwdriver" on the bar, picks up a silver dollar Mick has set down, rings up the sale and puts the change, a quarter, back on the bar.

"Thanks, Honey," she says as she brushes up against Mick while reaching over the bar to pick up her drink.

"Ah, err, um—you're welcome."

"So, what you white boys doing in a place like this?"

"Well, err, we came in to listen to the music."

"Looks like you got a little more than music."

"Ah, um—yeah."

"Well, take care of yourselves, and if you're around at closing time, look me up."

"Ah, yeah, um, ah, err—we'll do that."

She walks away, sipping her screwdriver through a short straw.

"You're lucky she didn't hurt you," Glenn says to Mick. "Go get her."

"You get her, big man on campus."

"She likes you. I don't want to cut in on your action."

"You can't cut the cheese."

"Let's get outta this place," Glenn says. "There's better action at the Four Lights—more girls. Come on." He heads for the door.

I stand there for a minute, and Glenn turns back and says, "Remember—you're riding with me, numb nuts."

"Yeah, I'm coming."

On the way to the Four Lights, we drive by the Stein Haus and see Gunner's car parked in front, a gold 1960 Ford Fairlane with the driver's side door and front-end smashed in, a result of a DWI. "Go see if Gunner wants to go with us," says Glenn. "I'll wait in the car."

Inside I find Gunner (Bob), John and Sig sitting at a table with Lesley, a girl Gunner has been interested in for the past few weeks. Gunner is putting the moves on Lesley and isn't interested in going to the Four Lights with us. John and Sig are getting left out of the action and need a ride home, so they decide to accompany us to the Four Lights.

"Glenn's waiting outside. He just got me served in the Ebony."

"No shit? Good work."

Glenn is driving his parent's car, a 1963 Ford Falcon—almost new. He guns the engine, pops the clutch and lays a patch of rubber as he pulls away from the Steiner. He hits second gear and sails down First Avenue North, crosses the Missouri River and drives to the top of the hill behind Black Eagle, a small Italian enclave adjacent to Great Falls.

We pull into the gravel parking lot of the Four Lights, slide to a stop and bailout of the car. A bouncer the size of the Jolly Green Giant, but black, checks our phony ID cards while we hold our breaths. He nods approval, we exhale and walk in. The Four Lights, an after-hours bar, strip club, brothel, gambling casino and jazz club, leaves little to the imagination. Outside the city limits and under the jurisdiction of the Cascade County sheriff, things are pretty loose here. The sheriff is paid off to ignore the illegal activities here, plus it stays open all night. It's still early in the evening, so we have the whole night ahead of us. The "girls" are lined up, the band is wailing, the dice are rolling, the drinks are pouring and the testosterone is flowing.

"I'm gonna ask that girl to dance," Glenn says, strutting over to a babe. "You wanna dance?"

"Sure, but you have to buy me a drink," she says.

This is how the bar makes money—charging high prices for soft drinks bought for the "girls."

"What, I gotta buy you a drink? No way. Let's just dance."

"No, you gotta buy me a drink first."

"No, I'm not gonna pay a dollar for a drink just to dance. "

"Okay—no drink, no dance."

"Come on, just one dance."

Suddenly, the Jolly Black Giant appears. He grabs Glenn by the shirt and starts dragging him toward the door. "You're outta here, and your friends, too." He shoves Glenn out the door, then turns around and glares at us. We meekly file out, hoping he doesn't toss our asses out.

"You dumb shit, Glenn. You got us kicked out."

"I wasn't going to pay a buck for a drink just to dance. Let's go back to the Ebony."

I call shotgun, jump in the front seat, and Sig and John get in the back. Sig lights a cigarette, rolls down the back window an inch and blows out a puff of smoke just as a dark figure appears on the front steps of the Four Lights holding a shotgun.

As Glenn guns the engine and spins the car around the parking lot, spraying gravel from spinning rear tires, we hear an ear-shattering boom and see a flash of light from the shotgun leveled at us. There is a split-second delay from the flash to the dull thud of buckshot hitting the side of the car.

Chapter 39

Black People Aren't Black, Dad's Lesson

During our senior year, my buddies and I become regulars at the Ebony Club. I'm feeling comfortable with all the black folks there. It seems natural to be around people who are different. I think I've always felt this way. Maybe it goes back to when I was a kid.

I remember being seven years old, and the circus came to our rural little town of Bridger, Montana, population seven hundred. On Saturday afternoons, parking places are scarce on the four-block Main Street. My dad, Frank, and my mom, Anna, like to visit and make friends with anyone who comes along.

Dad occasionally works repairing railroad tracks with a section gang, or "Gandy Dancers," made up of locals and a few immigrants. They are known as Gandy Dancers because the swing of their hammers synchronized to the cadence set by the lead workman creates a kind of dance rhythm. "Gandy" may have come from the Gandy tool company that made the hammers.

One of Dad's friends is Jimmy the Jap, who he works with on the section gang. In 1951, it was perfectly fine to call his buddy Jimmy the Jap. Jimmy knows my dad loves him and that his name is just who he is. Dad has also befriended other minorities like the Mexicans who come every summer to harvest peas, beans and sugar beets. They live with their families in small shacks on the farms but come to town on Saturdays squeaky clean and showing us all models of good family values. On Sundays, they fill the Catholic Church to the chagrin of some of the church members. Dad hangs out, drinks beer with them, or just sits on benches along Main Street visiting with them.

"Ah, Mr. Frank, come sit," Felipe says. The Mexican migrant workers usually call the local men by their first name with Mr. at the front.

"You hoe'in beans out on the Curry Place?" Dad says.

"Sí, we finish next week, go to Webber Place."

"Good, I'll be there next week too. We'll work together."

The three Mexicans and my dad are squeezed together on a small bench, feeling very comfortable sitting against each other. I don't realize the Mexicans are different than us. I have not learned prejudice yet.

Beans are one of the main crops in the Clark Fork Valley, but in the 1950s, much of the farm labor is done by hand. The weeds need to be hoed, and a good hoer can do up to eight rows at a time. As a kid, I can do just two rows. It is hot, dry, strenuous labor wielding a hoe from six in the morning to dusk. Pay is almost nothing, but for many, it means survival.

* * *

Being of German descent, my dad worked during World War II as a translator at the German prisoner of war camp on the outskirts of Bridger. German prisoners of war were shipped to small communities around the country. Because of the war, most farm laborers had been drafted into the army, creating a shortage of workers. The POW camps were established to provide workers for agriculture.

The Bridger camp consisted of canvas tents surrounded by a fence topped with barbed wire. Prisoners were assigned to work at different farms. Dad would accompany the soldiers and translate when workers were dropped off for the day. His parents had emigrated from Germany around 1900 and spoke mostly German. My grandmother hardly ever spoke English, and I never had a conversation with her or my grandfather.

It was forbidden to give the German prisoners food. My dad could see that the POWs were not being fed well enough to do hard farm labor, so he told the farmers they needed to secretly feed the prisoners if they wanted a good day's work. The farmers agreed and provided extra food. The prisoners appreciated Dad's efforts on their behalf and became friends with him.

"Tomorrow, we go to the Langstaff Place," my dad says in German to Klaus, one of the prisoners.

"Ya, sure. They always treat us right," Klaus answers in German.

"That's because you work hard."

"We work hard because we have no place to go. We miss our home. No need guards for us."

"Yes, many miles and much water to Germany."

"If not for Hitler, we would be home. He has ruined Germany—a crazy man! Why so many people believe him? We lose the war and our country."

Later, Dad tells me, "These Germans are stuck in the middle of Montana, and there's no place they can escape to. They didn't like Hitler and were all drafted into the German army. They just wanted the war to be over and to go back to their families."

For many years after the war, former prisoners would return to Bridger to show their families where they had been held prisoner during the war.

"Yes, they would come back," Dad explains, "and they would always find me so I could meet their families. They were good people, just like us."

Sixty miles from Bridger, near Powell, Wyoming, was another camp—but not for war prisoners. This one was for US citizens. Behind the same barbed wire fences, as used in the German POW camps, Japanese families are held—moms, dads, children and grandparents. The US government, fearful that these people might side with the Japanese government, took away their rights as US citizens.

"What happened to your home in California?" my dad asks Jimmy the Jap, his fellow worker on the section gang.

"It was all lost—our house, my father's food store. All gone, taken and given to white people. We got no money and no place to return to. That's why I stay in Montana."

"How long were you in the camp?"

"Three years. It was cold with bad food. It broke my mother's heart and her spirit. She died young," Jimmy says with a blank look.

Japanese families were forced to give up their property and spend up to three years in a frigid, barren, forsaken place. Ironically, when they turned eighteen, most of the young Japanese men volunteered for the army. A tragedy of justice, most of these "Japs" loved the USA and were not only harmless but loyal. Many of them had been US citizens for as long as most local Wyoming people.

I ask my Dad why Germans weren't put in camps like the Japs. "We're lucky—we're white," he says. I don't understand this until I got older because prejudice is subtle and hidden.

* * *

The summer of 1954 is Shangri-La for kids in Bridger, our farming community on the Clarks Fork of the Yellowstone River just thirty miles from the snowcapped Beartooth Mountain Wilderness. The Clarks Fork Valley, scrubbed out of the remnants of a pre-historic ocean floor by the river, is crowned by sandstone cliffs up to four hundred feet tall that run the length of the valley. The sandstone, originally the ocean floor, still houses fossils of long-extinct fish and shark's teeth. The valley, once covered with sagebrush, has been cleared by farmers and replaced with neat fields of corn, sugar beets, peas, beans and wheat. Irrigated by a series of canals, it is lush and productive.

At ten, I'm one of those kids in Shangri-La riding an oversized hand-me-down bike from my older brother. Dismounting is simple, just dive off while it's still moving. The wheels have playing cards clipped to the fender frame with clothespins. The cards vibrate against the spinning spokes and make a sound like a motorcycle engine.

First bike

Pulling sled behind car

We wear patched clothes and use cardboard to cover the holes in the soles of our shoes. In the summer, we run barefoot down the gravel streets to save on shoe leather. From river willows, we make bows and arrows so bent we can shoot around corners. I fish with a willow fishing pole using ten feet of twine tied to the end, a washer for a sinker, and a hook big enough for a worm the size of a snake. I catch rainbow trout, cutthroat trout, whitefish, catfish, ling, and occasionally a big sturgeon that creates so much excitement we almost pee our pants. Back at home, Mom hands me a knife and says, "You catch 'em, you clean 'em."

A crude pistol my dad carved out of scrap wood is all I need to win any pretend war. We don't have anything, but we have and do everything—ride a pretend motorcycle, shoot arrows at rabbits, shoot pretend bullets at my friends and pull fish out of the Clark's Fork River.

The Clark's Fork, named after William Clark of Lewis and Clark fame, begins where ice melts off the 12,808-foot Granite Peak high in the Beartooth Wilderness. The Beartooth Mountain Range is the largest wilderness in the lower forty-eight states and is bordered by Custer National Forest and Yellowstone National Park. It covers 10,000 square miles of stunning landscapes. A mile east of Bridger, the water runs so cold, clear and pure we regularly quench our youthful thirst, which is fueled by the running, jumping, climbing and swimming we do through our busy summer days. We share the river with horses, cows, beavers, muskrats, fox, deer, elk, bears, turtles, frogs and throbbing schools of fish.

My parents own a green 1941 Buick. It's ten years old, but for our family practically new. Camping is our only family recreation during the summer. Our favorite place is Yellowstone Park, seventy-five miles down a precarious, narrow gravel road that snakes its way to the top of the world. With no guard rails, a wrong turn can launch a car off a thousand-foot cliff to utter destruction.

My mother drives because she doesn't trust my dad to stay on the road, but the rest of the family doesn't trust her careless driving, either.

My father gives up the wheel to keep peace in the family. I remember many close encounters with the edge of the road with car tires spilling loose gravel over the side. According to my mother's faith in the Catholic Church, a St. Christopher Medal pinned to the headliner keeps us safe. Today on this drive, St. Christopher, the patron saint of travelers, works overtime.

We don't own a tent, cooler or any camping equipment. My father lays a large canvas tarp on the ground, layers it with blankets from our beds, and then folds the tarp in half over the top of us. We have a sleeping order—my dad on one end next to my mother, then my younger brother Steve, age three. I'm next at age seven, then my brother Arne, age thirteen. Finally, my oldest brother Gene, age fifteen.

The high mountain nights in Yellowstone Park are clear, crisp and piercing. We huddle together and keep warm and mostly dry when it rains. In the 1950s, the National Park policy for managing bears allows them to eat out of the garbage dump and from people's cars. Most days, dozens of bears stop traffic and hang out beside cars eating handouts of donuts and sandwiches. On a good weekend, we count up to a hundred bears.

The bears are always on the hunt for people food. Often, in the middle of the night, they wake us up by rummaging around our camp. My dad rattles a tin coffee can filled with a few rocks and shines a flashlight to run them off. We go back to sleep for a few more hours only to get up and run them off again.

We store our perishable food in mason jars in the cold creek. One night, a downpour raises the creek and floats our cache of food away.

"At least we got eggs left," my mother says, digging a dozen eggs out of the trunk.

Dad starts a fire, heats some water in a porcelain coffee pot and dumps a scoop of coffee grounds into it. When the coffee is done, he fills five heavy ceramic mugs with the brew and laces them with sugar and heavy cream. We all enjoy a cup. Mine tastes like dessert. Even my three-year-old brother Steve gets a sip from Dad's cup.

When the small circus comes to town this year, it features a couple of clowns with big floppy shoes, plaid pants and orange hair ballooning from their heads; a fire eater; a two-headed calf in a jar of formaldehyde; a boa constrictor that might eat a live chicken, which one can witness for twenty-five cents.

A beautiful female acrobat swings perilously on a trapeze wearing a tight-fitting swimsuit covered by what looks like diamonds. She is almost too much for the eyes of a seven-year-old boy beginning to notice the opposite sex. There are six white horses, the kind a cowboy hero in the comic books would ride. But the most interesting part of the circus to me is a man whose skin is black. Not dark like the Mexicans or tan like Jimmy the Jap, but black like coal or black paint. I have never seen a man painted black before. He feeds, waters and brushes the horses until they gleam in the sun. I'm very shy when I see this black man and wonder why my dad is talking and laughing with him.

I ask my dad, "What is that?" pointing to the man covered with what I think is black paint or coal.

"Oh—his name is Ray. He's real smart and knows a lot about horses. Got a good laugh." He never mentions the color of the man's skin, almost like he doesn't even notice it.

He takes me over to Ray, who is filling a bucket from a garden hose attached to the Mercantile Building. "Ray, this is my boy, Dan," he says. "Mind if he sits on one of your horses?"

"Glad to meet you, Dan," Ray says, sticking out his hand.

"Shake his hand," my dad says, demonstrating how.

Ray takes my small hand into his big, rough but amazingly tender hand and squeezes it firmly and gently, then shakes it up and down. It is my first real handshake, and I never forget it. Ray's hand is rough, but he isn't. He's as big as the giant in *Jack and the Beanstalk*, but his heart seems larger than his frame. A brilliant smile explodes out of his square face, sucking you into a safe place. His teeth look almost as big as the horse standing next to him and translucent white.

"Your pa knows a lot about horses," Ray says, then swings me up on a big white stallion so I can have a bird's-eye view of the entire circus. Dad and Ray pull the horse's lips wide open and look into its mouth. The horse doesn't seem to mind and stands still while they discuss its teeth. The animal is slobbering all over their hands.

That's all my dad says about Ray—"He's real smart and knows a lot about horses. Got a good laugh."

He doesn't say Ray was black or a "nigger," like some of the other white folks in town will call him. He is just another man who knows a lot about horses and has a nice smile. That's all I need to know.

When Dad was younger, he'd go up into the Pryor Mountains and catch wild horses, which were descended from herds brought by early Spanish explorers to Mexico. He would tame these mustangs to be ridden with a saddle or to pull a wagon, and then sell them to the local farmers. He could ride any horse that came along. If he says Ray knows a lot about horses, that's enough for me. It's the highest compliment Dad can pay someone.

I could tell that Ray and my dad trusted each other even if they had just met thirty minutes ago. That day, my dad said a lot without using any words. He told me that people are all the same even if they look different. He told me to judge a person by what they do, not how they look. He told me that every man deserves respect. He told me what my young heart already knew—that it was not Okay to be prejudice. He told me all this with very few words and a lot of actions.

From that day on, I have been drawn to people like Ray. Eight years later, in 1960, I finished my freshman year at Billings Central. After attending a boy's retreat with Fr. Henry from the Passionist's Order, I'm enthused to be a priest. My parents put me on the train, the North Coast Limited, and I'm headed to St. Louis to go to seminary. The train stops for a four-hour layover at the elegant Union Station in Chicago.

I have never been out of Montana before. Traveling alone by train and seeing a big city for the first time is a huge adventure for me. Union Station seems as large as the whole town of Bridger, but grand. I hardly know what "grand" means, but I know the station is different than anything I ever imagined. I see dozens of people who look like Ray, probably for the first time since I had met Ray at the circus eight years earlier. I am amazed by how many there are like him. I look across at a bench where an old man sits alone. My inherited instinct draws me over to him.

I sit down and say what I think my dad would say: "It's a big place."

The old man smiles and says, "Yeah, don't get much bigger. Where you from, son?"

"Montana. On my way to St. Louis to be a priest."

"Thaz so? Thaz a long ways for a young man to be goin' by hisself."

"Yeah, never been outta Montana before."

"Ever see a bear?"

"Yeah, lots. They come right up to your car in Yellowstone, and we feed

'em old bread out the window. Sometimes they try to stick their heads in."

"Sounds dangerous."

"Nah, that's nothin'. One time we went camping, and my dad put down a big canvas and laid blankets in it, and we all slept under it. In the middle of the night, a bear came, and Dad took a tin can full of rocks and shook it, then shined a flashlight on the bear, and it ran off. We had to run it off two more times that night."

"You scared?"

"Nope, but the bear was."

"Sounds like it."

My new friend is James. I tell him about Ray. "When I was little, a circus came to town. There was a man whose job was takin' care of the horses. Name was Ray and my dad said he knew a lot about horses and made friends with him. He was the first black person I ever saw."

"Sounds like your pa knew a lot more than just about horses."

"Yeah."

"Sounds like you got that from him."

"Yes, sir."

When the layover is about done, I say goodbye to my new friend and depart for the St. Louis Union Pacific Station, where I'm met by Father Gerard, the Dean of High School Boys at the Passionist Seminary in the small town of Warrenton. This is where I spend my sophomore and junior years studying for the priesthood. I'm allowed to go home for summer vacations, but I'm a long way from home.

During my junior year, my parents move from Billings to Great Falls, where my dad takes a new job as a custodian at Our Lady of Lourdes Catholic grade school. At the end of my junior year, I decide I don't want to return to seminary.

This creates a whole new anxiety.

Chapter 40

Where Did All the Girls Go?

Suddenly, I snap out of my daydream about childhood in Bridger and my time at the seminary in high school. I'm still in the parking lot where the Ebony Club once stood. My visit back to Great Falls has opened a flood of memories.

I drive to the Burger Master Drive-In and order a Ramp Burger with special sauce, forking over $1.25. With burger in hand, I park and watch traffic go down 10th Avenue South. I remember all the good times I had here. The last time I'd bought a Ramp Burger, it had cost thirty-five cents. This was the local hangout for kids— a place to meet, talk, argue, flirt and sometimes fight. It was a time when we were emerging as adults and trying to look cool, although hot on the inside around the opposite sex. Everyone was thinking about sex, but no one ever said what they were thinking.

I head down Central Avenue on my way to the west side of Great Falls and stop at the railroad crossing. As a train rumbles by, I remember my train ride from Billings to the seminary in St. Louis more than twenty years ago.

It's 1959, and I'm fifteen years old. I'm riding the North Coast Limited, a stately train when trains were still at their prime and air travel was for the rich. The Vista Cruiser cars feature a glass-covered dome on the second level allowing me to see for miles. This is my dream, traveling across the country, taking in every detail—people, animals, the landscape—and wondering, *what is all this*? There is so much to see, and I want to see it all. I want to get off the train and talk to the farmer riding a tractor down a dusty road. I want to talk to the lady getting her mail on a rural road. I wonder what the cows are thinking as they graze open pastures, if anything. I wonder what is going on behind closed doors as we pass through small towns. I wonder, I wonder…

The formal dining cars sparkle with white linen tablecloths and napkins, polished silverware, crystal glasses and engraved china. I watch the black porters at work in their white jackets, black bowties and polished billed hats with a brass "Pullman Porter" tag on the front. Later in life, I learn that all porters are called "George," a throwback to slavery. Another detail that escaped me as a naïve fifteen-year-old was that there are no black passengers on the train. I sit in the dining car with wonder, watching rich white people eating elegant dinners. I order a Coke, because I don't have enough money to buy food, and eat the snacks and sandwiches my mother prepared for the trip.

"Take your time, son, got lots of room for everybody," a smiling porter reassures me. "You kinda young to be traveling alone."

"Yessir, my first train ride."

"Where you from?"

"Montana."

"Ah, I love when we go through Montana. So beautiful."

"Yeah, lots of things to look at."

The trip takes thirty-six hours and covers 1,500 miles, but for me, it ends too soon.

As we lurch to a stop at the St. Louis Union Station, I spot a young priest wearing a black cassock and a black-and-white plastic heart pinned to his chest. This is the symbol of the Passionist's Monastic Order. Fr. Gerard fetches me for the ride to the seminary.

This country looks different. Unlike the Montana prairie, there are many trees here but no mountains. It's early September but still hot—and very humid. I'd never experienced humidity like this before, having been raised in the dry air of Montana. I sweat profusely and complain.

"You'll get used to it," Fr. Gerard tells me. "Is this your first time away from home?"

"Yes, never left Montana before."

"It'll take a while. You might get homesick, but it'll get better."

The next day, I begin two years of a disciplined life that includes two hours of prayer and meditation each day. This is a long time to settle a young mind, but over time things begin to sink in. I'm beginning to learn who I am.

My daily regimen looks like this:

5:45 – Rise

6:00 – Holy Mass and Meditation

7:15 – Breakfast in silence with religious reading

7:45 – Supervised Study

8:30 – Classes Begin

11:45 – Meditation in Chapel

12:15 – Lunch in silence with religious reading

12:50 – Study

2:00 – Recreation – Physical Education – Shower

4:15 – Class

5:00 – Supervised Study

6:00 – Spiritual Reading and Meditation

6:30 – Dinner

7:15 – Meditation in Chapel

7:35 – Supervised Study

8:20 – Recreation

9:10 – Meditation in Chapel

9:25 – Retire

First day arriving at my new home

The days sail by. During recreation time, we search the hills and surrounding area discovering ponds, cliffs, snakes, birds, handball, football and new friends. A bunch of boys isolated from the world find mutual bonds and support. We are all a long way from home, and all we have is each other—and a dream to become a priest.

I'm homesick for the first month or so, but I try to push forward, telling myself that someday I'll be a priest and things will be better. Most of my life up to now has been spent waiting for things to be better. I do a good job hiding my insecurity, never wanting others to think of me as weak or having problems, so I figure out how to look good on the outside.

I make new friends—Jim, Mike and Bob from Southern California, Carey from Chicago. The seminary has students from all over the United States. There are four years of high school and two years of college offered here. In the early 1960s, religious orders recruited kids at age fourteen to begin education for the priesthood. I'm one of those kids, just barely into puberty.

We lead fairly normal lives at the seminary, even though the routine is strenuous. I don't truly comprehend that I am just beginning a long process of education and discipline to become a priest. After high school, there will be two years of junior college, one year as a novitiate, three years of philosophy, four years of theology and one year of post-ordination studies. That's eleven years of college and university study. Perhaps this is the reason priests here at the seminary are solid, well-rounded and trustworthy.

The only nearby town is Warrenton, with 1,700 residents. Several times a year, we are allowed to walk into Warrenton as a group on a Saturday afternoon. On my first trip to the small village, I'm shocked to see racial segregation. About half the community are blacks who live with segregated drinking fountains, bathrooms, restaurants and churches warning black people to keep out. Blacks live in shanties on the south side of the railroad track. On Saturday afternoons, they sit on front porches enjoying the day and talking with each other.

Sleepy Main Street Warrenton

One day I wander across the tracks with Mike and notice how they all smile at us. I want to stop and talk to them, but Mike is a little nervous. In retrospect, part of their friendliness may have been because I smiled at them. In my mind, they were all like Ray. It made no sense to me that they lived in one part of town, separated from the white folks.

When we come back to the "white side" of the tracks, a white man in a straw hat and suspenders yells at us. "If I see you boys back on the other side of the tracks, you're going to get a whooping." He scares the hell out of us, so we run back to join the rest of the group. I'm perplexed that black folks are "out of bounds" and wonder what they had done.

I make more new friends as the school year goes on. The other students, a mixture from around the country, create diversity. Bob is the cynic of the class, a creative writer and a good basketball player from Los Angeles. Wheeler is the runt of the class, the last to enter puberty—but a good ballplayer and a quick wit. Carey, being from Chicago, is a Cubs fan and talks baseball whenever anyone will listen. Bobula, also from Chicago, is the intellectual and looks Jewish. Komenda, a Hispanic (or Mexican, as we call them in those days), is also from LA. He is one of the wild kids in the class, and periodically the priests have to reel him in a bit. Jesse is quiet and Afro-American. Jim knows some things about photography and printing, so I tag along with him to learn stuff.

We are all given jobs in addition to our studies. Jim and I work in the photo lab and printing shop. One benefit is that we sometimes see the magazines that come in the mail before the priests tear out the women's underwear ads to save us from impure thoughts. When you're fifteen-years-old in a seminary isolated from girls, a bra ad is about as good as it gets.

Jack, me and Jim

Guys without gals

The guys hanging out—me, Jerry and Jim

Holy Day at the Seminary

Each student is assigned a spiritual adviser. Mine is Fr. Randall, a tall, kind man who is good at listening and encourages us to think for ourselves. He likes me, but then most of the priests like me. I'm always portraying the good kid. In the background, though, I enjoy playing practical jokes and shifting the blame.

I'm homesick off and on during the next two years, thinking of Mom and Dad. I believe my mom really wants me to be a priest, so this keeps me going, even though I want to go home at times. During those lonely, cold mornings, in prayer and meditation, a lot of thoughts go through me, and eventually, I was "born again," as they say. To this day, that experience is still clear and real.

Let me paint the scene. The image of a large, life-sized crucifix—a cross with a plaster of Paris statue of Jesus hanging on it—hangs above the altar. At first, it seems like a dream, but I am awake. I poke Jim next to me to see if he sees it, but he stares blankly ahead, not aware of anything.

Jesus comes down from the cross and stands in front of me. I blink and then blink again.

Jesus says, "There is much I can't tell you today. I will return when you can understand. But for now, I am the way, the life and the truth. Be vigilant."

Jesus seems very human, and if I wasn't frozen in my pew, I could have reached out and touched him. But I'm not scared.

I look over at Jim, and he is still staring at the spot where Jesus is standing, but he doesn't see anything.

Then, in a flash, Jesus is back on the cross, but his eyes are looking at me.

I never tell anyone of this experience. Later on, when people talk about being "born again," I just smile and think, "Yeah—been there, done that."

It will be another thirty-two years before I understand what Jesus was trying to tell me. In the meantime, I keep looking, and looking, and waiting.

At the end of my second year at the Passionist's Seminary, my mind has shifted from becoming a priest to girls. It was probably on girls the entire time, but now girls have become a priority. Toward the end of the school year, despite my spiritual "rebirth" the year before, I visit Fr. Randall in his office.

"Umm, I think I lost my vocation." I stammer with guilt.

"What makes you think that?"

"I don't know, but I want to go home and do something different."

"Well, Dan, we all have to make our own life. I never thought I would live mine as a monk and a priest, but somehow it happened. It's been difficult at times, not having a family and children, but I make the best of it."

"But you seem so happy with your life."

"That's just how I look. We never know what goes on inside another person. That's why Jesus tells us not to judge and to forgive others. Sometimes it's easier than forgiving ourselves. You'll have to do this for yourself and decide how to be happy in life. When I make myself look happy, it helps me feel happy inside. I don't have any regrets. I made my own life."

"That's what my mother says, 'Just think yourself happy.'"

"Try to follow her advice. In the meantime, do what you need to do and go home. You have to make your own life."

He is understanding and doesn't make me feel guilty. I really didn't need any help feeling guilty anyway since I am doing a pretty good job of that myself.

So, at the end of my junior year, I leave Missouri to go to Great Falls. My parents have moved there from Billings during my sophomore year, so I will begin my senior year at Central Catholic High School. Little do I know at this point that North Dakota and another seminary are on the horizon.

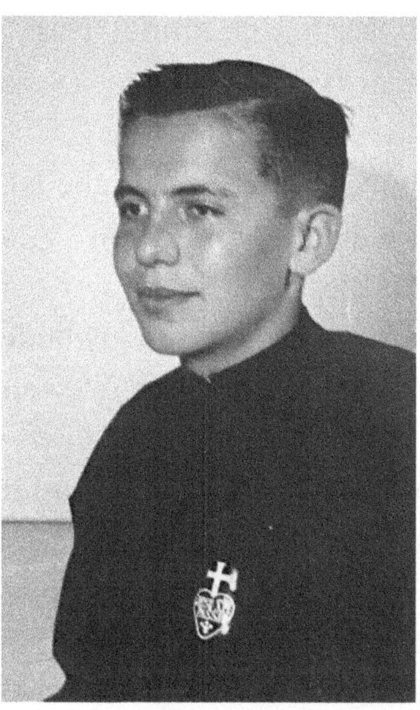

Just before I lost my vocation

Classmates at reunion fifty years later.

My memories of those high school years in the seminary will never leave me. I have always wondered what happened to my classmates.

Twenty years later, as I'm attending the National Rehabilitation Association Conference in St. Louis, I realize Warrenton and the seminary are just sixty miles away.

After the conference, I say to Tom, my buddy from Billings, "My old seminary is just sixty miles from here. You interested in a little road trip?"

"Sure, I'd to see where you lost your vocation," he quips.

Tom and I pick up a rental car and head west on I-70 for Warrenton. It's a gorgeous fall day, and the heavily wooded countryside flashes by dazzling shades of yellow and gold. It's been twenty years since I was at the Passionist's Seminary.

Today, Warrenton is a modern-looking town with double the population. I remember horse-drawn carts still in use when I was there and recall the segregation prior to the Civil Rights Act of 1964.

Today, things have changed so much I can't find my bearings. We stop at a gas station and ask for directions to the Passionist's Seminary.

"Oh, that's long gone, but the buildings are still down the road," the attendant says with a Missouri drawl. We head down Highway 47, and soon the familiar water tower of the campus comes into view. Turning off the roadway, I see that the large stucco seminary sign was replaced by one proclaiming the "Child Evangelical Center."

We drive down a long entrance road to a circular driveway and park in front of the old chapel—a church, really, with a tall spire. The door is locked, so we walk around to the monastery entrance. Inside, we inquire about the purpose of the Child Evangelical Center.

"We evangelize children," the man curtly answers.

"Do you mind if we look around? I used to attend school here and would like to see how things look today."

"Feel free, but don't go into any of the private rooms."

As we walk down a corridor, Tom remarks, "I ain't drinking any Kool-Aid in this place," referring to the mass suicide of 900 members of the Jim Jones cult in Guyana a few years back. "That guy looked like a troll guarding the bridge. I don't like this place."

"Me neither, this feels creepy. I have a bad feeling of what they might be doing with children here." While it is now called the Child Evangelical Center, there are no children here.

We walk past the dining room where we used to eat in silence and listen to readings on spirituality or from scripture. We walk past the classrooms where we squirmed, waiting for the bell to ring at the end of classes; the recreation room where we played cards, games and listened to records censored by the priests.

Today, the rec room is filled with huge printing machines producing brochures and letters asking for financial donations to save children. It looks like a money-making factory. I study a brochure filled with guilt-inducing language clearly intended to entice people into making donations. Reading between the lines, it seems like children here are taught what to think, not how to think—something I have never liked about organized religion.

At the end of the long hall is the dormitory where I lived for two years. Our next stop is the chapel. The pews have been removed, and lines have been drawn on the floor delineating a basketball court. The altar is still there but hovering above it is a basket attached to a pole. The beautiful, carved hardwood altar and wall panels are still intact, but the orange hoop hanging over the altar seems like blasphemy. The large crucifix of Jesus that once spoke to me is gone. This was where Jesus had told me that he had more to tell me and that I should be vigilant and wait. I am still waiting.

I walk toward the front and view the altar stone, a piece of marble twelve inches by twelve inches and one inch thick sitting flush in the surface of the altar. Embedded in it are relics, perhaps a piece of the original cross of Jesus, or a fingernail or bone of a saint. This is the stone where the priest lays the bread to be consecrated or transfigured into the body of Christ. This is the most sacred ritual in the Catholic Church. Even the most cynical of us boys were reverent during this moment in the Mass.

"Tom, it's the altar stone," I cry out. "We gotta save it from this place." I pry the heavy stone out of the fitted slot cut into the altar, feeling like King Arthur pulling the magical Excalibur out of pure stone. I stand there for a minute thinking of all the times I had made fun of religion—and now I'm the hero of the day trying to save this precious stone from blasphemy.

"How we going to get it outta here?" Tom asks.

"The window. If we get the window open, we can lower it out."

We struggle to open a stained-glass window, but they have all been permanently locked, and the chapel door is chained closed.

"Maybe I can hide it down my pants." I try putting it inside the front of my pants, but I can barely keep my pants up as I walk bow-legged.

"We're gonna get caught for sure," Tom says, "and then we'll be forced to drink the Kool-Aid. Let's get outta here." He searches the hallway for an escape. "The only way out is past that creepy guy."

"Yeah, he'll catch us. But I'll be back." I hide the stone behind the altar, making a promise to rescue it someday. Keeping that promise is another thing.

I leave feeling sad that the chapel has been downgraded to a basketball court.

On the flight home to Billings, I keep thinking about the altar stone and the precious relics lying behind the altar, now devoid of any reverence or respect. I think about my promise to rescue the stone, a promise that pretty much has already been broken.

Chapter 41

New Guys in Town, Sig, Gunner and Glenn

After leaving seminary in Missouri, I return to Great Falls, where my parents are. Two friends, Jim and Gunner from Billings, have also moved to Great Falls with their parents. I find Jim at home and suggest we go to see Gunner.

We cruise over to the north side of town. A black '49 Ford sits in the driveway. Lying beneath it are car parts, tools, open cans of Great Falls Select beer and two greasy bodies replacing a burned-out clutch bearing.

I look under the car. "Gunner, it's me, Danny."

"Danny, Griff—good to see ya. This is Sig, and that's Glenn over there."

We all nod at each other.

Thus, the beginning of new friendships and our year together at Great Falls Central. Now it is only a matter of time before we'll be engaged in the wonders of being seniors and at the top of our game—drinking beer, driving fast, wrecking cars, dancing to rock and roll, chasing girls, trying to be cool, chasing more girls and occasionally studying.

I am free of the Missouri seminary but not from the guilt of losing my vocation. And while I am happy to be back home, the guilt will follow me for the next twenty-five years. A few years after I left the seminary in Missouri, it closed due to the lack of young priest candidates. This was the beginning of the aging of the clergy in the Catholic Church.

Over the years, when priests retired or died, there were fewer replacements. The Church began shifting its ministry to laypeople. Because the seminary closed in 1969, there was no way for me to connect with my classmates who had scattered across the country. I had nothing but a collection of memories surrounding those adolescent years, but no one to talk to about my experiences there.

I wouldn't have any connection with that chapter of my life for almost two decades.

Chapter 42

Glenn's Daughter

Returning to Billings after my visit to the Vietnam Memorial, I can't stop thinking about Glenn, the Memorial and Teresa, Glenn's daughter. She is twenty years old now and living in Texas. The note with her number is burning a hole in my pocket, so I dial her number. The phone rings three times before someone answers.

"Hello."

"Hello, Teresa?"

"Yes."

"This is Dan Geiger, a friend of your dad's. We went to school together in Great Falls."

"You knew my dad?"

"Yeah, we were in the same class. I got your number from your grandparents last week when I was at their house."

"You saw my grandparents?"

"They gave me your phone number and send their love."

"Yeah, maybe I need to call them again. They're getting pretty old."

"I'm sure they would love to hear from you. Time goes by."

"So, you were like friends with my dad in school?"

"Yeah, we ran around together."

"He and my mom got divorced when I was a baby. I never knew him. My mom didn't say much about him."

"Yeah, I remember you at the funeral. You were little."

"All I knew was he was killed and drank a lot. Is that true?"

"Well, your dad drank like we all did when we were young, but he wasn't a bad person. He had a good heart and would always help others."

"Really?"

"Yeah, he liked people and had a good sense of humor. We had a lot of fun together."

"Is that true?"

"Yeah, a really good person."

"I like helping people too."

"It sounds like you have a kind heart, just like your dad."

"I always wondered about him. I wanted to believe he was a good person."

"It sounds like you have lots of good qualities from your dad. You can be proud to be his daughter. He was a brave man."

"Do you really think I have some of the same things as my dad?"

"Yes, I can hear it in your voice, you have a kind voice."

There is a long silence, and then, "I always knew there was good in him, no matter what people said. It was like he was talking to me, telling me I was good inside too. I so much wanted to believe that."

"I'm sure he's still talking to you today. You're still father and daughter, that never changes—it's simply different. You can help one another now. Listen to your heart, listen to him."

There is a silence followed by a deep sigh, "I can hear him."

Chapter 43

Back to Billings, continued

After making contact with Glenn's daughter, I return home to Billings, continuing to plow through life. It's the mid-80s, I'm divorced, and my daughters are six and eight. I try to be a part of their lives by having them stay with me on weekends, but I'm still an absentee dad. We do our best, but it's difficult for all of us.

The years click by, and soon my daughters are finishing high school and going off to college. I wonder where the years went. It has been twenty years since I was hanging out at the Stein Haus. During that stretch, my career blossomed, and I quickly worked my way up into administration, but inside I feel empty. I hide this from everyone, of course, and just keep looking good on the outside.

From my early travels from Montana to Chicago and St. Louis, I have developed a passion for adventure and travel. Over the years, I visit many countries, including China, the USSR, Thailand and most of Europe—always searching for something, perhaps for answers to who I am.

I am intensely attracted to people, cultures and religions. I read the Book of Mormon, study the Seventh Day Adventists, Jehovah Witnesses, Evangelicals, always finding inconsistencies in their teachings and moving on to the next one. While in Thailand, I spend time with Buddhist monks and appreciate their self-awareness and kind spirit, but feel I need a religion that focuses on serving others. I find the Hindu religion, with its mystical practices, fascinating. But I remain puzzled at the way various religions create and maintain conflict not only with each other but within their own ranks. Most all of them claim they are the one true religion, but how can this be? If there are 30,000 sects of Christianity, which is the true one? If there is one God, then why have His followers create so many different versions of what they consider the truth?

I keep looking.

Chapter 44

Where Did This Depression Come from?

I have many regrets, but not being there for my children is the most painful one.

When my first wife and I divorced, my daughters were too young to understand but not too young to be hurt. I tried to be a weekend father, to fill the gap of not living in the same house. As the girls entered junior high, their interests shifted to friends, school activities and becoming adults, so our time together was less frequent. While still in junior high, they moved to Seattle, where their mother had decided to pursue a new career, or perhaps just get away from me. I never really knew the reason, but the move broke my heart.

Now I'm in Seattle and anxious to see them, so I call. "Hi, it's Dad. I'm in town. I can pick you up in an hour."

"Okay, see you soon."

I drive to Kirkland and find the apartment building where they live. I'm here for the weekend and staying in a hotel in downtown Seattle where we settle in for the weekend.

The kids enjoy looking out the window from the twentieth story, which overlooks Puget Sound. It's a typical absentee-dad weekend—going out to dinner, walking in the park, shopping for clothes… and it ends too soon. A couple of days here and there just isn't enough to feel like I'm part of their lives.

My trip back to Billings is sad and depressing. All I do is reminisce morosely about the precious time we spent together when they were little children. Now that's all gone. I try to be grateful for the time I have with them now, but the empty spaces between visits are painful.

Because I had ignorantly signed away joint custody, I had no control over where my children lived. I thought seriously about filing for joint custody but decided not to, knowing this would create a difficult situation for my daughters. After two years, however, my ex returned to Billings with the girls. I felt as if I had lost two years of precious time in their lives but was happy to have them back.

Then I watched them grow up too fast, leave for college and become their own persons. Looking back, that time was a blur. We try to teach our children to be independent, but when they are, we struggle with it. My oldest daughter leaving for college out of state was one of those times.

Marie is beginning college at Colorado State University in Fort Collins. I'm driving her there from Billings. We load up the car and head across southern Montana, the high plateau of Wyoming and northern Colorado. It is 500 miles and a nine-hour drive. I enjoy our time together and realize she is rapidly becoming an adult and starting a life of her own.

We arrive on campus, find her dorm, unload the car and have a nice dinner together.

"So, what are you the most interested in college?" I ask her.

"I like writing and being on the school news magazine last year. Maybe doing PR and writing."

"Are you nervous about college?"

"Not really, I have a friend here from Billings."

"Think you'll get homesick?"

"Oh, I dunno—probably be too busy with college. Did you get homesick when you were in school?"

"Some, but there was so much new stuff I didn't think about it much."

"I'll probably get in a lot of activities and some new friends."

"You always made friends easy—and as Grandpa says, 'She's a good kid.'"

Laughing, Marie says, "Grandpa thinks everyone is a good kid."

"I think he really means it with you. I think so too."

The waitress comes to take our order. "What would you like?" she asks Marie.

"I'll take the tuna salad."

"Sounds like a healthy choice."

"Yeah, thanks to my dad."

After dinner, I say goodbye, "Have a great time at college. You going to be okay?"

"Sure, Dad, I'm fine. All excited to start. Thanks for the ride." She's bright, happy and excited—already making new friends in the dorm.

"Okay, see you at Christmas."

"Yeah, see you at Christmas."

I leave and realize she on her own, independent and happy with her life. I'm happy for her but feel a great sadness driving home. I am grieving the separation from my daughter, now a young adult.

* * *

This depression comes and goes over the years, but I seem to always bounce back. I consider suicide, though I can't pinpoint exactly what is ailing me. Life continues as a blur at times. I wonder where my feelings of insecurity come from. Everyone has them, but most hide those feelings and try to look strong. Others are complainers or whiners and seem to make their lives and those around them worse.

Every generation struggles with life. It seems every generation blames the previous one for the troubles in the world, and every generation comments on how easy the younger generation has it. We've all heard, "When I was a kid, we had it tough. Had to walk five miles through snow in twenty-degree-below temperatures stalked by mountain lions on the way to school."

For my parents' generation, most of this is true. I think for my generation, post-World War II baby boomers, it was one mile, ten below and stalked by house cats. For the next generation, it's walking across the parking lot at school after being dropped off by Mom in her Suburban with heated seats in temps around thirty-two-degrees while being stalked by Hello Kitty school backpacks.

Chapter 45

Roots, Standing Rock Indian Reservation 1992

I recall stories of my parents' days as children and wonder at the hardships they endured. My father was born in 1910 on the Standing Rock Indian Reservation in central North Dakota. A small colony of German settlers co-existed with the Lakota Indians in this remote and harsh location. In 1992, after listening to my father's stories of life out there, I decided to find the beginning place of my German ancestors when they arrived in America in the late 1800s. The directions are vague. "Just drive south of Bismarck about sixty miles," my dad tells me, "and you will find St. John Cemetery. My grandpa and grandma are buried there."

"How will I find it?"

"Oh, just ask around. Some farmer should know where it is. Has an iron fence around it."

With this information, I head east out of Billings on Interstate 94 toward Bismarck. For the next 500 miles and eight hours, I pass through a few towns, all too small to be called a city. Not much has changed around here in the thirty years since I traveled the highway on my way to Richardson to attend the seminary. The narrow two-lane highway, though, has been upgraded to a four-lane freeway. I can see the remnants of the old narrow, twisting highway now slowly being reclaimed by the prairie. I miss the old highway as it forced one to slow down to a pace closer to nature. Today the speed limit is eighty, and things whiz by unnoticed. I try to slow down and enjoy this sea of grass where the wind creates waves that flow and break across the landscape.

It's late afternoon when I arrive in Mandan, the sister city of Bismarck separated from it by the Missouri River. Mandan, population 15,000, has three motels and a dozen bars. I check into the TP Motel, which is clean, dated and quiet. A couple blocks away is Frieds Restaurant, a family-run business. I sit at the counter as a sixtyish waitress in a red wig asks, "What can I get you, Honey?" I look at the menu and like the name Frieds—everything on the menu is fried. I order the chicken fried steak with mashed potatoes.

After dinner, I walk back to the motel, turn on a local channel and watch a few minutes of Melrose Place. Paging through the phone book, I find eighty-four Geigers in the Bismarck-Mandan area. It's truly a hotbed of Geigers. I knew this but was surprised to see so many. Some are first and second cousins of my dad but not close enough to me to call relatives.

The next morning, I drive to Solen, population 87, which has three businesses—US Post Office, Hoffman's Garage and Last Chance Saloon. I inquire around town, but no one can give directions to St. John the Baptist Cemetery. The bartender at the Last Chance points northeast and says, "It's up thataway about ten miles."

I head northeast for about ten miles on gravel roads with ninety-degree turns that follow the surveyed section lines. Finally, I stop at a house and find a farmer lying under a tractor next to the barn.

"Howdy," I say cheerfully, "I'm looking for the German cemetery."

He lifts his head to talk but continues to lie under the tractor. "Just went past it. Go back a half-mile, and it's behind that hill on the left. Who you looking for?"

"Geiger relatives, Anton and Cecilia."

Hearing this, he struggles into a standing position. "We're related. Their son John and my dad are cousins. I'm a Kilwein. That makes us second cousins. What's your dad's name?"

"Frank."

"Yeah, I met him a couple of times when they came to visit relatives. Tell him hello from Martin."

"Will do. Nice to meet you. Thanks for the directions."

"You betcha."

I backtrack on the gravel road a half-mile and spot a fifty-foot hill on the left. Faint tire tracks across the prairie grass lead me to a small cemetery behind it. A large wrought iron gate and fence surround the cemetery containing about fifty graves. As I step out of my car into the early North Dakota spring, I'm immediately tattered by the unyielding prairie wind. I battle sideways through the gate and look down the rows of graves for Geiger markers.

A six-foot ornate cross with a figure of the crucified Jesus catches my eye because it's similar to the Jesus Who spoke to me when I was a fifteen-year-old seminarian. Gabriel, the guardian angel, kneels at the foot of the cross, and on a plaque above him is inscribed "Anton Geiger 1850-1916, Cecilia Geiger 1851-1929." My great-grandparents lie at my feet. As the wind continues to batter me, I wonder how they lived in this harsh environment.

I retrieve a couple of pieces of white paper from the car and do a rubbing of the plaque as a keepsake. As I hold the paper over the plaque, the wind shreds it.

I recall my dad's instructions for finding the house they lived in: "Just look northeast from the cemetery a couple of hundred yards, and you will see it, a rock house."

Looking northeast, I see the faint outline of a crumbled stone wall. I get back into my car and drive a couple of hundred yards across the prairie because it's too windy to walk. Stepping out of the car, I'm once again mugged by the wind, which steals my body heat.

I pace off the house my dad described. It's 14 by 16 feet and built from rock scrounged from the prairie and glued together with mud to form a wall about eighteen inches wide and six feet tall. A decayed cottonwood tree log about twelve inches across lies at the bottom of the rubble. I poke in there and find a shard of mirror four inches long and an inch wide. Maybe it's my grandmother's. My dad was born and lived here until the age of ten, at which time the family moved to Montana.

A 1920 census of Morton (or Sioux) County records these family members living in the Geiger household:

John, my grandfather, age 40
Anna, My grandmother, age 40
John (son), age 19, born 1901
Julie (daughter), age 15, born 1905
Margart (daughter), age 14, born 1906
Tony (son), age 12, born 1908
Rosie (daughter), age 11, born 1909
Frank (son) (my father), age 10, born 1910
Minnie (daughter), age 8, born 1912
Lillian (daughter), age 6, born 1914
Cecelia (daughter), died age 3 months, born 1915
Adam (son), died age 1 day, born 1916
Elizabeth (daughter), age 2, born 1918

My grandmother is pregnant with Martin, who would be born when they arrived in Montana in 1920.

I study the small rock structure and imagine my grandparents living in this tiny home with nine children. Where did they all sleep? What did they eat? How did they survive?

My dad told me, "In the winter, the kids would go down to the river and get buckets of water to throw on the walls and make ice to keep the wind out."

"Did you stay warm?" I asked.

"The Indians were warmer in their tepees. One of the neighbor kids fell through the ice, and they never found him. In the spring, the men walked up and down the river, but he was gone. Only eleven years old."

The Germans co-existed with the native Lakota Indians living here, but there was some friction.

"I wouldn't have blamed the Indians for not liking us," Dad told me. "The government stole their land for the homesteaders. We didn't treat them right."

Before my father's death, I wrote this story about his life here on the Standing Rock Indian Reservation. It still holds a place in my heart as an example of love and courage.

Sea of Grass

> Frank grew up being lost. At an early age, he was lost. Lost in a bundle of kids, just one face out of many. Lost emotionally with parents who knew or had the time to find him. Lost on a vast prairie, a small dot on an infinite land. But with all this against him, he knew one thing—he knew how to look out for himself. He would struggle against great odds and find a place for himself in this world. He would also help others find themselves.
>
> In 1918, Frank and his nine siblings clung to a meager existence on the Great Plains of North America in an area now known as North Dakota and Montana, where they wrestled with survival. His father and mother had escaped difficult times in Russia and Germany and sailed to America where they traveled to the Wild West. Here, they and a few other German farmers dug into the land.
>
> Like the old man of the sea who lived on a sea of water, they lived on a sea of grass. The tall grass waving in the wind looked like waves on the sea. For a thousand miles in every direction, the grass moved like a huge ocean. In the middle of this ocean, a few dozen German settlers lived with a tribe of Indians. These Indians were the famous Lakota Indians who had survived difficult times in America because of the injustices of the government. With many settlers coming from Europe, they were forced to give up their freedom and land. Now constrained by the government to a small reservation, they and the German settlers

lived together. The Indians lived in warm, spacious tepees while the German settlers lived in tiny houses made of rocks or grass sod. The winters were punishing, with harsh winds piling snow to the top of their huts and bitter temperatures of minus twenty degrees.

During these long winters, everyone hoped and prayed for spring to arrive. Two children, who were best friends, waited for spring. Their names were Frank and Many Waters. They were both eight years old. Frank was a German settler's son, while Many Waters was a Lakota Chief's son. Frank was light-complexioned with blue eyes, and Many Waters was dark-skinned with brown eyes.

By early March, the sun melted the snow except for large drifts hidden from the sun on the north side of the hillsides. Frank and Many Waters had a secret plan. They knew that summer would soon bring new grass almost as tall as them and would hide the floor of this great land. Now was the time to search through the grass for hidden meadowlark nests. Because there were few trees in this great land, the birds built their nests on the ground. When the boys found a nest, they marked it, sticking a long willow branch from the riverbank into the ground with a piece of white cloth tied to the top. They hurried to finish before the meadowlarks returned to their nest.

Soon, the meadowlarks returned from their southern winter homes. Their song is very distinctive, and when Frank and Many Waters first heard the song, they knew the birds were back. They ran to find the nests.

"Look," shouted Frank as he spied a hidden nest next to a willow branch with a piece of white cloth tied to it.

"Yes, I see it," squealed Many Waters, as the two carefully watched newly hatched meadowlarks reaching for the sky with open mouths. The two boys hid in the tall grass to watch the babies being fed.

As the summer continued, Frank and Many Waters enjoyed the best times of their lives, playing simple games of tag, throwing stick arrows and playing hide and seek. But some of the older people were not so sure about Frank and Many Waters always playing together.

The German adults talked among themselves, saying things like, "Perhaps Frank should spend more time with the other German kids. He always plays with that Indian boy. We don't know if this is good."

The Indian adults said the same things about Many Waters, "He always plays with the German boy. He needs to learn the Indian ways. This is not good."

One day when Frank returned home after a long day playing with Many Waters, his parents told him, "It is better you are with your own kind and learn the German ways. You must stay home now." Frank's heart broke when he heard this, but he didn't have a choice.

That night Many Waters' father told him, "It is time you learn the Indian ways and be with your own people. You cannot play with Frank anymore." Many Waters' heart was also broken.

The next day, Frank and Many Waters peered across the sea of grass, hoping to see each other. They did, but all they could do was wave.

Many weeks went by, and the Lakotas planned a big dance, or powwow. The dance was to honor God the Creator and to ask for a spring and summer that would bring abundant crops and successful hunting to provide food for the following winter. They built a large fire and danced around it for three days and three nights, giving thanks and praying to God, who they called the Creator.

The Germans were Christians who prayed in a tiny sod house they called a church. They prayed to God, who they called the Father. While the Lakotas and the Germans tolerated each other, they did not pray together. Each had their own religion that they thought was the only true religion.

When the day came for the Lakota's big powwow, the Germans watched from a distance. Suddenly, Frank could see his friend Many Waters dancing with his family. Many Waters was dressed in bright feathers and buckskins covered with beautiful glass beads. Frank wished in his heart that he could be with his friend.

So, he began running across the prairie to where the Indians danced in a circle. His parents shouted at him, "Come back, Frank. That dance is not for Germans." But Frank kept running as fast as his short legs could carry him. His father ran after him but could not catch him. When Frank got to the circle, he ran into the middle where his friend Many Waters was dancing.

"Many Waters, Many Waters," he shouted.

When Many Waters saw his best friend, he shouted back, "Frank, Frank, I have missed you so much." The two boys hugged each other and cried tears of joy. Frank's father ran into the circle, where he met Many Waters' father, the Lakota Chief. The two were touched by the boys' love for each other. Then, as the drums continued to beat, the two boys began dancing together around the huge fire.

The Indians were surprised to see a white boy dancing in the circle, but they could see the love between the two boys, and they knew it was good. Frank's father stood

> watching until Many Waters' father invited him to dance with him. The two men followed the boys' example and danced together around the fire. Soon, the other German settlers came and joined the Indians in a great circle, dancing and praying to the same God—God the Creator and God the Father—for good crops and hunting.
>
> That summer, the crops were many, the berries covered the bushes and the wild game ran plentiful. When fall came, the Indians built a great fire to dance and pray in thanksgiving for the abundance of food. This time, the Germans danced and prayed with the Indians, and again it was Frank and Many Waters leading everyone around the great circle. The spirit of Frank and Many Waters would continue to live in the hearts of those they touched.

As my dad told this story, tears filled his eyes.

I asked, "How did you talk to Many Waters. In German or Lakota?"

"Oh, we didn't need to talk. We knew what the other one was saying."

Chapter 46

Skywatch, Always Looking Over Our Shoulder, 1953

My dad's family left the reservation in 1920 and moved to Bridger, Montana. He married my mother in 1935, and they raised four sons. I was born at the very beginning of the baby boom and lived in Bridger through seventh grade until my parents moved to nearby Billings.

The post-war baby boom was fueled by young soldiers coming home from the war with four years of backed-up sperm as a result of being separated from most women except for an occasional pin-up poster. In turn, young women isolated from men with five years of wasted ovulation created the perfect conditions for a baby boom—or perhaps a "baby bomb."

It was a happy time, but peace after WWII was constrained because the United Soviet Socialist Republic (USSR), a former ally, quickly drew lines in the sand and stole half of Europe. With the USA and USSR developing Inter-Continental Ballistic Missiles (ICBMs), the Cold War was on. Paranoia permeated the country when these young baby boomers were at a tender age. Bomb shelters were sprouting deep in the back yards of Middle America. Atomic bomb alerts and air raid drills were regularly held in schools, with young children futilely diving under their desks for protection from potential nuclear blasts that would evaporate not only their desks but the school building and the city.

I remember this well. Huddling under our desks, we peer out and giggle at one another, feeling strange and thinking, "What are we doing?"

"Quick children, get under your desks," Ms. Green commands.

"Ouch, I bumped my head!" Linda says. She's right next to me.

"Don't talk, the teacher will get mad."

"Shush, yourself."

As third graders, we laugh out of anxiety and fear.

When we aren't huddled under our desks, we might accompany our parents to Operation Skywatch for duty in the Civilian Observation Corps. It is 1953, and I'm nine years old as my dad and I walk the four blocks from our house to the tiny Bridger Airport. It is a crisp, frosty morning, and I'm excited. It's like we are in the army and being called to duty to protect our country. As we walk down the snow-packed streets, I run and slide in my overshoes, pretending to skate. The buckles on my rubber boots jangle like spurs on a cowboy's boots.

The airport is a single gravel landing strip with a wooden tower ten feet square and two stories high. A wooden ladder on the outside allows access to the upper level. We climb the stairs, and when we're inside, my dad turns on a small electric space heater. His frosty breath wafts across the room, and he says, "Sit here next to the heater until it warms up. Russia has the bomb now, so we have to keep watch so they don't get through."

The small room has four large windows on each side that allow us to survey the countryside. While this is the official control tower for the airport, there is no radio to communicate with planes. The only air traffic in rural Montana in 1953 is an occasional single-engine Piper Cub owned by farmers or other locals. Twice a week, Frontier Airlines Flight 2420 from Billings to Salt Lake City rumbles overhead as the twenty-one-passenger, twin-engine Douglas DC-3 strains to gain enough altitude to clear the Rocky Mountains in Yellowstone National Park. The rest of the week, Bridger is a quiet farm town whose main sounds are crickets, birds, cows, horses, tractor exhausts, church bells, kids yelling down the streets and family fights.

Two planes tethered to the ground sit next to the control tower. A small hangar contains another plane and a small shop for making repairs on aircraft. We are now on official duty for Operation Skywatch. We're manning the front lines. Our job is to look for Russian bombers who may have snuck through our North American Radar System. Over 800,000 volunteers across the country from age seven to eighty-seven scan the skies hoping to prevent a surprise nuclear attack.

There is a small card table and two folding chairs in the tower. On the table sits a black rotary dial telephone, a pair of binoculars and a poster displaying airplane silhouettes and brown rings from coffee cups. In the event a plane is sighted, we are supposed to call the "Filter Center" located at the airport in Billings, about forty-five miles away.

My dad pours a cup of coffee from a thermos and laces it with sugar and thick cream skimmed earlier off a bucket of whole milk from our neighbor's cow. It is a big deal for a nine-year-old to drink coffee and be in the army with his dad.

"Here, have a sip. Don't tell your mom," he says with a twinkle in his eye.

"Sure is good."

I feel seven feet tall, but somewhere in my sub-conscious, there is a hidden fear—I'm feeling safe with my dad but unsafe from an unknown threat. After three hours, we think we hear a plane engine. My dad scans the skies with heavy WWII surplus binoculars and spots a Piper Cub north of town.

"It looks like Ralph Johnson coming home," Dad says. "Just coming back from Billings to get supplies for his farm. Better call Billings and report it."

Dialing up the direct line to Billings, I hear him say, "This is the Bridger Airport calling. There is a Piper Cub coming in to land. Looks like Ralph Johnson, don't think he's a commie."

The man on the other end of the phone doesn't get the joke but acknowledges the report.

Ralph lands in a cloud of dust, taxies the last hundred yards and parks his plane next to the small hangar. He kills the engine and climbs out the door, attaches a rope to a holding ring on the bottom of each wing and stops by to say hello.

"Howdy. Frank. Got your son helping you today?"

"Yeah, he's been a big help. Pretty quiet today except for you."

"Yeah, had to run into Billings to get some penicillin for one of my horses. Cut his leg on barbed wire. Nice clear day for flying. Well, better get home. Wife will be getting supper on soon."

"Say hello to Gladys. Hope your horse is doing better."

After four hours of watchfulness, we are relieved of duty by Joe Johnson, Ralph's brother.

"Saw Ralph today," my dad tells Joe. "Just got back from Billings."

"Yeah, one of his horses has a cut leg that's getting infected," Joe tells us.

"How you been, Joe? Everything going okay?"

"Yeah, just trying make a living like everybody else."

With Joe taking over command of Skywatch, we head home in the late winter afternoon. The sun, low on the horizon, casts a long shadow over us and the town. Long shadows of darkness and long shadows of doubt and fear follow us as I look over my shoulder, squinting against the sun for Russian bombers carrying "the bomb." How long would I carry this doubt and fear in my life? Probably years—until long after Skywatch and the Russians are gone.

Living in a small town, most everyone knows everyone and everything going on. Not much is missed—family fights, a flat tire, somebody staying at the bar too late and coming home drunk, a dog getting run over by a car, someone "stepping out." The latter rarely results in divorce because people up here just "put up with it." The idealistic picture of small-town America seen on the cover of *Life* hides many dark secrets of abuse and dysfunction. Things that in later years will be prosecuted by the law are now often ignored. Nobody wants to create trouble, and the common notion is to "just mind your own business." Unwed girls who get pregnant are shipped off to the Florence Critton Home at the state capital in Helena so their babies will be hidden from the community. Forced to give up their children, the mothers often suffer guilt for the rest of their lives. The father is usually forgiven, of course, because "boys will be boys."

Kids on Saturdays have the run of the town and countryside. It's usual for nine and ten-year-old boys to head out to the hills on Saturday morning carrying peanut butter sandwiches and a Mason jar full of warm grape Kool-Aid. The rules are simple—be home by supper time, don't get bit by a rattlesnake and no shootin' one another with your BB guns. We hunt rabbits, snakes and occasional birds, but most of the fun is harmless.

I remember walking one day about a half-mile to the town dump to look for treasures to drag home. Behind the dump, we climb the sandstone cliff above the drive-in theater.

"Woody, I'll go first on the 'Cat's Eye.'"

"Okay, be careful. Don't look down."

"Yeah, wait until I get to the other side."

The Cat's Eye is a thirty-foot shelf on the face of a sandstone cliff a hundred feet above the sagebrush. A second shelf about two feet above it extends about a foot out from the cliff requiring one to walk sideways and bent forward with no handholds.

"Are my feet okay?" I ask Woody. The second shelf blocks one view of our feet.

"Yeah, go slow."

I finally finish shuffling across. "Okay, Woody, your turn. Don't look down."

"I'm coming, watch my feet."

"Yeah, be careful."

"Don't worry."

Woody scoots across, and we scramble to the top of the three-hundred-foot cliff, not thinking how close we had come to death. Now we search for the "Worm Hole" cave, a top-secret hiding place that we keep for ourselves. Behind a twisted cedar tree growing out of a crack in a sandstone boulder is a small hole invisible to passersby.

"Here it is. You want to go first?"

"Sure," Woody says.

The entrance to the cave is about a foot in diameter, just large enough for nine-year-old boys to wiggle through. It's a special cave for us because adults can't fit through the small opening.

"I'm in," Woody says. "Hand me the candle and matches."

"Here, light it. Pull the knapsack through."

Woody lights the candle, and I follow the army surplus knapsack through.

Inside, the flickering candle casts ghostly shadows around the cave. We hope they are only shadows—our imaginations run wild.

"Do you think dead Indians live in here?

"I dunno, but if they do, we better make friends with them," I say.

"Look, our names are still here," Woody says, pointing to "Danny" and "Woody" scratched on the cave wall.

In later years, I wonder if those names are still scratched on the wall, but adulthood prevents us from going back to childhood, especially through a twelve-inch "Worm Hole."

We dig out our lunches and quickly down the peanut butter and jelly sandwiches, a couple of apples and the grape Kool-Aid. As the sun gets low, we head back across the Cat's Eye then past the town dump to pick up a broken fishing pole we'd hid earlier. Nearby, a coal seam smolders, lit some fifty years ago by someone burning garbage, or maybe by a grass fire. It will burn until the seam is exhausted.

Today was one like hundreds of others when boys explored the area protected by good fortune despite traveling with no sunscreen, no sun hats, no shoes and no fear. During many generations of kids climbing these cliffs, no one has fallen to their death or been dismembered here. The Cat's Eye, while treacherous, was kind.

Chapter 47

The Bad Guys United Soviet Socialists Republic (USSR)

As ten-year-old kids, we play cops and robbers, cowboys and Indians, and army, meaning we take on the Russians— commies, as adults call them. Our uniforms are patched jeans and tattered T-shirts with pots and pans for helmets. The commies are the bad guys, and we fight them to the last man.

Years later, when I visit the USSR in 1987, just before the breakup of the Soviet Bloc, I witness firsthand the ravages of WWII and communism on the proud country of Russia. What we imagined as our arch enemy is now a disheartened relic. The once-powerful country now lives in poverty except for the communist elite. This once-terrifying enemy of our youthful minds is now quite benign.

The front line of the Russian army, which we once fought with BB guns and wooden sticks, is now the babushka. In the Russian language, babushka has several meanings, but the most common is "grandmother" or "a colorful head scarf" that is folded into a triangle and worn like a small hood tied under the chin. The most sinister meaning of babushka is a female "guard" or "sentry," which is how I come to understand the term. With this meaning, babushkas are everywhere

I visit, the result of hundreds of thousands of women being widowed when thirty million Russian soldiers died in WWII. Compare this to the United States, which lost four hundred thousand troops. Babushkas are the glue of the USSR, making sure everyone obeys the rules.

I'm staying in an official "Inturist Hotel" in Moscow, a hotel designed for tourists. It's filled with dated carpet and wallpaper, shoddy plumbing, dark hallways, tired furniture and intrigue. In 1987, the Soviet government wanted tourists to see only the good face of Russia. Unfortunately, this tourist hotel is one of the best faces they can expose.

Cabbage is the centerpiece of most dinners. Tourists are monitored and tracked—we are not allowed to travel the city unescorted. The hotel is full of conspiracy, collusion and scheming. Western tourists rub elbows with prostitutes, black market dealers, KGB and the babushkas.

My travel group and I gather in the lobby, which is decorated with red flocked wallpaper, gaudy crystal chandeliers, elephant-sized leather chairs and a glass coffee table with large, red ashtrays.

An official wearing an army-like uniform speaks through a translator: "You must stay in the group with official tour guide, no photos of people or inside buildings, no buying on black market and only rubles from bank." He warns us not to leave the hotel alone as it is not safe. It is safe out there, of course, but his ominous warning is intended to keep us corralled.

We take our luggage upstairs, where I meet my first babushka, or sentry, on the fourth floor. She hands me the key to room 403 after I show my receipt. When I leave the room the next morning, I return the key to her for safekeeping. With the babushka on duty, there will be no funny business on the fourth floor. She is all business. It will take me two days to get her to smile and then an eternity to keep her from smiling.

I take the tiny two-passenger elevator to the lobby. Scanning for KGB, I slip out the back door of the kitchen and race down the alley.

After a couple hundred feet, I stop where a young man of twenty is sitting on a concrete step.

"Hi, do you speak English?" I ask him.

"Yes, you from America?" he answers with a Russian accent.

"Yes, at the Inturist Hotel. My name is Dan."

"I Sergei," he says, standing up and shaking my hand. He wears a drab grey shirt and fake blue jeans made of cheap polyester.

"Is this where you live?" I ask.

"No, I come to look for job but man is gone. Everyone in Russia supposed to have job but this not true, Live with parents. Where you from in America?"

"Montana."

"Ah yes, Marlboro Man."

"Yes, many cowboys in Montana."

"Will you trade dollar for ruble? I have ruble to trade."

Rubles for dollars is a common underground barter. The Russians don't trust the ruble. They believe it's better to have a hundred friends than two hundred rubles.

"How many rubles will you give me for a US dollar?"

"Thirty."

The official exchange rate at the bank is seven rubles for one US dollar. I remember the admonishment of the Russian officials not to deal on the black market. At thirty for a dollar, I quadruple my money.

"I'll take $50 worth," I say, handing him a crisp fifty-dollar bill. This feels like a Humphrey Bogart movie. Sergei is delighted, and I figure we both can make a profit. We make plans to meet again tomorrow.

"What else do you have besides rubles?" I ask.

"Many things. What you want?"

"A big Soviet flag and souvenir from Olympic team. We can trade US dollar or other things."

"Yes, we make a deal," he says.

"Okay, see you tomorrow."

"Yes, good to meet you."

I walk back to the hotel, hoping I'm not missed by the tour guide. I like Sergio, a kind young man. I instinctively trust him.

I realize the other Americans on our tour are exchanging US dollars at the official rate of seven for a dollar. I see a profit to be made and begin selling my rubles to my fellow tourists at fifteen for a dollar, doubling my money but still helping my travel mates.

The next morning, I find Sergei sitting on the same cold, damp step. A package wrapped in brown paper and tied with a cotton string sits next to him. I carry a plastic bag from K-Mart stuffed with two pairs of Levis and a Yellowstone National Park T-shirt with a grizzly bear on the front.

"You come back," Sergio says, clearly relieved.

"Yes, why? Were you worried?"

"Things happen, things change in Russia. We never know."

"I see you have a package."

"Yes, I have flag and coat," he says, opening the package. "Hold the corner." I stand holding the corner of the flag as he pulls it open. It is ten feet wide, six feet tall and made of red silk. A gold hammer crossed with a sickle is positioned beneath a gold-bordered red star in the upper left corner.

"Where did you get this—off the post office?"

"I have connections," he says, laughing. I don't ask any more questions.

We fold the flag and put it back in the brown paper wrapping. He then hands me a blue warmup jacket with the Russian letters "CCCP" (meaning USSR) printed on the back below five overlapping rings, the Olympic emblem.

"Jacket worn by Olympic basketball player," he tells me.

I put the jacket on. "It fits!"

"Look good," he says, grinning. "We go to my parents' home now. When we close other people not to talk English. It better if no one know you from America."

"Okay, I have jeans and a shirt for you. Is this a good trade?"

"Yes, yes. This very good!" He almost venerates the goods, feeling the fabric and carefully folding the items back into their original shapes.

We walk down the alley to a broad avenue and wait at a bus stop. After a few minutes, a sturdy but uncomfortable bus screeches to a stop. We board, and Sergei gives the driver one ruble, about fifteen US cents. Passengers stare silently during our thirty-minute ride across Moscow. It feels like they are staring at me.

Hundreds of identical four-story, square, concrete buildings with small windows line every street. Leaving the bus, we walk ten minutes to Sergei's home, a concrete block apartment building with small windows and narrow stairs. A tiny two-person elevator groans up four floors.

Inside the 600-square-foot two-bedroom apartment, Sergei finally breaks the silence with laughter.

"People on the bus look at you believing you are Olympic basketball player."

"Oh, I forgot I have the jacket on."

"Yes, it mean many, many to me that you visit my home. I never have friend from America."

"I've never had a Russian friend."

The small, barren apartment feels sterile. Sergei's bedroom is sparse, containing only a single bed, a wood chair, a dresser and two photos—of him in his army uniform and the other of his brother and parents, who are not at home.

"We have nothing," Sergei explains. "My parents live here since they were young and will die here. Russia like a great tree with pigs eating the roots."

We ride the bus back to the hotel. We don't talk much on the bus, but it is understood that we have become friends.

"Is this your wedding ring?" he asks.

"Yes, I'm married. My wife went with the tour guide today."

"Maybe someday I be married. Are you happy to be married?"

"Yes, marriage and children are a big part of life."

"All I have is my family. We have nothing else. Life in Russian is empty. Without family, I would be dead inside."

"Someday, you will find a wife and have a family. Be patient and believe."

I give him a hundred-dollar bill in exchange for rubles and another twenty-five dollars for his part of the profit I made selling rubles to my American friends.

"We partners, you get some of the profit," I tell him.

"Yes, like capitalism."

"Yes, like capitalism. We meet tomorrow, yes?"

"Yes, I will come to same place," Sergei says, excited.

The next morning, I slip out the back door of the kitchen. The cooks smile at me as if we are friends now. I find Sergei waiting, but he looks disturbed.

"This last time I see you. The KGB watch me now. They not arrest me because I have good record with army. Now I have to be careful."

I give him another hundred dollars for rubles and another twenty-five dollars for his share of the profit.

"Thank you. You good friend who help me. I never forget" He says this with yearning in his eyes.

"I learned much from you, Sergei," I say. "I wish you success in finding a job and wife."

We part, and I feel the sadness of losing an old friend even though we have known each other for only three days. I realize I am fortunate to have comfort and safety in my life. I am fortunate on this trip to peek through the Iron Curtain and find a friend halfway across the world. I learned a lot from Sergei— about trust, gratitude, friendship and faith.

Over the years, I correspond with Sergei and occasionally send him a crisp fifty-dollar bill wrapped in black carbon paper in a plain envelope using a postage meter rather than a stamp. I pray the letter is not stolen before it is delivered. His letters to me are full of gratitude. I admire that he never complains about his dismal circumstances.

As the years pass, Sergei marries. He and his wife find a two-bedroom concrete apartment three blocks from his parent's home, and he strives to make a life for himself.

Chapter 48

Failed Again, Is It the Same As Sinned Again?

The 1980s roll into the 90s, and my second marriage to Joyce is in trouble. We married in 1985 and did well in our first four or five years, but things have started to change. I become concerned about our drinking. On occasion, I decided to quit by myself. This usually lasts for a few weeks, but then I find myself back at it. I start counting the beer cans in the garbage and making pencil lines on the scotch and gin labels to monitor how much booze we are going through. It's way too much.

Joyce is an accomplished watercolor artist and works for a small oil exploration company. She runs the office for Dick, an oil land man, and Jack, a geologist. I become friends with these two and enjoy learning about the oil business.

Joyce and I camp in the summer and ski in the winter. Joyce is beautiful, spunky, vibrant, kind, generous and adventurous. We are a good fit on this level.

I work at Social and Rehabilitation Services as the Regional Manager for eastern Montana, supervising a dozen rehab counselors. I am also on the board of directors of the Rehabilitation Association and served one year as president for the Great Plains Region. I travel to most of the states on business and as an excuse to party.

Joyce has become unhappy and wants out of the marriage. She makes this clear one evening during one of those uncomfortable husband-wife conversations.

"I don't feel like we are on the same path," she begins.

"What do you mean?"

"Just that we seem to be going in different directions."

"What can I do?"

"I don't think there is anything you can do, it's just how it is. I really need to move out for now—to think things over."

"Err, okay," I say, trying to support her. But I'm dying inside.

"We've had some great times together, and I thought this would be forever."

"Me too."

She moves in with a friend and suddenly the house to too big and too quiet. I'm not only alone but lonely too.

I spend the next year trying anything and everything to save the marriage. I probably try everything except to really listen to her—and perhaps I try too hard and push her even further away. I cry almost every day—a deep, wrenching, hopeless kind of sobbing. I cry in my car, at work, at the store, in bed. I cry and cry and cry.

I begin attending a healing group, Beginning Experience. It helps divorced and widowed individuals get through the grieving process. I meet Diana, a facilitator who is kind, caring and a wonderful sounding board during this time. I am still hopeful my marriage can be saved and hang on for another six months. Diana supports my commitment to get back together with Joyce. After almost a year from the time Joyce moved out, I finally give up and let go.

Joyce and I part as friends, sort of, but it is painful to occasionally run into her for many years to come. Each time, I try to put on a happy face, but inside I'm dying. We finally divorce in March of 1994, but the marriage had ended much earlier than that.

It's painful, almost too painful. Suicide enters my mind. I brush it away, and it creeps back in. One afternoon, I drive my '63 Impala that

I've driven for the past thirteen years to the top of Sacrifice Cliff on the north side of Billings overlooking the Yellowstone River Valley. I park near a place where a small band of Crow warriors rode their war ponies over the cliff as a sacrifice to protect their village from smallpox. I consider driving over the cliff, imitating those warriors, but the images of my children keep my wheels on firm ground.

Sanity prevails for now, but I continue to struggle.

Chapter 49

Ravens, Please Go Away

The year 1994 continues to chip away at my resistance to change. My marriage to Joyce has ended, and I'm still looking for a spiritual home. One day, I find a dead raven lying next to my car in the office parking lot. Its distraught mate paces nearby. The asphalt parking lot is not a proper place to die, so I place it under a bush. The mate hops closer to me. I leave, thinking about the surviving mate who had been left alone. In some ways, I understand its sorrow.

The next morning, I find a raven feather lying on the floor next to my office desk. I have no idea how it got there. Neither does my staff. There are two doors and a waiting room between my office and the outside, making it impossible for a bird or a feather to make its way into my office. I lay the feather on my desk, puzzled.

Several days later, as I'm walking through the neighborhood near my office, a curious and noisy raven starts to follow, hopping on the ground and scolding me with an annoying squawk. I wonder if it's the mate of the raven that died earlier.

Over the next few weeks, a day seldom goes by that I don't have an encounter with a raven, sometimes perched in a tree nearby, hopping on the ground, or sometimes overhead with a persistent squawk. It's enough to make me wonder why I am such a draw for ravens.

Fall comes, and my thoughts turn to my Native American Crow mother, Josephine Prettyweasel, who had adopted me into her family and the Crow Nation. I remember meeting Josephine in 1973 when she applied for a job as a counselor aid in our office at Crow Agency.

"So, why do you think you can do this job?" I ask in our first interview.

"Because I've been there, seen it all, did it all. I know the people's pain."

I listen, but as a young counselor myself, I don't really understand what she is telling me.

"You know, we Indians have a saying," she tells me. "'You don't know someone until you walk in their moccasins.' I've walked in a lot of moccasins."

"What are some of these moccasins?"

"You know—the poor, the sick, the little ones, the handicapped."

I know from this moment that Josephine knows more about life than I do.

"So, can you start work on Monday?" I ask hopefully.

"Yes, I'll show you some of those moccasins."

"Great, I come down to Crow Monday."

This is the beginning of a great friendship that will last for twenty-five years.

I'm standing next to Josephine in her wheelchair

Adoption has been a custom for Native Americans from early times. It comes from the days when tribal members lived in small nomadic villages scattered across the prairie. By creating extended families, a traveler could always find family and refuge in a village. This connection with the Crow Tribe has allowed me to learn a new culture, a new way of thinking and a new way of looking at life. Over the years, my birth parents have come to know Josephine and her husband, Leonard, so it is like having two sets of parents.

It has been a year since I last saw Josephine, who had moved to Medford, Oregon. After living her entire life on the Crow Indian Reservation in southeastern Montana, she announced one day, "I'm going to get off the rez and go to Oregon for a while."

Josephine was always an independent, self-reliant person who survived a rough life for many years on the reservation. Life is difficult there, as on most US reservations, because of limited resources, high unemployment, alcoholism and a loss of identity.

The US government finally realized that if it were going to succeed with its policy of Manifest Destiny and expand throughout North America, it needed to get rid of the Indians. The attempt at extermination was purely an act of white supremacy over Native people who had lived on this continent for hundreds of generations. The plan basically called for taking 99 percent of the land and relocating the Indians to small reservations to be segregated in poverty.

Even Hitler praised the US government as performing the best example of genocide in the history of the world. Not only did we reduce the number of natives through warfare and disease, but we also decimated their culture, self-worth and identity by separating children from their parents in boarding schools. I'm always amazed that Josephine survived and even developed a love and tolerance for white folks after what the government did.

The Crows tried to work with the government and signed several treaties. The Crows sided with the government in the Battle of the Little Big Horn and worked as scouts. That historic battle took place on the Crow Reservation. It was a rare instance in which Native Indians can claim a victory over the US Government's one-hundred-year crusade to eradicate the Indian population through disease and outright slaughter of men, women and children.

On June 25, 1876, the Seventh US Cavalry, under the command of the egotistical Colonel George Custer, was defeated by Sitting Bull and Crazy Horse, who led Lakota, Northern Cheyenne and Arapaho warriors. Today the Crows and six other tribes live on small reservations in Montana. The Crow Reservation once covered ten million acres and was reduced to one million acres through a series of broken treaties and promises. The Crows were eventually pushed into smaller and smaller areas. Today they live in poverty, separated from their true selves through a series of US Government programs designed to eradicate their culture. Of the 350 treaties signed by the United States Government with native tribes, all were broken by the government.

* * *

It's autumn, and I'm on a road trip to visit Josephine and her daughter, KJ. I begin the 900-mile drive to Medford, Oregon, following the Yellowstone River to its source at Yellowstone Lake. In the fall, the park is vibrant with color and wildlife—buffalo, elk, deer, bear, and of course ravens. I take Lolo Pass across the Rocky Mountains into Idaho. Lolo Pass, a winding road cut into the side of mountains, forms breathtaking cliffs on the north side of the road and sheer drop-offs on the south side. I enjoy playing race car driver on the sharp curves, pushing my car to its limits.

As I round a corner, a deer walks into the path of my speeding car. On the left is a 500-foot drop into the Lochsa River, and on the right, a sheer cliff cut out of the mountain. My instinct is to swerve, but better judgment tells me to hold the course and drive into the deer, so I don't go off the cliff.

When my car is just a few feet from striking the deer, a raven sweeps down with eagle-like talons and flies into the face of the deer, causing it to back up. I narrowly squeeze by. In the side mirror, I see the car come within a few inches of the deer's nose.

I've never before seen a raven make an aggressive move at another animal. What is it with these birds? They seem to be following me. I decide to slow down.

As the miles roll by, I listen to the bluesy, throaty sounds of Van Halen on the stereo and start composing a song, trying to imitate his voice. One hundred miles later, I have this song scratched on the back of a manila folder. It's about me, but I don't want to admit it.

Just sittin here talking to myself
Saying the things I love to hear
And changing the subject
When the truth gets near

Just sittin' here scared
Trying in my mind
To hang on to my life
As it continues to unwind

I'm thinkin', yea, been thinkin'
About changing my way of thinkin'
But I just keep puttin it off
Puttin it off for another day

Just sittin here, blaming the devil
With truth closer than my life vein
Maybe time to accept a new revelation
And end this lifetime of pain

Just sittin here in the same old place
And when I can't seem to win
I go back and do things I never did
In places I've never been

I'm thinkin', yea, been thinkin'

About changing my way of thinkin'
But I just keep puttin it off
Puttin it off for another day

But I'm thinkin
I should change my way of thinking
But just puttin it off
Puttin off truth for another day

But if I keep on thinkin'
Maybe I can change my way of thinkin'
And quit putting off the truth
And finally end this lifetime of pain

But I keep thinkin' it's time
It's finally time for the truth
And the truth is just me
And now I can finally be free

The sound of Van Halen escorts me to Portland, where I stop for a few days before driving south to Medford. Here I visit Joyce's sister, Cryss. I still consider her family. I remember another old girlfriend from college, Shirley, who lives in Portland, so I call her parents back in Browning, Montana, and get her phone number. I haven't seen Shirley for a long time.

She answers my call by saying, "Do you call all your old girlfriends every thirty years?" We have an enjoyable dinner together. Shirley is an accountant, and one of her clients is a business that employs psychics. They do a lot of work helping law enforcement find lost persons and solve other crimes.

The next day she calls me. "I came into work this morning at the psychic group, and one of the women asked if I had visited with an old friend. I told her about having dinner with you. She suggested you call Renee, another psychic lady she knows. I'm not sure why, but they're always doing things like this."

"Sounds intriguing, I'll give her a call. Thanks for the great visit last night."

I'm curious, so I call Renee. That afternoon I'm visiting with her at her home. She is very unimposing and modest regarding her psychic skills. Though she's from Louisiana, she has no trace of an accent.

"I'll just tell you what I see," she says. "It may or may not be true. You'll have to decide for yourself what the meaning is. My grandma was a seer and realized when I was a little girl that I also had this ability. She encouraged me to develop it."

We sit at the kitchen table. There is no crystal ball or tea leaves, just her talking matter-of-factly from her heart.

"You are a very outgoing person who loves people," she says, "but you hide your true self from others. They only know you on a superficial level." I immediately think of Georgina and Suzie's description of me as the "pretty boy in plastic."

She continues: "There are two women who love you. One walks with a bouncing stride, has long wavy blond hair and loves the color red." Immediately, I know she is talking about Joyce and find it interesting that she still loves me.

"The second woman is hidden in the shadows," Renee says, "so I can't tell you anything about her."

I'm puzzled at this mystery woman and begin thinking about who it could be.

"You are on a very unique spiritual journey. It is so unique I can't tell you anything about it. I have never seen a spiritual path like this before. The first woman may or may not want to go with you on this journey. If she is not interested, you may have to go alone." She pauses, then adds, "I see you in a very ancient place and with a book like no other book."

With this statement, I begin to cry. Somehow, I know these tears are a deep mourning for something long lost, something I'm searching for. "Where is this place? And what is this book?" I ask.

"I can't tell you anything about the book. It is something I have never seen before and something the world has never seen before. I know it is important and encourage you to pay attention. Stay open to new ideas and truths."

The meeting with Renee has stirred me up. As I drive toward Medford to see Josephine, visions of ravens, a mysterious book, an ancient place and a spiritual journey run through my head. What does this mean? I think back over my life and the regrets of wasted potential. There were so many opportunities I had let slip by out of fear or indifference. Is this the time to realize my potential? Is this what I have been searching for? Is this what Jesus was trying to tell me thirty years ago?

I find Josephine at home. "So, I saw a psychic lady in Portland," I tell her.

"We call them medicine women. What did she tell you?"

"She talked about a spiritual path, something new, something she had not seen before."

"What does it look like?"

"I don't know—that's the mystery. She couldn't tell me anything except that it's unique."

"Anything else?"

"Yes, she mentioned a special book and an ancient place are on this path."

"Sounds like you should pay attention."

"Oh, and the ravens have been after me, almost every day."

"Ahhh, ravens. Ask Hartford about the ravens, he can tell you."

Hartford, a Crow medicine man, camps next to us at Crow Fair, the big pow wow in August each year. I consider Hartford a brother.

"Yes, I'll ask Hartford."

"Maybe it's time to do things different. I had to change my ways. It was for the better. Don't hide from these things, they are trying to talk to you."

"Who is?"

"They."

"Who is *they*?"

She laughs and says, "Oh, you'll find out if you stay awake."

I'm beginning to understand the wisdom of Native American culture and how we European settlers lost the opportunity to understand things on a deeper level. Being of German descent, I was steeped in pragmatism and encouraged to ignore my feelings. Now, I'm running out of answers and excuses.

Chapter 50

Back to the Medicine Man

I leave Medford and return to Billings, where the ravens are waiting for me. They're beginning to get on my nerves, so I make the hour-long drive to the Crow Reservation and find my adopted brother Hartford. He lives in a small house a few hundred yards from the Little Big Horn River.

The Little Big Horn Battlefield, where Custer was defeated by the Lakota in 1876, sits on a plateau above the river. White grave markers of the buried soldiers are visible from Hartford's backyard. Hartford is one of four medicine men in the Crow Tribe. Over the years, I have witnessed his amazing ability to heal people. A miracle, the doctors would say, after their CT scans and MRIs couldn't find any evidence of disease after he had healed their patients.

I had experienced one of Hartford's miracles. A few years ago, Hartford was smudging me in preparation for entering a sweat lodge in his backyard. While wafting sage smoke over me with an eagle feather, he quietly said, "You have a kidney problem. It is not serious now, but it may be when you get older. I can fix it."

Previous blood tests had revealed abnormal kidney and liver function, so I decided it couldn't hurt to have Hartford work on me.

"How do you fix it?'

"Bring me four things—a black scarf, red earth paint, sweetgrass and a flickertail feather."

I believed the first three items would be easy to find, but the feather was another thing. A flickertail is a small, reddish woodpecker that lives in the Montana river bottoms.

"Where can I find a flickertail feather?" I ask.

"There are many out there," he says, pointing toward the giant cottonwood trees lining the river banks.

Over the next couple of months, I spent time walking the river banks looking for a flickertail feather. Finally, after I had quit looking, one appeared. Perhaps it was at that moment that I gave up my pragmatic German thinking.

A few days later, I went to Hartford's home with a black silk scarf, red earth paint, sweetgrass and a flickertail feather. He was sitting in the backyard tending a small fire. He seemed distracted as if in another world. He greeted me, then filled a cast iron frying pan with hot coals and motioned for me to follow him into the house.

His wife Sylvia was in the living room, and an empty three-pound Folgers coffee can sat in the middle of the floor next to a small wastebasket lined with toilet paper.

"Here, sit," he told me. "Take off your shirt."

His only other words seemed to be prayers in the Crow language. His eyes were wide and dilated, his movements jerky. Sylvia stood to make sure he stayed in the room, not physically but spiritually.

He placed the cast iron pan with hot coals on top of the coffee can to keep the floor from getting burned. Then he tied the black scarf diagonally across his chest, painted red lines on his temples, lit the sweet grass on fire and wafted the smoke with an eagle feather into the four corners of the room, purifying it. He smudged Sylvia, then me, and finally himself.

The room also contained a grey, upholstered couch, two easy chairs and two kitchen chairs. A few photographs of family members and crayon drawings by grandchildren hung on the wall with a single flickertail feather stuck into the frame of each photo.

Hartford worked himself into a trance, chanting a melodic prayer to the Creator. He then picked through the hot coals with his bare fingers.

"Yes, this good one," he said, holding one the size of a golf ball. He placed it in his mouth, leaned close to my lower back near my kidney, and blew. I felt the heat from the hot ember penetrating my side. Then he tossed the hot ember back into the pan.

I felt a slight feather touch to the same area on my back. And then he placed his mouth over that area and sucked out what appeared to some vile fluid from my side and spit it into the wastebasket. He did this three times, gagging each time. A few minutes later, he came out of his trance and said, "There, now it's done."

The next morning, I noticed a faint scar on my side where he had touched me with the feather. I was perplexed by the scar, so I called my mother. She said I never had surgery or any injury in that area.

The scar disappeared in a few days. Several months later, when I got my annual physical, the blood tests showed that my kidney functions were normal.

Today, I'm coming to see Hartford for a different reason, those incessant ravens. I park in front of the house and walk to the back door. Inside, Hartford is sitting at the kitchen table drinking coffee. Sometimes Hartford is quiet, and sometimes he says many things.

This time Hartford quietly says, "Aho," and pushes a chair toward me. "Coffee?"

Without waiting for an answer, he fills a cup and slides it across the wooden table marked by crayons, markers and pencils.

"Thanks," I say.

"You okay?"

"Good, and you?"

"Yes, but they tried to kill me."

"Who?"

"The other medicine men—wanted to test my medicine."

"How did they try?"

"They don't use guns or knives. They got other ways. Things fly around, they got their ways. It didn't work, my medicine was strong. Every now and then, they test me, but my medicine is good. It is from the Creator."

Over the years, I have listened to Hartford talk about medicine, and gradually, I've begun to understand what he is saying. Today I understand, but there is still much I don't understand.

"How did you become a Medicine Man?" I ask.

"One day, it just came. I didn't want it. I had a government job in administration with the Bureau of Indian Affairs. The medicine just came to me, like a light turned on. The Creator decides all these things. I didn't have a choice. The next day, the other medicine men began to test me. I didn't tell them, they just knew. For one year, the tests went on. They tried to kill me to see if my medicine was good. Things fly around. Things move. Shadows move. It's not a good job. You take the sickness out of a person, and if you don't get rid of it, you get sick. Over the years, I've carried the sickness of others. Now my health is not so good. It catches up with you."

He takes a sip of coffee and asks, "Why you come to Crow?"

"To visit and ask a question."

"That's good."

"The ravens have been after me," I explain, knowing it sounds pretty strange. "Almost every day they come—for many months now. They fly over me, perch on a tree, everywhere. I saw one today by Fly Creek—sitting in a tree watching me drive by."

"That's good. They are trying to wake you up. The medicine of the raven is white medicine, not black medicine. It is good medicine to get you to think at a higher level. Maybe it's time you changed your way, a new way, a new path. Keep your eyes clear for this path, and don't miss it. It will be your medicine to help people—different than my medicine. The ravens are trying to help you. We are the Apsáalooke people, children of the large beaked bird. The white man make mistake and call us Crow, but Raven is large beaked bird."

I sit and think about the book, the ancient place, the mysterious path Renee talked about. Is this what the ravens are trying to tell me?

"The ravens are noisy and annoying sometimes," I say.

Hartford laughs. "That's good. Things fly around. They got their ways. If you are weak, you will lose and not see this new path. Don't go past it. Clear your eyes and your head."

Hartford has given a lot to help people. His home is poverty-level. His wealth is family, community and service.

Hartford and Me

I leave by the back door and look south toward the Big Horn Mountains. I can see seventy-five miles of open land. The Montana prairie hasn't changed much in the last thousand years. Now it is dotted with occasional farms and ranches, but is not much different from when the Native Americans lived here freely. The huge herds of buffalo are missing, slaughtered by the white man to cripple the Natives. So much was stolen from them—freedom, culture and identity. Hartford hangs on to a thread of all this with his medicine, but what will happen when he is gone?

I drive back to Billings, trying to piece together the mystery of the ravens, the book and the ancient place Renee spoke about. I remember what Jesus said when I was fifteen years old: "There is much I can't tell you today. I will return when you can understand. But for now, I am the way, the truth and life. Be vigilant."

Chapter 51

How Did I Get Here?

Back in Billings, my friend Diana has invited me out for coffee. She has been a facilitator in my Beginning Experience support group for divorced folks. On my way to the coffee shop, I realize I don't know very much about her personal life. I have an uncomfortable feeling that she is a "born again Christian," and her motive for inviting to meet is to "save" me.

In previous discussions with "born agains," they have seemed upset that I don't believe exactly as they do. The idea of someone deciding that another person needs to be "saved" has always troubled me. As I recall, the Bible says, "Judge not lest thee be judged."

At the coffee shop, Diana says, "You seem uncomfortable today."

"A little. I have a feeling that you want to talk about religion, and I don't want to talk about it."

"No—I hadn't planned on that at all. But since you brought it up, what do you believe?"

I hadn't ever been asked this question before and had to think for a moment. I took a deep breath, and for the first time, laid out my belief system as best I could.

"Well, I was raised Catholic and always believed in God and Jesus," I began. "As a child, we were told that only Catholics would go to heaven. Even the other Christian sects were not the "true church." But

I never really believed that, and when I questioned it, I was ignored or punished emotionally by the priests, nuns, even my parents. I was told just to believe it and not ask questions.

"As a small kid, I always believed that God spoke to all the people of the world, not just a few select ones. You know, like in the song we sang, 'Jesus loves the little children of the world, red and yellow, black and white.' So, if God is All-Just, then it seems to me he wouldn't leave anyone out. I've traveled to many countries and found many religions that were much different than Catholicism and Christianity, but when I watched people pray and talked to them, they all described God the same. I think God spoke in the east through Buddha for the Buddhists and Krishna for the Hindus. The island people have their own religions, and they seem to worship the same God. Just like the Native Americans here, they all worship the Creator. Maybe Jesus appeared to everyone, or maybe God sent more than one Jesus. Every religion has a book or tradition that says the same thing as the Bible. Every religion believes they are the true one."

Diana simply says, "Yes, that's what I believe."

"Really?"

I had never met another person who believed in this oneness of religions idea. I always thought I was an odd duck. Anytime I had a discussion about religion, I'd usually end up being lectured about how "their" religion was the true one. If this is so, how many true religions are there? And why do they disagree with one another?

"So what religion are you?" I ask.

"Bahá'í."

"Bahá'í? What's that? I've never heard of it."

"The Bahá'í Faith believes in the oneness of religion and the oneness of humankind," she answers and then switches to another subject. No follow-up lecture.

Interesting, I think.

Then she asks me, "Have you always lived in Billings."

"Well, I was born in Bridger and moved to Billings for the last year of grade school and my freshman year in high school, then I went to Missouri to a Catholic seminary my sophomore and junior year, but I finished my senior year in Great Falls because my parents moved there. I lived there for ten years from 1960 to 1970 when I moved back to Billings."

"What did you do in Great Falls?"

"After high school, I went to the College of Great Falls and worked for Osco Drug as a manager trainee."

"Which Osco store?"

"The one at West Gate Shopping Center."

"Did you know Gladys Burt?"

"Yeah, she was the manager of the cosmetic department."

"That's my mother. She used to come home from work and tell me about this college kid who was a real joker. She wanted me to come down to the store to meet you."

"Really! She was a lot of fun to work with."

"Wow, my mom would talk about the jokes you played on them. She kept bugging me to come down to the store, but I didn't want to meet some old college guy who worked with my mom."

"Yeah, right."

"I was a junior in high school, so I brought a friend with me. I looked like the model Twiggy—short hair, skinny legs and a short skirt."

"I kinda remember the Twiggy look and you coming in."

"My mom introduced us, and I just said, 'Nice to meet you, Mr. Geiger.' We left finally, but we did what my mom wanted."

"So you weren't that impressed."

"No, you were too old."

"Yeah, right."

"When I saw you at BE, I thought you looked familiar. That's why the twenty questions."

"Boy, small world. So, where is your mom now?"

"In Great Falls. She retired from Osco."

"Well, tell her hi."

"Oh, I will. She'll be happy to know I met you."

"So, what's this Bahá'í?"

"You said you didn't want to talk about religion."

"Oh, right."

I leave the coffee shop thinking how small the world is and how people are connected on many levels. This idea she talked about, the oneness of mankind and religions, fits with my thinking. I'm intrigued that other people believe this too and that there is a religion that teaches these principles.

I drive back to my office to find two ravens sitting in a tree near my parking place. One of them squawks at me.

"Yeah, yeah, I hear you," I squawk back. "Leave me alone, I'm still trying to figure out my life."

Chapter 52

Sun Dance, It Ain't Rock and Roll

A few weeks later, I see Hartford again. "Go down to The Sun Dance, maybe you'll learn something."

The Sun Dance is part of the Native American tradition of the Plains Indians dating back to ancient times. It was banned by the US Government in 1883 and revived in 1936. During these fifty years, natives were prohibited from worshipping except for Christian rituals. The government understood little about the Sun Dance as a method of prayer and making a connection with God through nature. It was seen as a pagan ritual. In most indigenous cultures, there is not a word for atheist or agnostic, as this is a foreign concept to them. Everyone believes in God. It's us white guys who came up with the idea of no God.

I observed a couple of Sun Dances in the last few years, and I'm always intrigued by the piety and sacrifice of the participants. A big part of the Sun Dance is learning respect for women and seeing them as equal participants in a relationship—a much different belief than my ancestors held, and then the current patriarchal views of society.

The sacrifice of fasting for three days is dedicated to the healing of family and friends. It takes months of emotional preparation, and I'm working my way up to the idea of participating.

This summer, there are four different Sun Dances on the Crow Reservation. The Plains Indians often begin the Sun Dance with the summer solstice on June 21. This one is scheduled in the Wolf Mountains near the border of the Northern Cheyenne Reservation and the Crow Reservation. It's held on August 3, 1993, and I drive from Billings to the Wolf Mountains.

My 1969 Ford van purrs along the first eighty-one miles of Interstate 90, a ribbon of pavement cutting through the almost deserted plains of Montana. The scene is the way it was in the 1800s. The only things missing are the massive buffalo herds. My Ford van has served me well over the years. I bought it in 1971 and converted it into a small camper I call my "poor man's Winnebago."

At Lodge Grass, a reservation town of less than 500, I exit the Interstate and head east on a gravel road toward the Wolf Mountains, also known as the Wolf Teeth Mountains by the Crow People. The mountains are only 4,500 feet in elevation but have the jagged appearance of teeth. The gravel road gives way to a bumpy, rutted dirt road. My van bounces along, but this is not new. I've had this van in such remote places that if it broke down, I'd need a helicopter to lift it back to civilization. The final ten miles takes an hour.

Sun Dances are usually held in remote places. Visitors are welcome if they come with a sense of reverence and respect. As I round the final corner, I look down on a green meadow bordered by a small stream. A few dozen cars and pickups are parked near a dance arena about fifty feet in diameter. A half dozen tepees and camping tents house the individuals who are there to support the dancers.

A shade arbor—a structure constructed of three-inch diameter Lodge Pole pine trees for the outside wall and roof then covered with leafy cottonwood tree branches—creates a circular sunshade around the dance arena. In the middle of the arena is a twenty-foot cottonwood tree trunk about six inches in diameter. Transported from the river bottom and buried in the ground to keep it upright, the trunk is the centerpiece of the Sun Dance. A buffalo head, like one mounted on a museum wall, is placed on top of the Sun Dance pole. A mounted bald eagle keeps the buffalo company on the pole. Brightly colored prayer ribbons—cloth strips and flags made by the participants—flutter from the pole. The ribbons represent the ascension of prayers toward the heavens.

I park my van and quietly sit near the circle in the shade of a cedar tree. I don't know who the Sun Dance chief is, but I'm sure I'll be noticed soon. After a half-hour, Joseph walks by and says, "Aho. Are you here to dance?"

"No, just pray and watch."

"That's good."

Joseph, a big man in his mid-70s, wears a handsome straw cowboy hat, blue plaid western shirt and Wrangler jeans that drape over his pointed cowboy boots. The focus of his outfit is a five-inch silver belt buckle adorned with a cowboy on a bucking horse and engraved, "Saddle Bronc Champion—1956." As he walks off, he says, "Come tonight. We put on a feed." It's an invitation to dinner, Crow style.

I spend the afternoon praying, thinking and watching people and birds. Around six o'clock, people gather at eight-foot tables under a stretched canvas cover. Beef steaks sizzle on a gas barbecue, corn on the cob boils in a large kettle and baked potatoes in aluminum foil roast in an open fire pit. Dessert is canned blueberries in a thick syrup coming out of a commercial-sized gallon can.

I ask one of the women for a knife and cut up my watermelon, stacking the slices on a cookie baking pan—my contribution to dinner. Lou, the woman who gave me the knife, looks at the slices and jokes, "You're a good cook."

The other five women laugh at this, and Lou asks, "Are you Josephine's boy?"

"Yes,"

"How is she doing?"

"Good, still tough as nails."

More laughter follows.

Lou adds, "You better be a good boy," and the laughter gets louder.

Joseph is the patriarch for the dance, but his wife Rosie is the matriarch of the camp. Joseph sits at the end of three eight-foot folding tables smoking a Marlboro. Rosie sits at the other end near the barbecue and food table, supervising her daughters, a son and grandkids in the preparation of the food.

I sit next to Joseph. "Thanks for the invite."

"It's good you are here. We can always use extra prayer. Have you thought of dancing?"

"Hartford thinks I should dance," I say.

"I know Hartford. You know him?"

"Yes, he has strong medicine."

"I hear this but never see it."

"I've seen his medicine. I'm Josephine Prettyweasel's son."

"I know, I see you in her camp at Crow Fair. Are you the one the ravens are after?"

"I guess so."

"That's good."

Not much goes unnoticed on the reservation. Clans watch out for themselves and one another. Sometimes I feel at home on the reservation, and sometimes I feel like I'm being watched. Either you pass the test of being accepted, or you are suspect. If you are invited to dinner, you know you are accepted.

The dance starts tomorrow, so this will be the last day of feasting until the dance is over in three days. Because the dancers fast and neither eat nor drink during these three days, the other members of the tribe will eat and drink in private.

Crow dinners are predictable—small jokes, teasing and lots of laughter. People tell about the time someone fell off a horse, when a car broke down, when the home team won a basketball game—such things always brings laughter. I wish this laughter existed in my white man culture. We Germans are way too stoic.

That evening, I take my sleeping bag to a nearby hill and lay under the stars listening to murmured laughter from camp. Noisy toads and crickets join in the laugher with their croaking and chirping. At two in the morning, I wake up to utter silence and a sky of stars like flashlights. I lie here thinking about how fortunate I am to be part of a sacred Sun Dance and to have my own special place on top of a hill remote from the rest of the world. To feel so alive. I feel that my true self is nearby but yet to be discovered.

As the sun rises over the Wolf Mountains, I awake to hear the first sounds of the Sun Dance. The high-pitched tweeting of eagle bone whistles slices through the sagebrush up and to the hillside where I lie. About thirty dancers had slept under the shade arbor in the Sun Dance arena last night. They begin the Sun Dance ceremony this morning when the sun first peeks over the mountain.

The dancers stand in a circle around the arbor and face toward the Sun Dance pole in the center. To the rhythmic, high-pitched tweeting of the whistles, they methodically dance twenty feet toward the center pole, but just before reaching it, they dance backward to the outer circle again. They repeat this for hours. The back and forth dancing and other rituals will continue for three days. Most dancers will repeat this Sun Dance four times over the course of a few years. Four is a sacred number in native religion, symbolizing the four directions, four colors, four seasons, four winds, etc.

For the next three days, I sit quietly in the shade of a small cedar tree near the edge of the arbor, taking a few long walks up coulees that snake into the Wolf Mountains or helping the women with camp chores. The dancers continue to fast even though the August days are hot and dry, with daytime temperatures around ninety-five degrees F.

At noon first day, the whistles quiet, and the first three of a dozen people are brought into the arena for a healing ceremony. They chant prayers and guide those in need of healing into a circle around the Sun Dance pole. One lady is pushed in a wheelchair.

At mid-afternoon, the first dancers to be pierced come to the center of the arena. Long narrow strips of leather suspended from the top of the Sun Dance pole are attached to their chest by pinching a finger of skin and piercing it with a needle-like bone. They attach the leather strip to this bone, and the dancer backs up to the outside of the arena until the strips are stretched taut between the pole and the dancer's chest. The dancers lean back on the straps until the skin on their chests stretches a few inches out from their rib cages. The dancers endure the pain as a sacrifice for someone's healing. In a final act, they will lean back and tear themselves free, pulling the bones through the skin.

Late afternoon clouds build the first sign of a thunderstorm. This weather is typical on hot days on the western plains. The rolling white clouds grow larger and darker until some are ten miles tall. Suddenly, the clouds seem to burst, dumping rain in dense sheets across the plain.

Rain is just one aspect of thunderstorms. Their notoriety comes from dramatic lightning and thunder. Night falls as the rain pounds the plain, and I take cover in my van, listening to what sounds like ten thousand buffalo stampeding toward us across the plain. As the stampede rolls into camp, the thunder is deafening, and the lightning strikes so numerous and close I could read a book by the light.

I am hesitant to roll the window down to take a picture because the lightning could come through and strike me. The thunder doesn't rumble but clashes like orchestra cymbals clanging against my ears. I think of the dancers huddled under tarps in the arbor, not as protected as I am. The prairie shakes for thirty minutes, then the storm moves on, and a coolness comes over the camp as if God had tested the spiritual intentions of the dancers. The camp slips into a quiet sleep with a sliver of a moon hanging on the horizon.

Morning sun brings warmth, and by mid-day, the land has dried along with its inhabitants. The eagle bone whistles continue their high-pitched tweeting until noon when a second piercing takes place. This time, the skin of two dancers' backs is pierced with bones fastened to leather straps tied to a large buffalo hide weighted with nine buffalo skulls. The two dancers drag the buffalo hide around the arena, which tears at the skin on their backs. It's difficult to watch. The hide leaves a trail of dust around the arena adding to a ghostly and mystical atmosphere.

For the duration of the Sun Dance, I steep in the dancers' fortitude, watching the methodical two-beat dance step moving inward and outward toward the Sun Dance pole and back again. These movements are repeated countless times while the sun bakes the dancers. Lost to this culture for many years, the Sun Dance has returned with hope and purpose for a suffering people. Today, I admire those doing their best to bring healing to themselves and others.

Sunday night, the ceremony closes. The dancers—weary, thirsty, hungry and with an exhilaration that only sacrifice and service can bring—finally feast. It's a happy, festive time with plentiful food and drink laid out on long tables cobbled together in a crooked line on the uneven ground. Talk and laughter waft through the canyon, like the sweetness of a lilac bush. There are stories of dancers coming to the brink of giving up, only to find new strength from a hidden reservoir that only faith can explain—faith in a Creator, a mystery that befuddles our feeble finite minds.

I lie in my sleeping bag on the top of a nearby hilltop, keeping company with my friends, Mr. Toad and Miss Cricket. A dream-filled night nudges me in a direction that will become clear in the days to come. The sky above and the lumps below me remind me I'm human.

The long shadows of early morning begin to retreat and uncover me as I contemplate how I arrived at this point in my life—how life's tests, experiences, resistance to change and God shapes our character, sometimes for the better, sometimes not. The one thing I know for certain is, "I'm here." But then my memory begins to reclaim a similar experience I had in Thailand a few years ago.

Chapter 53

Niran Ain't Exactly Nirvana

Buddhist temples are a magnet. They pull with an invisible force. I'm in Thailand and intrigued by the monks who live a life of simplicity, few possessions and reliance on others for their daily food. Their early morning chanting pulls me out of deep sleep and down a narrow street in the tiny village of Sop Rauk. I know little of Buddhism but enjoy the humility of the monks.

It is June of 1988, and I follow the Pied Piper of melodic chanting toward a small Wat or temple near the Golden Triangle, where Thailand, Burma and Laos intersect on a small bridge. Here, the Rauk River flows into the mighty Mekong, intersecting the three borders of these countries. The Piper leads me into the courtyard of the Wat Pra That Pukhao, a Buddhist monastery. I sit in the courtyard on a stone bench, looking down at dusty footprints on the stone tiles. The chanting stops, and two dozen saffron-robed monks exit the temple in a cloud of quiet murmuring. They are a mix of old men, young boys and everything in between.

A man in his thirties approaches and says in very good English, "Good morning."

I'm surprised at his fluency. "Good morning. Is it okay I'm here?"

"Yes, everyone welcome, my name is Niran. Would you like some tea?"

"Yes, that would be very nice."

Niran takes me to his small room in the monastery. Inside, Niran's possessions are a straw mat and blanket for sleeping, a tiny charcoal stove for heating water for tea, a teapot, three cups, a large bowl, a small bowl and a spoon. A small bamboo chest contains an extra saffron-colored robe and a few more personal items. Niran serves up two cups of green tea and asks me, "Why you come to Thailand?"

"I'm just a tourist. I enjoy meeting people and learning about religions. How long have you been a monk?"

"One year. My wife divorced me, so I came here to discover why she left me."

"How much longer will you be here?"

"Until I discover my purpose, maybe a week or maybe many years. Depends how much I resist the truth. Besides people and religion, why you come here?"

"Maybe also to find my purpose."

"Have you been looking long?"

"All my life, since I was a child."

"Yes, finding purpose, a path can take time. Depends how much we resist."

"I don't think I resist."

"If you didn't, you would have found it many years ago."

"Guess I don't think of it that way."

"Not many do, many just think and think and not let go of mind."

"What do you mean?"

"Mind can't do this, only heart."

"How do you let the heart do this?"

"Ah, now you begin to understand, but some things I can't tell you."

"I wish you could."

"Perhaps you should stay here in the Wat. You can stay three days and then you have to shave your head. After three days, you will know if this is right for you."

"I don't know… maybe."

In midafternoon, I say goodbye to Niran, knowing I won't be staying for three days. I admire the life of a monk but know it is not for me to be isolated from the community and lead a solitary life. I have always enjoyed being part of a larger community and finding ways to interact with people, especially those less fortunate.

As I walk out of the ornamental gate topped with a twenty-foot figure of Buddha covered in gold leaf, Niran says, "Your true purpose in life is coming. Pay attention, or you will miss it."

The long shadows on the hilltop near the Wolf Mountains shorten, and the bright sun transports me back to Montana. It's been six years since I saw Niran. I wonder if he found his purpose, and I remember his admonishment to not miss mine.

Chapter 54

Too Much at Once, You Name It, It's Happening

I return to Billings and discover that Joyce has moved out of the house to live with a friend. I knew this was coming, but I am still surprised and heartbroken. She probably left emotionally months ago, and I didn't realize it. Denial is a strong attribute, especially if it keeps you from feeling pain.

I spend the next year in a state of numbness. I find myself crying every day, wrenching sobs from deep in my gut.

Joyce moves back home for a few weeks over Christmas, but there is no connection between us. She is gone, and the distance continues to grow. She carries resentment, and I carry sadness.

I remember Niran and his admonishment. I'm almost fifty and wonder if I will ever find my purpose. Maybe it's to keep seeking truth. My life has been moderately successful on the surface, but I've managed to keep my insecurities hidden. I've always managed to look good to others. "pretty boy in plastic" description has been accurate most of my life. I wonder if other people also put up a façade and feel like they're bluffing their way through life the way I do.

I continue to be concerned about my drinking. About fifteen years ago, my drinking buddy, Don, called from a treatment center. I remember the call like it was today.

"Hey, it's Don. I'm at the drunk farm."

"Where?"

"The drunk farm."

"What?"

"The drunk farm in Glasgow."

"Oh, I get it. You quit drinking?"

"Yeah, guess it's time. The sauce caught up with me."

"How is it going there?"

"It ain't a picnic. Can't pull any shit on these guys. You either come clean, or they don't leave you alone. I don't like it, but for the first time, I'm being honest with myself."

"Hang in there. When you get out, we will have to think of something new to do besides get drunk and wreck cars."

"Thanks, pal, appreciate that."

"Hey, that's what pals are for. I admire you pulling the plug on booze. Maybe I'll do it someday."

"Yeah, everyone has to figure out their own deal."

"Been thinking about it."

"Later, I'll call you when I get out."

I hung up, thinking that if Don had a problem then maybe I had one too. But I put this idea on the back burner for a few more years.

* * *

The next fifteen years whirl by quickly, and now I'm living alone and attending a recovery group for divorced and widowed individuals every Friday night in a church basement. About thirty of us get together and talk about our struggles. Everyone is hurting, so misery has company. After our discussion, some of us meet up at a coffee shop to hash over the night and avoid going home to an empty house. This evening, I head down to the Brew Pub, a local watering hole, and meet my buddy, Keith.

As we sit at the bar, he asks, "Did you quit drinking or something?"

"Why?"

"I dunno—I see you drinking a soda water instead of scotch."

"I hadn't thought about it until you mentioned it."

I remember toasting the bride and groom at a wedding in Alaska last summer and setting down a half-empty champagne glass and not finishing it. That was my last drink.

"Maybe I have," I tell Keith. "Kinda weird, it just went away."

"Yeah, that is weird. What's next? You going to find religion and be saved?"

"I doubt that. Was saved once in high school—don't need saving again."

"In your case, being saved again wouldn't hurt," Keith says, laughing.

I don't laugh.

Instead, I go home and lie in bed, wondering what to do with all the booze in my wine cellar and thinking about that last drink I had at the Alaska wedding. Was it really the last one?

In the coming weeks, Joyce and I file for divorce, amicably split up our assets and show up at the courthouse. I don't want the divorce and still hope that someday we can get back together.

The New Year, 1994, rolls in, and I'm wondering what it will bring. I'm doing everything I can to limp through this painful time—writing poetry from a very dark place, listening to the ravens squawk at me, doing sweats on the Crow Indian Reservation and thinking about a Sun Dance. My fellow workers at the counseling center are perplexed as I continue to grieve, often in public. I'm a mess. Feeling this way is new, but maybe it's good.

I see my friend Diana, the Bahá'í, and ask her a few more questions about her faith.

"So, is the Bahá'í Faith all the religions rolled into one?"

"No, it's the newest religion that brings a new message for today's modern world."

"What about all the other religions that came before?"

"If you think about it, they all teach the same basic spiritual principles. But every thousand years or so, God sends a new Manifestation to update the social laws and help an advancing civilization understand things that previous societies couldn't comprehend."

"So, what are some of the teachings for today?"

"Well, in a few words, the main ones are the oneness of religion and race, equality of women and men, and the responsibility for each individual to independently investigate truth for himself. Or herself."

What she said was very appealing to me—everyone should think for themselves. It bothers me that there are good and bad clergy that can lead people astray. In my mind, that would be a good reason for a new "Manifestation"—a Moses or Jesus or Mohammad—to appear now and then to help us with a kind of course correction, a "resetting" of what's true and essential.

Diana's answers confirm my lifelong beliefs. Maybe I'm not quite such an odd duck when it comes to religion.

I ask a few ministers about the Bahá'í Faith, and they tell me to beware. It is probably a cult, they say. But none of them has firsthand knowledge about it. Their opinions are based on hearsay from others.

I want to understand from the source what this faith is all about, so I begin reading the original Bahá'í Writings. Many of the teachings are similar to the Bible, but there are many new and revolutionary truths. Some of the familiar concepts involve the nature of the soul, the belief that there is life after death, and the mystery of God and creation. But there is much more, and I'm intrigued with these new teachings—especially the Bahá'í belief that our souls will continue to progress in the spiritual realm after death. This seems refreshing compared to the notion of heaven and hell, which asserts that each of us earns an "A" or an "F" for our performance on earth, which seals our afterlife fate forever.

As I continue to read, I realize there is much more to this faith than just a simple belief system. It's a whole new way of looking at the world. There is a promise of peace on earth. Rather than the earth being destroyed, it promises that a great peace is coming. As Jesus told us to pray, "Thy kingdom come, Thy will be done, on earth (too) as it is in heaven."

Best of all, there is no guilt from original sin in the Bahá'í Faith. Rather, we are created "noble" to be responsible for our own decisions and conduct, not that of our ancestors. I was always troubled trying to imagine an innocent infant and as tainted from the start.

I spend the next eight months devouring the Writings of Bahá'u'lláh, the founder of this faith. In August of 1994, I'm sitting at a picnic table in a park near my office when a raven lands on the far end of the table and squawks at me.

"Yeah, yeah—I hear you," I tell the raven, hoping no one will see me talking to a bird.

Suddenly, in an aha! Moment, I flash back to 1960 when I was in the chapel and Jesus came down from the cross and told me, "There is much I can't tell you today. I will return when you can understand. But for now, I am the way, the life and the truth. Be vigilant."

Everything becomes clear to me, but I realize it is impossible to describe my epiphany to another person. What's clear is that I don't have to abandon Jesus. Christianity is my foundation. It is a pillar of the Bahá'í faith, just as other prior religions are. The only word I can think of is "grace."

At that moment, I realize that I'm a Bahá'í. I'm not sure what to do with this knowledge, but it feels right. Suddenly, the raven on the table is quiet. I almost miss the insistent squawking. Maybe all that squawking was encouragement to find the Bahá'í faith. I find myself in an extraordinarily quiet, peaceful. The wait that Jesus described is over for me.

That weekend I drive to the Sun Dance in the Wolf Mountains. It has been a year since I last participated. My '69 Ford Van bounces over the same gravel road, inching deeper into the mountains. Joseph watches me drive up. "Aho," he says, "you come to dance?"

"No, just to pray. I have new prayers." I show him my Bahá'í prayer book. He slowly pages through it, then stops and reads one of the prayers, partially in Crow and partially in English. The prayer breathes life through the valley with sweetness and steadfastness. This is that prayer.

> Create in me a pure heart, O my God, and renew a tranquil conscience within me, O my Hope! Through the spirit of power confirm Thou me in Thy Cause, O my Best-Beloved, and by the light of Thy glory reveal unto me Thy path, O Thou the Goal of my desire! Through the power of Thy transcendent might lift me up unto the heaven of Thy holiness, O Source of my being, and by the breezes of Thine eternity gladden me, O Thou Who art my God! Let Thine everlasting melodies breathe tranquility on me, O my Companion, and let the riches of Thine ancient countenance deliver me from all except Thee, O my Master, and let the tidings of the revelation of Thine incorruptible Essence bring me joy, O Thou Who art the most manifest of the manifest and the most hidden of the hidden!

Joseph reverently closes the book and hands it back to me, saying, "This is good. Say this prayer for us today. Someday we will not have Dance, this prayer will be all we need. For now, this is what we do. Someday it will change."

I spend the next three days quietly sitting on the outside circle of the arbor enjoying the eagle bone whistles and the rhythmic steps of the Sun Dancers. I feel at peace and begin to make sense of my life's twists and turns.

On the drive back to Billings, I stop at Crow Agency and find Hartford sitting at his table nursing a cup of Folger's coffee. On a hill across the Little Big Horn River, the white tombstones of the Battle of the Little Big Horn shimmer in the afternoon heat.

"Aho, you come to Crow?" Hartford says.

"Yes, I'm on the way home from the Sun Dance."

"That's good. Did you dance?"

"No, just prayed." I hand Hartford the Bahá'í prayer book and open it. "This is a prayer Joseph told me to say."

Hartford slowly reads the prayer and then looks up at me and says, "This is good."

I tell him about becoming a Bahá'í, and we discuss some of the principles of the faith.

"Now you are getting it," he tells me. "We Crow have known these things for long time." He then goes on to explain the progressive revelation of religion from his own perspective. "There is the Yellow One and the Red One and the Black One. Many other colors too. They come to all the places on the Mother Earth and to all the people. Same beliefs but different colors."

"Who is the Black One?" I ask.

"That is Jesus. The Yellow One is Buddha, the One in China. They are all the same and appear everywhere, but only the color is different. It is believed they are all the same color, but this is how we understand them. We have our own, for the Indians. The people who live on the islands have their own, but each one belongs to everyone. People don't understand this, but when they do, there will be no more fighting among the religions. But for now, they still fight one another."

I sit in wonderment at the depth of his understanding of religion, and I realize how we white folks have missed having a broader view of the world. When I came to Hartford's home, I felt that I was bringing him new ideas, but he already knew them. Perhaps this is how we whites too often think we know everything.

Before I leave, he tells me one more time, "It has taken many years, but now you are getting it. This is good. Now you have more work to do. Your work is like a medicine man—but a different medicine, not mine."

He doesn't say what kind of work, and I don't ask. It's understood that this will become clear in the future.

I return to Billings to sort out the changes in my life, but it's a better feeling I have now. Maybe I've finally moved beyond the song, "Been thinkin' about changing my way of thinking."

For the past year at Beginning Experience, Diana has been helping me cope with the loss of Joyce. Even during my divorce, she has been supportive of me reuniting with Joyce. I admire her for this and for maintaining the boundaries of our relationship while I am married.

I remember Renee, though, the psychic woman in Portland who told me there was a second woman who loved me but who was hidden in the shadows. Suddenly, it is clear that Diana is this woman. Diana is also my Bahá'í friend who has quietly and respectfully answered my questions about the Bahá'í Faith. I don't say anything about this to Diana, but I know in my heart that she is the one.

The next time I see Diana, I drum up some courage and ask, "Would you be interested in going out on a date?"

"What about Joyce?" she asked. "I thought you wanted to get back with her."

"It's been a year, and I've had to let go. She has no interest in getting back together."

"What did you have in mind for a date?"

"Maybe get a cup of coffee?"

"We do that anyway. What would be different?"

"I'm not sure. Just knowing it was a date, I guess."

"Sounds okay."

Diana and I have the same dream to travel and explore the planet. And, of course, we share a common spiritual belief in which we see the world and its people as one family. For the next several months, we enjoy each other's company and grow more fond of each other.

We married in January of 1995. The following year, I retire from the counseling center and try to live my new life as a Bahá'í.

The ravens are still quiet, and I am certain now that I've found my purpose in life. Perhaps I have been saved a second time. Maybe this is what Jesus was trying to tell me back in 1960 when he spoke to me at the seminary. I remember his words, still clear in my heart and mind: "There is much I can't tell you today, but you will understand some day."

Chapter 55

Holy Land Calls, Better Answer

In 1998, Diana and I move to Haifa, Israel, where we volunteer at the Bahá'í World Center. The prophet of the faith, Bahá'u'lláh, is buried here, and the administrative center is also located here on Mount Carmel. We love living in Israel and make friends with local Arab Muslims, Christians and Jews.

At the World Center, there are 850 volunteers from about a hundred countries. Because volunteers come for only a few years, there is a constant rotation of staff. During our three years there, we meet people from virtually every country in the world.

Before coming to Israel, I went back to school and learned hypnotherapy. I like this approach to mental health better than counseling or talk therapy because it is less intrusive and more effective. In Israel, I have the opportunity to develop my practice with people of many cultural backgrounds. And Diana and I have the opportunity to immerse ourselves in the culture of the Middle East.

We buy a used Subaru station wagon and begin traveling the backroads of Israel. To our surprise, Israel is a very safe country to live in, contrary to what one hears on the news. The crime rate is almost nonexistent, and Diana feels safe walking home late at night in Haifa, a city of 200,000 people. Terrorism is localized to the area around the Gaza Strip and the West Bank.

Some weekends we camp near an Arab Muslim village, other weekends near a Jewish kibbutz and sometimes in the Negev Desert with the Arab Bedouin Nomads. It all feels safe, and the people are friendly. I remember the first time I drove into an Arab village, parked my car and locked it, then realize I was the only one in the village with a locked car.

I'm beginning to understand what Hartford told me about the different colored Ones. I don't see other religions as the enemy anymore. Living in Israel creates a new awareness of culture, religion and people.

* * *

In March of 1999, I receive an email from KJ, the daughter of Josephine, my adopted Crow Indian mother. The message is short. "Mom is sick, and we don't know if she will make it. You might want to come home to see her before it is too late."

Three days later, I am visiting Josephine at St. Vincent's Hospital in Billings. She doesn't look very good, but her sense of humor is still there.

Josephine worked for me in the 1970s and 80s as a counselor on the Crow Reservation, helping people with disabilities make a life for themselves. When I traveled to the rez, I would always take Josephine with me as a bodyguard. When she was with me, the Crows trusted me. "Leave him alone, he's my son," she would command.

Josephine had stabbed a guy in a bar several years before I'd met her because he had tried some "funny business."

I had asked her, "Did the police do anything?"

"No, they knew he had it coming," she had told me. "I didn't kill him, but it taught him a lesson." Then she laughed.

Today, in the hospital, she still has that laugh. Then, out of nowhere, she says, "You know, when you became a Bahá'í, it changed you for the better. I could see a difference."

"Really? What?"

"Oh, I don't know. It made you a better person, less a jackass." She laughs again.

Josephine was a devout Christian and knew the Bible forward and backward, so I never said anything to her about the Bahá'í faith. I didn't want to upset her.

I am surprised, then, when she tells me, "I want to become a Bahá'í. I still believe in Jesus, but I think there is more. He said there are many things he couldn't tell us while he was still here. How can I become a Bahá'í?"

"Well, it's pretty simple. You just need to recognize the messenger for today, Bahá'u'lláh. Everyone does this in their own way. There's not much more I can tell you other than to investigate it for yourself."

With this, she closes her eyes and quietly rests for a few moments, then opens her eyes and says, "Okay, I know Him. He came down through the top of my head and out the bottom of my feet. All the pain is gone."

With that, she gets up and goes home from the hospital.

I have always wondered what happened during those few moments when she had her eyes closed. Afterward, she started telling people she was a Bahá'í.

I visited her a few days later at her home. A revival tent across the street was hosting an evangelical congregation from Texas that comes every year. Over the years, Josephine has become friends with two Christian women, Ellie and Betty, who come to visit her. They enjoy reading the Bible together. Today, while I am visiting, they stop by as usual, and the conversation quickly turns to the Bible.

I am enjoying the conversation when Josephine tells them, "You know, I became a Bahá'í. I like the way it teaches that all religions and people come from God."

Suddenly, there is a cold silence in the room. Then Betty responds, "Bahá'í? How could you do this? Your soul will be lost to hell. Who told you about this?"

"Dan told me, but I saw it with my own eyes and heart."

Betty turns to me and firmly "reminds" me that Bahá'ís are bound for hell. After about ten minutes of lecture, they leave.

After they are gone, Josephine smiles and says, "Just let them go do their thing. They don't understand yet. You know, Jesus tells us not to throw pearls before swine. That's why I didn't say anything to my friends. They don't get it, but it's not their fault."

She sits back and smiles. "God is always trying to talk to us, but for some reason, we don't like to listen. Maybe because I was so sick in the hospital, I couldn't do anything but listen. That's good. It's good when we can listen."

I leave Josephine after a week and head back to Israel, remembering her words and trying to listen when God speaks to me.

Back in Israel, Diana and I drive through the Negev Desert on our way to Masada for the weekend. Driving south on Highway 90, the silver-gray color of the Dead Sea blends with the pre-dawn sky. Only the brightest stars and planets are still visible, their fainter peers having retired for the coming day. The desert mountains on the distant shore of the Dead Sea signal the presence of Jordan. It is five-thirty in the morning, and the desert breezes blow cool before the sun heats up this part of the world.

Highway 90 follows the great rift carved through Israel down to Africa. Two continental shelves parted company millions of years ago, creating this deep fissure, the lowest point on the planet. Highway 90 glides along 1,274 feet below sea level, keeping pace with the Dead Sea for its entire fifty miles.

Our destination this morning is the Ruler of the Dead Sea, Masada. The desert highway offers few clues to what is ahead. Signposts compete with mirages, keeping travelers guessing. Most signs are in Hebrew and Arabic. But one, with a small arrow, faintly blinks "Masada" as we purr by.

The filtered pre-dawn light begins to reveal a detailed fortress created by man and God. It's a remote, natural plateau standing 1,430 feet above the Dead Sea. At seven hundred yards long and three hundred yards wide, it makes it a perfect place to hide and be protected.

For 3,000 years, Masada hosted a series of people looking for a safe place. For centuries, the only access to the top was the Snake Path. We stand at the bottom of the Snake Path.

"Maybe we should go now before it gets too hot," I say.

"Yeah, it's quite a ways up there.

"I can see why they call it the Snake Path."

We fill a pack with water and snacks and begin the long hike up. At about eight that morning, we are sweating at the top of Masada and looking out over a desert landscape of dunes, rock ridges and eroded gullies accentuated by long shadows of the early sun. A few miles away, the Dead Sea ripples with glimmers of heat ghosts.

From the flat top of the plateau, we follow a maze-like path through thousands of years of history. Ancient everyday living quarters provide a glimpse into the lives of people who were not so ordinary.

First, a complex water system channels water into underground cisterns during the short rainy season to provide water for the entire year. The cistern supplies a bathhouse with a courtyard surrounded by Roman columns, a gymnasium, dressing room, swimming pool, cold room bath, warm room bath and a hot room bath.

Next, we sit in a synagogue where scroll fragments of Deuteronomy and Ezekiel had been discovered. A modest hall with a small altar and stone benches allow about fifty people to be seated. We wonder who sat here before us.

Adjacent to the synagogue, we marvel at soldiers quarters, stables, living quarters, a three-story palace, a columbarium for raising pigeons, a Byzantine Church, storerooms, villas, mosaics and water cisterns.

Masada has always drawn people despite its remoteness and difficulties sustaining life. It is a beacon in the desert that requires persistence and sacrifice to visit. For centuries, people thrived on Masada without technology. They had opulent palaces and lavish baths. Diana and I are curious about who they were and how they lived here.

I read this passage from a tour guide: "Flavius, a Jewish historian, gives us this description of Masada, '...fortified by Heaven and man alike against any enemy who might wage war against it.'" One of the last holdouts on Masada were the Jewish rebels known as Zealots who fought the Roman rule to the end.

Prior to this, Masada was the showcase of Herod of Jerusalem. Herod, a Jew, ruled Israel but never trusted Mark Anthony and the Romans. He discovered Masada by chance when he sent his wife and children there during turbulent times. He realized it was a perfect hiding place and fortress.

Herod died in 4 AD, and a few years later, the Zealots holed up here trying to escape from the Romans. They did pretty well until 72 AD, when the Roman army decided to put an end to this nonsense. The Romans showed up with 15,000 men and began a siege. The Zealots tried to wait them out, trusting the natural defenses of Masada to protect them.

As we look down on the valley below, we can still see small rock huts, evidence of the Roman army camps. But most startling is a large breach in the wall of the fortress. The Romans built a huge earthen ramp from the valley floor to the brink of the rim of Masada. Constructed by 10,000 Jewish slaves over several months, it allowed the Roman siege machines to break through the wall.

The Zealots, realizing there was no hope, decided to take their own lives rather than live as slaves. Seeing the end coming, Zealot leader Elazar Ben-Yair delivered his most famous speech: "... God has given us this privilege that we can die nobly and as free men... Come! While our hands are free and can hold a sword, let them do a noble service! Let us die not enslaved by our enemies, and leave this world as free men in company with our wives and children."

Ten men were chosen to slay families as they lay side by side. These remaining ten men cast lots to choose one to slay the final nine and then turn his sword on himself. The result was 964 Zealots died while one mother and her two children hid in a cistern to tell the tale of this final act.

Masada has long been a symbol of bravery and inspiration for the people of Israel and the whole world—the stand of a few against the many, the weak against the strong. This took on a new meaning today as an Israeli tour guide and former army soldier carefully instructed us in strong and demanding English: "The Israeli army comes here to take its oath of loyalty—'Masada shall not fall again.' But it is not right to think we must fight all the time. It must change, the attitude must change, the fighting must end, and we must find another way to peace. Do you understand? Do you understand?" He repeats this phrase several more times. "The world must become a different place so they will not have to take this oath. We must find a new way, do you understand?" he says again. "Peace can only be made at the table, not on the battlefield."

The American tourists are silent as the Israeli plants into their hearts the idea of peace without war. Behind him on the horizon looms Jordan and Syria.

We stand there, joining our tour guide in his hope of finding a new way, not the Masada way.

Chapter 56

Home to Montana from the Holy Land, the Long Way Around

After three years of service at the Bahá'í World Center in Haifa and an additional year and a half traveling around the world, we return home to Montana. I write a newspaper article titled "Around the World in 80 Beds," referring to the eighty-seven different beds we slept in during our trip—the beds of eighty-six Bahá'í families and one Hindu friend. The purpose of our journey was to serve people in many ways—providing hypnotherapy for individuals and groups, speaking to groups on the topic "Is Peace Possible in Today's World?" and picking strawberries and tomatoes.

We arrive home in 2003, finding our parents doing well. They watched and worried as we traveled around the world and are happy to have us home safely. My dad is in his mid-90s and somewhat frail now. He's lost his stride.

In January 2004, I answered my phone and hear my dad tell me. "I can't get out of bed."

"What's wrong?"

"I don't know, I just can't get out of bed."

I jump in my car and drive to Prairie Towers, an assisted living high-rise in Billings. Dad is in bed, disturbed and frustrated.

"What's wrong?"

"I don't know. Here, I'll try to get up again. Don't help me."

He struggles to sit up, but he's too weak. I call his doctor, whose diagnosis is short and to the point: "He just ran out of gas."

"What?"

"His heart is weak, and the valves are leaking a little, so he's not getting enough oxygen. We can put him on oxygen—that may help. Unfortunately, it wouldn't help very much to replace the valves, and at age ninety-four, it would be risky. You can explain this to him, or I can."

"Okay, I'll do it."

I go back into Dad's bedroom. "The doc says you just ran out of gas."

"Yeah, feels like it."

"He says oxygen might help."

"No—no oxygen, no ambulance."

"No ambulance?"

"Yes. Promise you won't call one if things get bad."

"Well—okay. Are you sure?"

"Yes, it's okay now. I've had a tough life, but the last years have been good. Mom and I are doing the best we ever have. I don't want to die in a hospital, just here with mom and you boys."

Suddenly, I understand my dad has lost more than his stride. He's ready to go. I call hospice, and a nurse and social worker arrive within a few hours. The nurse teaches me how to care for Dad, which entails changing his diaper, bathing him, changing his position and making sure he gets enough water and nourishment.

As the weeks roll by, I watch my dad go through the process of letting go of this world. I'm sleeping on the couch and spending every day with him and Mom.

In the beginning, our routine is to watch a little TV, then I'd read the newspaper to him and we'd play cards or dominoes visit. After a couple of weeks, he asks me to take the TV out of the bedroom, but I continue to read the paper to him each morning. After another week, he asks me to read only the obituaries and the weather report—and to take down the wall calendar.

"I don't really need to know what day it is, and I can see the weather out the window," he says.

A week or so later, he asks me to take the clock out of the room. "I can see if it's day or night by looking out the window," he tells me.

I watch him detaching from the material things of this world.

"In life, your circle gets smaller and smaller as you get older," he says. "Now my world is this bed. Get those slippers out of the closet and see if they fit you."

I try on the sheepskin slippers he has worn for many years. "Yes, they fit."

"Good, take them. See that red striped tie hanging with my suit? That's my favorite." He doesn't need to say anything more. That's the tie he wants to be buried in.

For the next couple of months, I slip my shoes off at the door and into these warm comfy slippers. He takes notice that I am wearing them. I think it makes him happy.

I've done a lot of things in my life—explored the back roads of more than fifty countries, flown an ultra-light plane, bungee-jumped, skied off mountain head walls and driven 140 mph—but all of those things were easy compared to learning how to change my dad's diaper and clean him.

He jokes, "When you were a baby, I changed your diaper, so now I guess it's your turn." He keeps his dignity, and I try to hide how difficult it is for me. As the days continue on, it gets easier, but I don't know how well I hide my struggle.

For the next couple of months, I listen and learn. One morning he says, "The most fun thing was snowballs—you know, having a snowball fight."

As the sun sets one evening, he says, "It's beautiful, it's just beautiful. It's so beautiful."

One day, as he is staring out the window, he says excitedly, "Look, a bald eagle."

Sure enough, a majestic bald eagle makes four turns next to our window. It's very unusual to see one in a metropolitan area.

"I wonder what it's doing so close to us," I comment.

"I don't know, but my Indian friends always told me that is a good sign." He laughs. "I hope they're right."

During the last two months, he gets weaker and loses weight. We try to pump him up with protein drinks, but he isn't interested in eating and drinks them just to please us. There are times when he goes into a deep slumber, but it isn't sleep—it's as if he has left his body and his soul steps into the next world. I can sense this as there is an energy in the room radiating from him. At first, it is strange, but then it is comforting. When he comes back to consciousness, he looks around and says, "Am I still here?"

"Yes, you're still here," I tell him.

He looks disappointed and almost frustrated.

I ask him, "What's it like? What do you see?"

"I can't tell you. There are no words."

I ask him this same question every time, and he always tells me the same thing. Finally, one day he says, "It is like the most beautiful flower—but it is not flowers."

This explanation of the spiritual realm is one of the most beautiful I have ever heard. Dad's description conveys deep meaning with simple words. Of course, there are no words for describing a spiritual realm. Our finite minds create metaphors to describe an infinite world.

In the days following, Dad increasingly spends time in the next world. When he is there, being with him is like sitting next to a radiant heater. I just enjoy knowing he is at peace.

One day, he points behind me and says, "Your uncle Tony is here. He has been coming almost every day now. He and I were real close. He was my only brother or sister who treated me right. He died young, and I've missed him for many years. Now he is waiting for me. There are others who come too."

I look around to look but can't see Uncle Tony like my dad can. But I tell Dad that I can sense him there with us.

"Yeah, he looks happy," Dad says. "Always had a big smile. He says I'll go with him when I'm ready. You know, on the other side, there is much we don't know here. Jesus is there, but there are others like Him. I couldn't understand why you became a Bahá'í, but now I do. You've always been the one to help us and now taking care of me. You don't get all the credit, but you get most of it."

This is all I need to hear from my dad. All those years of yearning for him to discuss philosophy and psychology are suddenly moot. I'm beginning to understand his deep sense of wisdom and the many things he taught me about life through action, not words. He didn't know many big words, but the small nuances of gesture and doing what is right were real treasures.

As a son, I always wondered whether my parents understood me. When we were off living in Israel and traveling around the world, my dad would say, "I don't understand why he doesn't settle down." But today, I think he understands me, and this is all I need.

On his last day, he is excited. "It was like a dark room, and then there was a bright light, brighter than the sun and angels," he told me. "They looked like what you would think—they were beautiful, and the light was so bright, but not like the light we see here."

"Can you tell me more?"

"No—no words can tell it. I thank the Lord that everything is settled. I ask God to bless my family and friends and bless me too that I can go now."

His sister comes to visit, and as I leave to give her a ride home, my dad says, "I'll be okay, take your aunt home."

Twenty-five minutes later, I return to the apartment where I'm greeted by mom. "Dad left us," she says. "I went in to check on him, and he told me he would be okay and that he loved us—then he left. It was 4:35, and the sun was shining."

Now I understand the greatest lesson he taught me. Dignity in death comes from dignity in life. Death is a struggle between the body and the spirit. The art of dying comes from the art of living. Honesty in death comes from honesty in life. Dad certainly demonstrated this—his true qualities shone brightly during times of struggle and allowed him to triumph in the end.

We clean his body and dress him in a clean shirt, then call the family to come. We pray the rosary. My mother loved the rosary, and I was happy to pray it with her. I call Smith Funeral Home to pick him up.

At nine that evening, we put my father in a plastic bag. I zip it up, and we wheel the cart down to the van waiting outside. I remember Dad saying, "Jesus is waiting, but there are others too."

Tonight is three months since he called me to say he couldn't get out of bed. There were times when I selfishly wished he would pass on, saving me the emotional struggle of caring for him. But now I see that this time with him was one of the most significant periods of my life. I feel both gratitude and guilt.

At the visitation, many family and friends come to say goodbye. My brothers are uncomfortable with death. They are also uncomfortable with praying the rosary, even though we grew up praying it almost every night. They are "born again" and no longer see the Catholic Church as the one true church.

How many true churches are there? I think asking Jesus's mother to help can't be bad. It doesn't diminish His stature in any way. For me, it's more about what makes Mom happy at this moment.

My mother does well for the next year. She is a strong woman, thinks positive and makes the best of every situation. I visit her often. She and Dad were married sixty-nine years. The last ten years were the best of their marriage, partly because Mom mellowed out and let Dad be Dad.

During their last decade together, they were like two love birds. When she lost her wedding ring at the hospital, he bought both of them new rings. He had never had a wedding ring of his own because in those days, there wasn't money to buy another ring. My mother was so touched when they placed the rings on each other's hands. We all cried tears of happiness for them.

In May of 2005, I stop by on Tuesday for a routine visit. Mom is sitting in her favorite chair wearing a rose-colored dress, a little make-up and her favorite wig to cover her thinning hair. She looks good. She is strong and alert. Quietly and unexpectedly, she says, "I think I'm going to go be with Dad."

"Really?" That's all I could say.

"Yes, I'm done here. I don't have anything left to do."

"Okay—would you like to move in with us for the summer?"

"Yes, that would be good."

"Then I'll set up a bedroom for you."

Two days later, I finish putting together a room for her in our home. I call my brother to bring her over, and he tells me that he doesn't think she can be moved.

"She's too weak to come down to the car," he explains.

"Just get a wheelchair from the office."

"I don't think that will work."

"Why not?"

"She's too weak to get out of bed."

"Well then, just call an ambulance."

An hour later, an ambulance delivers Mom to our house. I go out to greet her. She looks very gaunt and weak.

"You're leaving, aren't you?" I ask here.

"Yes," she answers faintly.

In two days, she has quickly slipped closer to departing this world. I call all the family and friends to come say goodbye.

People stream in to say goodbye. On day seven of her announcing, "I'm going to be with Dad," our daughter-in-law brings Lila, our five-month-old granddaughter, to her bedsides and sits her on the edge of the bed supporting the baby's head. My mother, whose eyes have dried shut and who has not spoken or moved for four days, gently reaches over and picks up the sweet infant. With perfect support and safety, she draws Lila to her breast. At this moment, there is some kind of intimate exchange between them that only they understand. Then Mom carefully hands Lila back to her mother.

On day nine, Mom lies quietly in bed. I assume she can still hear me, so I carry on one-sided conversations with her.

"You know, Mom, everyone I called has come to visit, and you can go now if you want."

In my mind, I think, *Perhaps she will go now in a day or two*. Once again, my mother's determination surprises me. She takes one more breath after receiving my permission to leave, and then she is gone. I'm shocked, but feel a warm glow in the room, and deep peace.

Chapter 57

Still Thinkin'

As I sit here today at seventy-six, thinking of the many years, miles and experiences of my life. I feel at peace with myself, the Catholic Church and life in general. Joyce passed away six years ago at age sixty-two, and we were able to say goodbye in peace.

My office phone rings, so I answer.

A timid voice on the other ends says, "This is Debbie. I hope you can help me. I woke up this morning and found your website. I'm suffering from panic attacks, and I'm fearful for my baby, that I can't take care of her properly. I don't know what to do. The panic attacks are getting worse. Does your therapy help with this sort of thing?"

"I wouldn't be surprised," I tell her. "I've seen lots of people with this, and they got better. I think there is hope for you."

"I don't have any money to pay now… but maybe I can pay you later? I can't find anyone to help me."

"Don't worry about the money. Let's make a time for you to come in. How about this afternoon at three?"

"Yes, yes, I'll be there. Thank you so much! You don't know how much this means to me."

"Okay, see you then."

I hang up, wondering what I could be doing at this moment that would be more meaningful for me? Maybe I've found my purpose.

At three, I open my office door and greet Debbie.

"Hi—thanks so much for seeing me," she says. "I can give you twenty dollars when I get my check from Burger King. Can my baby wait with my girlfriend in the car?"

"That's fine—whatever you can afford. And yes, your baby is okay in the car."

Debbie's story is one I've heard dozens of times. She blurts out, "My dad was either gone or drunk and when he was at home, he was angry. I hid from him in a world of my own. Lots of things happened that are hard to talk about. My mother died when I was six, and I went to live with an aunt and uncle. I was happy to get away from Dad, but my aunt and uncle were worse. I got married when I was sixteen to get away from them and got pregnant right away. My husband was nice until we got married. Then he changed—got to be like my dad. Now he threatens to kill me and the baby if I leave him."

Her anxiety is so high she can barely sit in the chair.

"The worst is over, you'll be okay," I assure her. "There's hope, lots of hope for you."

"I hope you are right."

"The therapy I do is different than counseling or talk therapy. There is a part of you that knows what is wrong and can help you to heal. I call it the Inner Spirit, but it has many names. You know, that intuitive part of us," I say, pointing to my heart.

"Yes, I know. When I was a little girl, it was my best friend that kept me safe."

"It is still there. You can find it again."

After forty-five minutes in a deep state of hypnotherapy, Debbie opens her eyes. "Yes, I found it. I'll be okay now. And the panic is gone."

"You'll be just fine. Right now, though, we need to get you to a safe place. There are people who will protect you and your baby, and we can continue to work together to heal your heart of all those things that happened."

"Yes, thank you so much."

As I watch Debbie's car follow a police officer to a haven for women, I open the drawer on my desk and find Glenn's pocket knife in a tray with assorted pens and markers. I pull it out and place it on my desk next to a plastic model of my white '63 Impala.

It's time to find Glenn's daughter, Teresa.

Post Script

Scrolling through the names on the Virtual Vietnam Memorial, I find Glenn's name and leave a brief message: "You are a good buddy. Won't forget you. Thanks for your sacrifice. Dan Geiger."

Five years later, I receive a short email from a man named Scott. It reads, "I read your remarks about my Great Uncle Glenn on the Vietnam Memorial website. Thanks—I didn't know him, as I was only five years old when he died. Scott."

Below his signature is a phone number in Alaska. Surprised and excited, I call him.

"Scott, this is Dan Geiger. I just got your email about your Uncle Glenn. Thanks for contacting me."

"Sure, happy to learn more about my great uncle. We don't know much about him or what happened."

We talk for about ten minutes, and I share some things I know about Glenn. Then I say, "I'm looking for his daughter, Teresa. Any idea how to find her?"

"Not really. The family hasn't had much contact with her over the years. Let me ask my mother. She may know something."

A few weeks later, I receive a text message from Scott's mother with a photo of an old Rolodex file card with the name of Teresa and her last name with a Great Falls, Montana, phone number. This is the only information Scott's mother has. I spend the rest of the day searching the internet for phone numbers and addresses but find nothing.

Facebook turns up no clues until I search for Betty, Glenn's ex-wife and Teresa's mother. I finally find Betty, who agrees to have Teresa call me.

The next day, I answer my phone. A woman's voice says, "Hi, this is Teresa. My mother said you wanted me to call you."

"Yes, thanks for getting back to me." I say. "I've been trying to find you for several years now. I was your dad's high school friend. Do you remember talking to me when you were in Texas?"

"Not so much. That was a long time ago."

"Yeah, thirty years."

"So, you knew my dad?"

"We ran around together in high school. Had lots of fun together."

"I'd like to know more about him. I don't really know much."

"I'm coming to Great Falls on Memorial Day. Can I come by and meet you?"

"That would be great."

"Maybe Saturday afternoon around two?"

"Yes, looking forward to it."

I hang up look over at Glenn's pocket knife on my desk, the one I got from his dad fifty years ago. I put it into my pocket.

On Memorial Day, Diana and I are driving around the south side of Great Falls and pull up to a tidy suburban home.

My wife Diana says, "I'll wait in the car. You've been waiting for this for years. Enjoy seeing Teresa."

I nod and approach the door. Teresa greets me, and we enter her living room. It's a little awkward at first. I'm not sure what to say.

"Thanks for letting me come by" is my lame attempt at conversation.

"Sure, glad to meet you."

I can see a lot of Glenn in Teresa—his dark distinguishing eyebrows, the sly smile.

"Come in, have a seat." I feel more comfortable now, just like I did around her father.

"So, you went to school with my dad?"

"Yeah, we ran around—a bunch of us kids. I told some of our classmates I found you. They wondered what happened to you."

"That's nice to know. I don't know much about him or his friends, just a little what my mom told me, but she didn't talk about it much."

"Yeah, I suppose it was kind of an awkward situation. They weren't together very long."

"No, I'm not sure how long, maybe less than a year."

"Yeah, it was strange to see him go off to Nam and leave you behind. I think it was real hard on him, but he didn't know how to talk about it."

"Suppose not. Nobody said much about the whole thing."

"Funny how seeing you makes me remember how good a buddy he was. Still some sadness."

"Hope I didn't upset you."

"No, not at all. It's good to finally catch up with you."

I've been waiting for years to find Teresa. I don't know her, but I do know she is Glenn's daughter, my only connection with Glenn. I'm not sure how I feel—happy to find her or sad remembering Glenn is long gone. After fifty years, one would think there is nothing left to feel. I guess time heals our hearts but doesn't erase our memories.

"So, did you knew my dad pretty well?"

"Yes, we were good friends our senior years in high school at Central and then when we were going to college. He went to Missoula, and I went to the College of Great Falls, but we would see each other on weekends and during the summer."

"What was he like?"

"Well, we worked together at Buttrey's our senior year as carry-out boys. There were about six of us guys from Central, so we had a good time working together. When I started, he helped me learn how to do things."

"I didn't know he worked there."

"Yeah, we worked hard but had lots of fun playing pranks on one another. Your dad was kind of a joker."

"What do you mean?"

"Well, our sense of humor was kind of warped. We would think up stupid things to do to each other, but it was all in good fun."

"Sometimes I've got a weird sense of humor."

"Probably got that from your dad."

Teresa opens a cardboard box sitting on the couch.

"Here are some things I got when my grandparents died," she explains.

We begin to explore the early years in Glenn's life up to the time he was killed. Things come out of the box in the order they have been resting there—a letter for his varsity football jacket, a high school diploma, photos of his childhood, a birth certificate, baptismal certificate, death certificate, memorial service program and a newspaper clipping of his obituary. Actually, there are about a dozen news clippings, probably given to the family by friends. I wonder if anyone kept a clipping for themselves.

I pull the pocket knife out of my pocket and hand it to her. "Here, this is your dad's knife. Your grandpa gave it to me."

She looks it over and calls for her son to come up from downstairs.

A stocky teenage boy comes into the living room and she hands him the knife. "This was your grandpa's."

He looks over the knife.

"It's yours now," I say.

He smiles.

"I went to school with your grandfather," I tell him. "He was a really good guy. We were kinda crazy in high school, but we didn't get in any big trouble. I'll tell you some stories if you promise not to do the same things."

"Okay," he says with the kind of mischievous look I used to see on Glenn's face.

I tell them about the car wrecks, the egg fights that landed us in detention, about skipping school early to go play pool. "Remember, just because we did this doesn't mean you can. Kind of a double standard, I know."

He smiles again, probably wondering who this stranger is and who his grandfather was.

I get ready to leave, and Teresa says, "Oh, I have these letters my dad wrote from Vietnam." She hands me a half-dozen letters, the last four dated during the three weeks just before he was killed. I'm surprised at this last find.

"Wow, this is a real treasure!" I slowly read through the letters, a story of bravery, fear, anger and pride unfolding before me. It's the last piece of the puzzle. Finally, all the wondering about what had happened, the struggles with his death and the guilt of Vietnam are quietly laid to rest.

"Thanks for sharing all these things. It means a lot to me to meet you and see all this stuff."

"Thanks for coming by," Teresa says. "You can take the letters with you. Sometimes I want to talk about my dad, and sometimes I don't. It's kind of confusing."

"Yeah, it's confusing for me too, but it helped talking to you today."

"It helped me too," she says.

"Maybe we are both glad and sad at the same time."

"Yeah, both."

We end our visit, Diana and I return to Billings. That night, I read through each letter again in chronological order. It's another tale of wasted lives in a lost war. Young men killing young men. I feel sad, but I think of his grandson carrying his memory and the bounty of meeting Teresa.

I share the letters with a few classmates and finally return them to Teresa with a note telling her how her dad's old friends had enjoyed reading the letters. She sends back a note saying, "Knowing they remembered him makes my heart sing."

Letters from Glenn

Sat Night - Aug. 3rd
Dear Mom & Dad

Hello from hells corner. How is everything back in the world? I'm just getting used to everything now but still is quite a change. My permanent base camp is called Tan Am on the My Tho River. This is located about 50 miles South of Saigon right in the middle of the Mekong Delta. Right now we are in the middle of the monsoon season and we will be over about the end of October. It rains every day from about 3:00 in the afternoon to about midnight. This rain is not like home because it is just like a cloudburst for that length of time. In the morning it is very hot & cloudy usually around 100 degrees.

I'm going to try & tell you how it is over here. I'm not exaggerating or feeling sorry for myself but want to tell you exactly how things are. I've been assigned to the 9th Infantry Division 2nd Battalion 39th Infantry. Our job is strictly protecting all the small villages here keeping the Viet Cong out of the area. Believe me there is a lot of them down here.

I have been down here about a week and am running a Squad. Things are not exactly too rosy here. This area is pretty hot at times. I have been out in the field once. We were out for 2 ½ days & let me tell you it was hell. This area is all water - ⅞ rice paddies, canals and rivers infested with V.C. "Uncle Charlie". He never hits us unless he knows he can win. When we were out there we never saw him in person but could tell he had been all around. I'm still pretty green & and need 2 more weeks before I can be confident of myself. We were only fired at once and that was a sniper about 500 yards away. Those rice paddies are hell to walk in plus everything is all water because of the monsoon.

The Delta is heavily populated, ½ the population of Vietnam. People are all around but they are scared to say anything because they are scared the Viet Cong will kill them and burn their houses. It is a shame the way these people live but it seems they want to come on our side, but are scared if they do. In our operations we have to search every village making sure it is not Viet Cong controlled. Little kids always come out to where we are begging for food and candy. They are so cute you hardly refuse them but maybe their dad is a VC. That is the bad part about it, you cannot tell who the V.C. is from the regular South Vietnamese.

Well, I guess I better go. Please write as soon as possible. I only have 348 days left.

Love, Glenn

P.S. I have enclosed $200. Please save.

Saturday Morning - Aug. 10
Dear Mom & Dad:

It's about time to get another letter off because we are going back into the field today. I hope you received my other letters O.K. and am still waiting patiently for a letter. They say it takes about 2 weeks the first time.

I am at a different place for a while. I am now at Rack Kein right outside of Saigon. This town just was overrun by Viet Cong. We are going out today to get it back. It might take us one hour or 1 month but we will get it back. I'm pretty used to everything now and I guess you can call me a hard core veteran. We have been pretty close to Saigon lately keeping the out-lying areas clean.

Last Wednesday was my first real fire fight. We were sent to Dung Tha just to check out the area. When we landed we were hit. I spent 5 hours behind a rice paddy dike. I was scared but when you see everyone else doing what has to be done you haven't a chance to get scared. We killed 12 V.C. without anyone in our Co getting hurt. So much about war stories.

I'm still waiting for the day to come home. I forgot all about white sheets and a clean place to sleep. All we care about here is a dry place to sleep and that isn't very often. I want to buy a camera and take pictures but I don't know where I would put it to keep it dry but will try to find some way. We are leaving at 1:00 so don't know when we will be back. Hope everyone is in good health, I am fine and everything is O.K. Love Glenn

Friday - Aug. 16
Dear Mom & Dad:

Its time again to write from Vietnam. Everything is fine as well as can be expected. We are still at Roak Kein and it looks like we may be here for some time because it is so close to Saigon. The people are glad that we are here since we chased the V.C. away. I have my own woman that does my wash and cleans up where I sleep but that is the only civilization here except a small village. We have no facilities such as a PX or beer hall but have access to the small bars in the town. There is really nothing to do now but just pull guard on the town. These people have a rice whiskey that you can buy for 80 cents a quart. This stuff is bad but that is the only enjoyment we get. I sure would appreciate it if you could send me some books or magazines to read. We have none of that here. OK.

Tuesday I had to write something I never wanted to do. I lost one of my men in my squad. He was killed by a Russian made RPG rocket and is a custom of the Army for the C.O. to write a remembrance letter. In our battalion each squad leader has to add a little bit. All I could say was that he died doing something he didn't like but something he had to do. We all feel that way and I can say I have one of the best squads in the Company. Everyone works together out here. If one guy has a pack of cigarettes we all get one, and when we come back from an operation we all get drunk together. Everyone is just like a brother to each other, there never is a harsh word said.

Very shortly I will be sending home my first war souvenir. It is a North Vietnamese patch strip with Russian Ammo. I got this Monday off a dead N.V.A. I saw my first horrible sight that day. Kids 13-14 years old belonging to the North Vietnamese Army. When you see these kids lying face down in these rice patties it makes you sick. I couldn't sleep for 2 nights. This kind of thing will never get back to public back home but it is definitely more than what you read. We lost 10 men alone in our Company Monday night and you will probably hear 1 man killed back there.

Don't worry about me. I'm with one of the best units here. We are definitely winning the war and will be home in 331 days. Hope all of you are fine at home.

All my love
Glenn

Sat. Aug. 24
Dear Mom & Dad

I received your last letter today. I sure appreciate that when you write. I can't express in words how much better I feel when I hear from home.

Everything is about the same over here. The last couple days it hasn't rained which is very unusual. They claim this is the driest monsoon they have seen. Of course it is still wet & muddy which will be until October.

You were asking me about my squad. I have only eight guys now because I lost another one yesterday. He was shot in the shoulder while walking toward a bunker. After we put him on the helicopter he was just fine. He will probably go home now. All the rest are guys my age. Three of them are married and two of them are from Puerto Rico. There is one colored guy and two kids are nineteen. They will do anything for me. We all get along fine and I don't think we'll ever have any problems.

We still are at Rock Kein yet and will eventually move toward Saigon. We are out in the field everyday sometimes every night. They cannot keep us out in the field more than three days because that stagnant rice paddy water will start rotting your feet. We make contact with the enemy just about every day. Every time we do he gets beat. I just can't see how he keeps on going.

I am sick of these people. They make me sick. Half of these people that live in this village are probably V.C. but there is nothing that we can do about it because they are protected by our government. At night they are V. C. but in the day they are innocent people. I would like to kill them all. These people never had it so good. All of them are making money off of us. This war will never end because of this fact. When we go into the field if we suspect V.C. are there we burn their houses, kill their animals and tear everything up. If I had my way all of Vietnam would be in flames.

Everything is fine - sure do appreciate your letters. Hope all of you are the same.

Love Glenn

Three days later, August 27, killed in action.

Acknowledgements

I want to thank all those people who have come into my life even if it was only for a moment. You all made me who I am today, and I am grateful for the bounty of knowing you whether it was a positive or not so positive experience. It helped me learn who I am and my purpose in life. If you weren't mentioned in the memoir it may have been there were just too many people to mention everyone, or I might have blended you into one of the characters. You are certainly not forgotten. If you knew me, you are part of the book.

Thanks to my wife Diana for her encouragement and Bonnie the palm reader who reminded me for years that I had a "writing fork" in my palm and needed to write. And thanks to my friends Mary, John, Paul, Russ, Roberta, Shelley, Alida, Renee, Jack and others I have missed, for reading the manuscript and giving me your valuable insights.

Some names, places, events have been changed or shifted to allow my story to flow better. Some events and people may be clouded by time, alcohol or vain imaginings. This is how I remember things many years and miles after they occurred.

About the Author

Dan Geiger, MS, a native of Billings, Montana, has lectured and practiced psychology for the past forty-five years in fifty countries on six continents. Specializing in hypnotherapy he enjoys an international private practice. Growing up in rural Montana he became fascinated in exploring the world after taking a ride in a small plane at age ten and seeing the unending horizon. He continues to explore the back roads of the planet enjoying culture, people and food. After writing a series of travel vignettes, he completed his personal memoir and maintains his home base in rural Montana enjoying downhill skiing, backpacking and family.

Printed in the USA
CPSIA information can be obtained
at www.ICGtesting.com
LVHW091319131223
766179LV00028B/72